Jerusalem's Temple Mount

BOOKS BY HERSHEL SHANKS

The Copper Scroll and the Search for the Temple Treasure

Jerusalem: An Archaeological Biography

The Mystery and Meaning of the Dead Sea Scrolls

The City of David: A Guide to Biblical Jerusalem

Judaism in Stone: The Archaeology of Ancient Synagogues

The Dead Sea Scrolls After Forty Years (with James C. VanderKam,
P. Kyle McCarter, Jr., and James A. Sanders)

The Rise of Ancient Israel (with William G. Dever,
Baruch Halpern, P. Kyle McCarter, Jr.)

The Brother of Jesus (with Ben Witherington III)

BOOKS EDITED BY HERSHEL SHANKS

Ancient Israel: A Short History from Abraham to the Roman
Destruction of the Temple

The Art and Craft of Judging: The Opinions of Judge Learned Hand

Christianity and Rabbinic Judaism: A Parallel History of Their Origins and Early Development

Understanding the Dead Sea Scrolls

Archaeology and the Bible: The Best of BAR, 2 vols. (with Dan P. Cole)

Feminist Approaches to the Bible (with Phyllis Trible, Tikva Frymer-Kensky,
Pamela J. Milne, Jane Schaberg)

Recent Archaeology in the Land of Israel (with Benjamin Mazar)

The Search for Jesus (with Stephen J. Patterson, Marcus J. Borg, John Dominic Crossan)

Frank Moore Cross: Conversations with a Bible Scholar

Abraham & Family: New Insights into the Patriarchal Narratives

Aspects of Monotheism: How God Is One (with Jack Meinhardt)

Jerusalem's Temple Mount

FROM SOLOMON TO THE GOLDEN DOME

Hershel Shanks

continuum

NEW YORK • LONDON

The Continuum International Publishing Group Inc
80 Maiden Lane, New York, NY 10038

The Continuum International Publishing Group Ltd
The Tower Building, 11 York Road, London SE1 7NX

www.continuumbooks.com

Printed in Malaysia

A catalog record for this title is on file with the Library of Congress.

Contents

Acknowledgments

This book is the product of many helping hands.

The entire production was under the sure direction of Biblical Archaeology Society president and *Biblical Archaeology Review* publisher Susan Laden.

An early manuscript was superbly edited by Molly Dewsnap Meinhardt. She was succeeded by the equally competent Dorothy D. Resig, who also collected the pictures, wrote the captions and created the maps and plans. Bonnie Mullin carefully supervised the text production and reviewed what must have seemed like endless endnotes.

Kathleen E. Miller and Meghan Dombrink-Green ably undertook specific research assignments in connection with the manuscript.

The book was tastefully designed by Rob Sugar, assisted by Chris Komisar, Jason Clarke and Jinna Hagerty of Auras Design. The result is here for all to see and admire.

Production for printing was smoothly supervised by Heather Metzger.

The jacket design and final publication of the book were overseen by Continuum International and placed in the capable hands of Senior Editor Frank Oveis and Publishing Services Supervisor Gabriella Page-Fort.

The germ of this book was planted two or three years ago by columnist Charles Krauthammer and David Makovsky of the Washington Institute for Near East Policy, who urged me to write a small pamphlet on the history of the Temple Mount because it would likely be the center of controversy in the years ahead. I think they were envisaging the final issues in peace negotiations between Israel and the Palestinians. As things have turned out, final peace negotiations seem further away than ever. And their suggestion has turned into a full-fledged book. I hope the matters I discuss here are still relevant and interesting, despite the current political outlook.

We at the Biblical Archaeology Society could not exist were it not for the support of the academic community. That is particularly true of this book. The towering reputations of the scholars who reviewed my draft add a new luster to the book and give it an authority it would not otherwise have. Oleg Graber of the Institute for Advanced Study in Princeton, New Jersey reviewed Chapter Two dealing with the Dome of the Rock. The entire manuscript was parsed by four distinguished Israeli scholars and friends: Yoram Tsafrir of The Hebrew University, Ronny Reich of the University of Haifa, Gabriel Barkay of Bar-Ilan University and Dan Bahat of the University of Toronto, Canada. They saved me from innumerable blunders. Those remaining are attributable to my obtuse refusal in some cases to follow their guidance.

May the day be soon when all can visit the Temple Mount in brotherly peace.

Hershel Shanks
Washington, D.C.
May 2007

Jerusalem

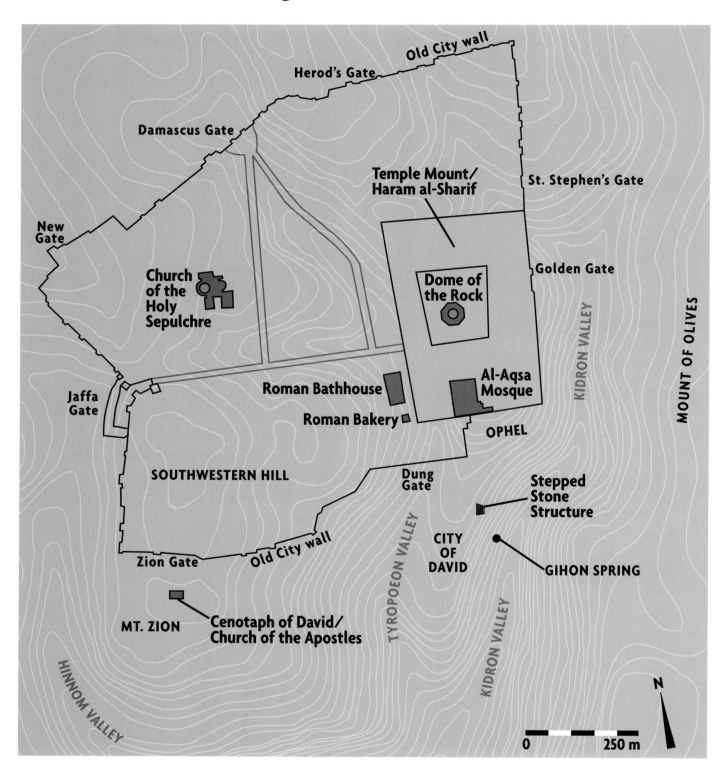

Time Line

	YEAR	EVENT
PRE-SOLOMONIC	c. 1850 B.C.	Jerusalem mentioned in Egyptian execration texts
	14th century B.C.	Jerusalem mentioned in El-Amarna letters
	late 13th century B.C.	Israel mentioned in Merneptah stele
	c. 1000 B.C.	David conquers Jerusalem
SOLOMONIC	c. 1000–920 B.C.	United Monarchy of David and Solomon
	mid-9th century B.C.	Tel Dan inscription mentions House of David
	late 8th century B.C.	Hezekiah pays tribute and Sennacherib withdraws from Jerusalem
	597 B.C.	Nebuchadnezzar attacks Judah and sieges Jerusalem
	586 B.C.	Babylonians destroy First Temple
EXILES' RETURN	538 B.C.	Edict of Cyrus allows exiles to return to Jerusalem
	536–515 B.C.	Exiles rebuild Temple
	175–164 B.C.	Antiochus IV Epiphanes rules Judea and desecrates Temple
	167–164 B.C.	Maccabean rebellion; Hasmoneans recapture and purify the Temple
HERODIAN	63 B.C.	Hyrcanus invites Pompey's assistance (end of Jewish sovereignty)
	37–4 B.C.	Herod reigns (starts rebuilding Temple in the 18th year)
	66–70 A.D.	First Jewish Revolt against Rome
	70 A.D.	Romans capture Jerusalem, destroy Temple
ROMAN & BYZANTINE	130 A.D.	Hadrian decides to rebuild Jerusalem as Aelia Capitolina
	132–135 A.D.	Second Jewish Revolt against Rome
	312 A.D.	Constantine victorious at Battle of Milvian bridge
	324 A.D.	Constantine becomes sole Roman emperor
	4th century A.D.	Constantine builds Church of the Holy Sepulchre
	361–363 A.D.	Julian the Apostate is Roman emperor
	361 A.D.	Failed attempt to rebuild Jewish Temple
ISLAMIC	638 A.D.	Arab conquest of Jerusalem
	692 A.D.	'Abd al-Malik builds the Dome of the Rock
	1099 A.D.	Crusaders conquer Jerusalem
	1187 A.D.	Saladin captures Jerusalem

I

Why This Book?

ACCORDING TO THE HEBREW BIBLE, KING SOLOMON BUILT A TEMPLE to the Lord in Jerusalem on a threshing floor that his father, King David, had purchased from Araunah the Jebusite for 50 shekels of silver. "No other building of the ancient world, either while it stood in Jerusalem or in the millennia since its final destruction, has been the focus of so much attention throughout the ages."[1]

In this sense, it is arguably the most important building in history. For although it is no longer there, it still has and has had enormous meaning for Jews and Christians, as well as for Muslims. It is, or was, for all three religions the home of God on earth.

Tradition—Jewish, Christian and Muslim—holds that Solomon built his Temple, dedicated to the Israelite God Yahweh, in the southeast corner of what is now Jerusalem's Old City, on a platform known to Jews and Christians as the Temple Mount and to Muslims as the Haram al-Sharif (the Noble Sanctuary).

Recently, in the context of the Israeli-Palestinian conflict, some Palestinians have claimed that no Israelite Temple ever existed. This book considers that claim. But it also includes much information that relates not to the limited question of the Temple's existence, but to the fascinating context of that existence.

Abraham is said to have been willing to sacrifice his son here, as God requested before staying the patriarch's hand. Even this is not the mount's first association with a biblical figure, however. Indeed, according to tradition, Adam

The Temple Mount in Jerusalem is a holy site for Jews, Christians and Muslims. Archaeological excavations are not permitted on the site, but it is possible to trace its history for thousands of years from both texts and archaeological finds.

1

With the Dome of the Rock looming in the distance, archaeologist Gabriel Barkay and his team are sifting tons of earth removed from the Temple Mount and dumped into the Kidron Valley by the Muslim Waqf.

himself is buried here. Then marching through history came people such as King David and King Solomon. Jesus came to the Temple built here by Herod the Great. Muhammed is said to have ascended to heaven from this spot.

Today, the site is adorned with the Dome of the Rock, one of the most glorious structures on earth. On the southern end of the Temple Mount, or Haram, sits Al-Aqsa mosque. The Haram is the third holiest site in Islam, after Mecca and Medina.

This book is a comprehensive archaeological history of the Temple Mount as it has come down to us through the ages—through constructions and destructions, through wars and peace, from sacred to profane, from buildings and rebuildings, culminating in the most disputed spot on the face of the globe, both in antiquity and today.

At the outset, it must be acknowledged that not a single stone can be claimed with certainty to have come from Solomon's Temple, known in Jewish tradition as *Beth Yahweh*,* the House of Yahweh, God's dwelling place on earth. (That

*Yahweh—YHWH, as it is spelled without consonants in the Bible—is the personal name of the Israelite God.

may be the single most widely quoted sentence from this book in some of the Arab press. Another voice: Don't flatter yourself; this book will be ignored by the Arab press.) With how much confidence, therefore, can we assert that Solomon's Temple ever existed on this spot?

To address this question, we will proceed backward in time like an archaeologist digging deeper and deeper into the past—from the structures presently existing on the Temple Mount, or Haram, to the wasteland of the era when Christians dominated the city, to the Roman tribute to Jupiter, to the magnificent Temple built by Herod the Great, to the modest Temple built by the Jews returning from the Babylonian Exile and to Solomon's Temple built on the threshing floor of Araunah the Jebusite. Then we'll dig down even further, to the days before the Temple.

The Palestinian claim denying the existence of the Israelite Temple is both vague and ambiguous. The claim is made quite generally—that the Jewish Temple never existed on the Haram. Sometimes it seems to refer only to Solomon's Temple, sometimes to any Israelite Temple, sometimes only to the location of the Israelite (Jewish) Temple.

For example, at Camp David, Yassar Arafat told the American negotiator Dennis Ross, and others, that even if Herod's Temple did exist, it was not in Jerusalem, but in Nablus, a city about 30 miles north of Jerusalem.[2] Arafat was referring to the Samaritan Temple on Mt. Gerizim (in Nablus). The Samaritans are a Jewish offshoot, and Mount Gerizim is their holy mountain, just as the Temple Mount in Jerusalem is for Jews.

Kamil Hatib, vice-chairman of the Islamic Movement, which works closely with the Muslim religious trust known as the Waqf, admits that a "Jewish temple may have existed but not in Jerusalem."[3]

Arafat admitted to President Clinton at Camp David that his faith forbade him from recognizing the existence of the Jewish Temple: "I am a religious man," Arafat said, "and I will not allow it to be written of me [in history] that I have ... confirmed the existence of the so-called temple underneath the mountain."[4]

On the other hand, even Arafat admitted the existence of Herod's Temple: "The Jews have no claim to the whole area of the Haram al-Sharif. They [the Israelis] excavated everywhere and they didn't find a single stone from the Temple [of Solomon], just some stones from the Temple of Herod."[5]

This clay seal impression was discovered in the piles of dirt removed from the Temple Mount. The form of its archaic Hebrew script dates the seal with which it was made to the First Temple period. Based on a similar example, this inscription has been reconstructed to read, "Belonging to Gaalyahu son of Imer."

Palestinian Authority (PA) Minister Nabil Sha'ath, a chief negotiator of the 1993 Oslo Agreement, has referred to the Jewish Temple as "fictitious."[6]

Mahmoud Abbas (Abu Mazen), president of the Palestinian National Authority, has stated: "[Israel] should not claim that the [Jewish] Temple is underneath the Haram ... I challenge the assertion."[7]

Similar statements have been voiced by many high-ranking Palestinians, including Abu 'Alaa, the former prime minister (before the Hamas victory).[8]

The Israeli newspaper *Ha'aretz* reports that "In public discourse among Arabs, participants regularly add the word *'al-maz'um'*—that is, the presumptive or fabricated—when referring to the Jewish Temple."[9]

PA Mufti Sheikh Ekrima Sabri told the German newspaper *Die Welt*, "There is not [even] the smallest indication of the existence of a Jewish temple on this place in the past."[10] "The Temple ... was never there."[11]

Even some Palestinian academics take this position. Hamed Salem, a lecturer in archaeology at Bir Zeit University near Ramallah, is quoted as saying: "There is no archaeological evidence that either [Jewish] temple existed. It's self-evident that the First Temple [Solomon's Temple] was fiction. The Second [Herod's

Muslim workers for the Waqf pave over the southeastern corner of the Temple Mount (left), making it impossible to examine what lies beneath.

A recently dug stairway inside the southern wall of the Temple Mount (the silver dome of Al-Aqsa mosque is visible at right) leads down to an underground mosque. To open this broad new entrance, thousands of tons of earth were excavated and removed without archaeological supervision.

Temple] also remains in the realm of fantasy."[12]

Some historians deny the existence of Solomon's Temple based on what *Nature* magazine calls the "dearth of direct evidence," which leads them "to argue that Solomon's Temple never existed and that the Jewish state thus has no legitimate claim to the sacred hill."[13]

In March 2005 archaeologist Gabriel Barkay, who had excavated a silver amulet in Jerusalem from the First Temple period containing the oldest biblical text ever discovered (a variation of the priestly blessing from Numbers 6:24–26), responded to a statement by an Arab member of the Knesset (Israel's parliament) denying the existence of the Temple. Barkay accused the Palestinians of waging a "cultural intifada" against the Jews. As I write, Barkay is sifting tons of earth excavated illegally by the Waqf (the Muslim religious trust) on the Temple Mount, searching for whatever might be left after some Arabs dumped it into the neighboring Kidron Valley.[14] (See Chapter IV.)

The question of the Temple's existence obviously has political implications. Archaeology in Israel has always been politicized by one side or the other. As author Gershom Gorenberg has written in *The Jerusalem Report*, "Dig a centimeter beneath the debate over antiquities, and you hit a debate over whom the [Temple] Mount belongs to, a centimeter beneath that is the war over whom the entire country belongs to."[15]

Time magazine has called the Temple Mount "potentially the most volatile 35 acres on earth." Had they deleted the word "potentially," the statement might have been even more accurate.[16]

Kiriath-jearim, just outside Jerusalem, where the Ark of the Covenant rested for 20 years before being brought to the Holy City.

Not long after the beginning of the first intifada (Arabic for uprising) in December 1987, riots from the Temple Mount became a regular feature following Muslim prayers each Friday.[17]

On September 25, 1996, Israel opened an exit from a tunnel adjacent to the western wall of the Temple Mount. The tunnel began at the Jewish prayer area and proceeded northward. The exit opened onto the Via Dolorosa. Although the tunnel itself had been excavated years before, Muslim rioting followed the opening of the exit. Over 1,500 were wounded and more than 70 died.[18]

A visit to the Temple Mount on September 28, 2000, by then opposition-leader Ariel Sharon sparked the second intifada in which nearly a thousand people were killed in the next year.[19]

More recently, Israel announced the rebuilding of the ramp leading up to the Maghrabi Gate high up on the western wall of the Temple Mount. The old ramp had become unsafe as a result of a minor earthquake and an unusual snowstorm. It had already been replaced by an unsightly wooden ramp. The Maghrabi Gate is the only gate to the Temple Mount that the Waqf (the Muslim religious trust that controls the Temple Mount) will allow non-Muslims to use. It is the only gate by which tourists can ascend to the mount. Sheikh Ra'ad Salah, a leader of Israel's Islamic movement, called for a new intifada in response to the Israeli announcement that the temporary wooden ramp would be replaced with a more permanent one.[20] Sporadic violence predictably followed. Whether the new ramp will be built has not yet been decided.

Given the recitation of Palestinian claims I have rehearsed above, the reader may expect this book to be a political tract. While I do disagree with the Palestinian claim, I shall do my best to avoid a political discussion. I hope what follows is a recitation of historical evidence.

But it is more than a demonstration of the Temple's existence. The Palestinian claim is just my excuse for writing a book about the Temple Mount that I wanted to write anyway. The reader will soon discover that there are numerous sideways and byways in my text. Often my criterion for inclusion or exclusion was simply whether the excursus was sufficiently fascinating. Only if the answer was yes did I include it.

According to the Bible, the Israelites built a portable sanctuary in the wilderness called the Tabernacle (Hebrew, *mishkan*),* which housed the Tablets of the Law containing the Ten Commandments that Moses brought down from Mt. Sinai. They were contained in the Ark of the Covenant, a box of acacia wood overlaid with gold and surmounted with two cherubim. The Ark of the Covenant was placed in the Tabernacle. The Tabernacle itself is elaborately described in Exodus 25–40. When completed, the "Presence (*kavod*) of the Lord [or Glory of the Lord] filled the Tabernacle" (Exodus 40:34). The Israelites took the Tabernacle with them as they traveled through the wilderness to the Promised Land.

When they reached the Promised Land, the Tabernacle resided at Shiloh (Joshua 18:1, 19:51; Psalm 78:60). For a time, it was also at Gibeon, according to later sources (1 Chronicles 16:39, 21:29; 2 Chronicles 1:3–6,13). Then it remained in Kiriath-jearim (modern Abu Ghosh, just outside Jerusalem) for 20 years (1 Samuel 7:1–2). From there, it was brought to Jerusalem to reside in Solomon's Temple.

But that's starting at the beginning. In this book we will proceed from the opposite direction—from the Dome of the Rock backward.

---

*Also called the Tent of Meeting (*ohel mo'ed*), which may be a different kind of structure, described (in Exodus 33:7–11) in a different authorial strand of the text; it is sometimes referred to simply as "the Sanctuary" (*miqdash*).

II

Dome of the Rock

THE DOME OF THE ROCK—*QUBBAT AL-SAKHRA*—HAS BEEN CALLED "the most beautiful and perfect achievement of Islamic architecture."[1] It is not only the earliest dated extant Muslim building, but—*mirabile dictu*—it has retained its original structure and artistic scheme for more than 1,300 years.[2]

The brilliant, golden dome—more than 65 feet in diameter—dominates the modern skyline of Jerusalem from both near and far. As one approaches the city from the south, it sits on the horizon, only to disappear as one nears the city. Still invisible to one climbing the immense podium on which it is located, it bursts into glorious view as one reaches the summit.

The building itself is octagonal in plan. The lower exterior walls are covered with black-, red- and cream-colored marble inlays. Spectacular glazed tiles—in royal blue, white, yellow and green—cover the upper portion of the walls. Most of the tile decoration is geometric in design, although lengthy quotations from the Qur'an wrap around the building.

Inside the building, every surface glimmers, with polished marble and porphyry, stained-glass windows, golden mosaics and gilded woodwork. Two arcades (series of arches supported by columns and piers) enclose the rock mass in the center of the floor that gives the building its name. The outer arcade is octagonal in plan, the inner circular.

Paradoxically, this jewel of the Temple Mount was the conception of a Muslim Arab who was influenced by—and reacting against—Christian architecture. The Dome of the Rock was to be the visual rival of the Church of the Holy

The golden Dome of the Rock dominates the Jerusalem skyline. The Church of the Holy Sepulchre with its two silver domes can be seen in the background.

9

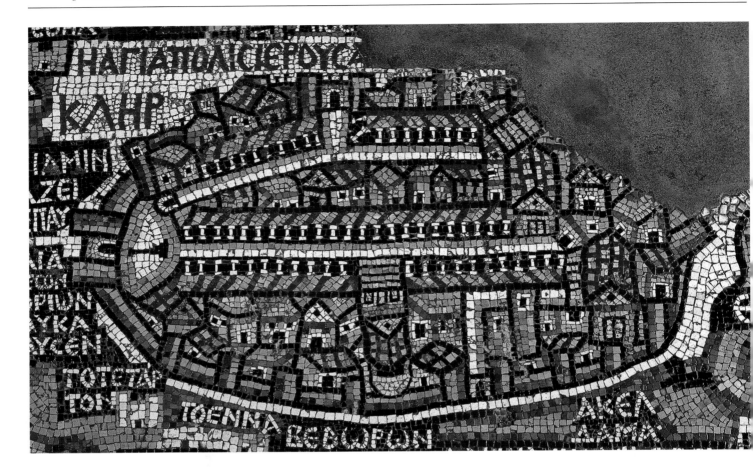

Byzantine Jerusalem is depicted within an oval in this sixth-century mosaic (above) known as the Madaba Map, located in a church in Madaba, Jordan. The entrance to the city is through a gate at left (the Damascus Gate). Inside is a plaza with a column. The cardo, the city's main north-south street, runs across the map. In the center of the cardo is the Holy Sepulchre complex (shown inverted).

Sepulchre, which was built on the spot where Jesus Christ was buried.

Prior to the Arab conquest of Jerusalem in 638 A.D.[3] and the subsequent building of the Dome of the Rock in 692, the Church of the Holy Sepulchre was the religious focus of the city. It was not the Holy Sepulchre we see today, which is the product of several destructions and rebuildings, most recently by the Crusaders. In the Byzantine period, when it was first built, the Holy Sepulchre complex was graced by two separate structures constructed on a site identified by Emperor Constantine's mother, Helena: one, a rotunda with a dome marking the tomb of Christ, and the other, a basilical church.[4] The rotunda and the basilica were separated by a courtyard enclosed in a columned portico. The basilica fronted on Byzantine Jerusalem's main street, the Cardo. This is all illustrated in the famous Madaba map, a sixth-century mosaic floor from a church in Madaba, Jordan.

Fragments of the original columns of the rotunda over the tomb of Christ have been retained in the columns in the present rotunda, so we can assume the original rotunda was even more impressive, with columns taller than the ones we see today. The fourth-century church father Eusebius reports that Constantine ordered the rotunda over the tomb of Christ "of a magnificence worthy of his wealth and of his crown."[5] As a modern commentator has described it: "Set up

This detail (right) from the Madaba map shows the layout of the Holy Sepulchre complex when it was built in the Byzantine period. The columned portico of the cardo (at bottom) is interrupted by four steps that lead up to the triple entrance of the red-roofed basilical church (the middle entrance is slightly larger). Beyond the basilica, separated by a courtyard, lies the golden rotunda that was erected over the tomb of Christ.

over the Tomb of the Lord, to exalt the glory of His Resurrection, [the rotunda] expresses the idea of triumph."[6]

It was this idea to which the builder of the Dome of the Rock was responding.

When the Muslims built the Dome of the Rock, the intention was to move the religious focus of the city away from the Church of the Holy Sepulchre (a sixth-century Christian pilgrim's account described the church as being "in the center of the city")[7] and to restore it to the Temple Mount, the site of the long-destroyed Jewish Temple. The move was part of what one scholar calls the "competition, almost a confrontation, between Christianity and Islam or, perhaps more accurately, between Christians and Muslims."[8] The dome on the Muslim structure was intended to eclipse the dome of the rotunda over the Tomb of Christ.

A leading scholar on the Muslim structures on the Haram al-Sharif notes that these buildings were "conceived in a manner and setting meant entirely to overwhelm and overshadow the Christian shrine."[9]

In the words of the Arab historian Muqaddasi (985 A.D.), "Is it not evident that ʿAbd al-Malik [builder of the Dome of the Rock], seeing the greatness of the *martyrium* of the Holy Sepulchre and its magnificence was moved lest it should dazzle the minds of the Muslims and hence erected above the Rock the Dome which is now seen there?"[10] The inner measurements of the domes on the Dome of the Rock and over the Holy Sepulchre are virtually identical: a little more than 65 feet.[11]

The Arabs referred to the Church of the Holy Sepulchre by a different name, using a pun in Arabic. In Christian tradition the church is widely known as the Church of the Resurrection—*al-Qiyama* in Arabic. The Arabs changed its name to *al-Qamama*—Church of the Dung.[12]

The Muslim attitude toward Christianity is further reflected in a remarkable mosaic inscription that is part of the decoration inside the Dome of the Rock. It is inscribed in a narrow strip on both sides of the octagonal arcade inside the building. The inscription is nearly 800 feet long and is the earliest example of Arabic script used as part of a decorative scheme, a feature of Islamic art widely employed to the present day (see photo, pp.14–15). The text, however, can be read as an anti-Christian polemic:[13]

Believe therefore in God and his apostles, and say not "Three" [that is, the Christian trinity] ... God is only one God. Far be it from his glory that he should have a son.

In short, "the idea promulgated in the building inscription of the Dome of the Rock is the exact opposite of what is commemorated in the Church of the Holy Sepulchre."[14] As one scholar has stated, the Muslim program of building on the Haram was an attack in what amounted to an "ideological 'cold war' " between the Christian and Muslim empires at the time."[15]

This inscription, by the way, also tells us who built the Dome of the Rock: the Abbasid caliph Al-Mamoun, who lived in the ninth century. For centuries, some investigators gave Al-Mamoun credit for this accomplishment. There's only one problem: He had nothing to do with it. It was actually built by the Omayyad caliph 'Abd al-Malik in the late seventh century. The Omayyads and the Abbasids were bitter enemies. The Abbasids successfully revolted and replaced the Omayyad dynasty in the mid-eighth century. Omayyad accomplishments were simply erased from the historical record. (Four imposing but previously unknown Omayyad palaces, also erased from the historical record, were discovered at the foot of the Temple Mount in Israeli archaeological excavations begun in 1968, after the 1967 Six-Day War; the Omayyad palaces were constructed largely of Herodian stones from the Temple Mount destroyed by the Romans.) "Erase" was precisely what the Abbasid caliph did to the identification of the builder of the Dome of the Rock: He erased the name of 'Abd al-Malik in the inscription and replaced it with his own name. Al-Mamoun made a mistake, however. He neglected to change the date.[16] The inscription states that the building was constructed in the 72nd year of the Muslim era, that is, in 691/2, when 'Abd al-Malik was caliph.

Not only was 'Abd al-Malik's dome meant to surpass the dome of the Christian rotunda, but the overall scheme of the two major Islamic monuments on the Haram imitated the scheme of the Christian complex. On the southern end of the Haram is Jerusalem's other monumental Islamic structure, Al-Aqsa mosque (see photo and drawing, pp. 20–21). Unlike

The interior of the dome of the Dome of the Rock glimmers with the beautiful gold, red and green geometric designs that circle the rotunda.

Polished marble and mosaics cover the ceiling of the Dome of the Rock. .

the Dome of the Rock, however, little of the present Al-Aqsa is original. The current mosque, in general a reflection of the original, is considerably narrower. Some scholars say that the original Al-Aqsa mosque resembled the basilical church in front of the domed rotunda over the Tomb of the Lord.[17] Moreover, the architectural alignment of the tomb and the church is repeated in the alignment of the Dome of the Rock and Al-Aqsa mosque. "In a manner of speaking, the Islamic application of the Temple Mount exaggerates the scheme displayed in the Holy Sepulchre."[18]

The Dome of the Rock also reflects another possible Christian influence: Its octagonal shape suggests that it was designed in conscious imitation of a Christian *martyrium* (memorial). *Martyria* commemorate particular events in the life of Christ or other biblical figures. They are customarily round or polygonal in plan, so that they enclose equally on all sides the site of the event being memorialized. For example, both the original chapel enclosing the traditional site of the Nativity in Bethlehem and the church built over the house of St. Peter (where Jesus stayed in Capernaum; see photo, p. 22) are octagonal structures. And so is the Dome of the Rock.

So, what did the Dome of the Rock memorialize?

One popular tradition suggests that the building commemorates Muhammed's flight to heaven. According to this later Muslim tradition, while Muhammed was sleeping in Mecca near the sacred Ka'aba (a rectangular, gray stone structure 50 feet long and 33 feet wide into the wall of which is embedded the sacred Black Stone, which Muslim pilgrims kiss), the angel Gabriel came to Muhammed and took him away, mounted on a winged steed with a human face named Buraq.

After a night journey to Jerusalem, they ascended to heaven from the rock (*al-Sakhra*) at the center of the Dome of the Rock (see photo, p. 31).

Although the Qur'an itself makes no explicit mention of Jerusalem, the following enigmatic passage is said to refer to this night journey and ascent to heaven:

> Glory be to Him, who carried His servant [Muhammed] by night from the Holy Sanctuary [in Mecca] to the Further Sanctuary (*al-masjid al-aqsa*) the precincts of which We have blessed, that We might show him some of Our signs. (*Sura* 17:1)

Whether the "Further Sanctuary" actually refers to a site in Jerusalem is a matter of scholarly dispute, however, as is the development of this tradition.

The earliest dated extant Muslim building, the Dome of the Rock has retained its original structure and artistic scheme for more than 1,300 years. The lower walls are decorated with marble inlays, while the upper portions are covered in colorful faïence mosaics and elegant script containing lengthy quotations from the Qur'an.

Some say there is proof that Muhammed did indeed ascend from the rock mass in the center of the Dome of the Rock: A cavity in the rock bears the hoofprint of the steed Buraq as he pushed off on the ascent to heaven. Until very recently (when non-Muslims have had difficulty gaining access to the Dome of the Rock), tour guides would regularly point out this imprint in the rock.

As in so many cultures—Muslim and otherwise—differing, even conflicting, traditions often coexist. Some say it is the footprint of Muhammed himself on the rock, not that of his steed Buraq. Consonant with this tradition, the Prophet (or Gabriel) put his foot down to restrain the rock as it tried to follow Muhammed to heaven.[19] Another legend, preserved in Jewish lore, interprets the cavity in the rock as the imprint left by God's own foot when, after completing creation in six days, he departed from his worldly throne—the rock mass in the center of the dome.[20] Egeria, a fourth-century Christian pilgrim, interpreted what was apparently this same footprint as belonging to Jesus. According to Egeria, the impression

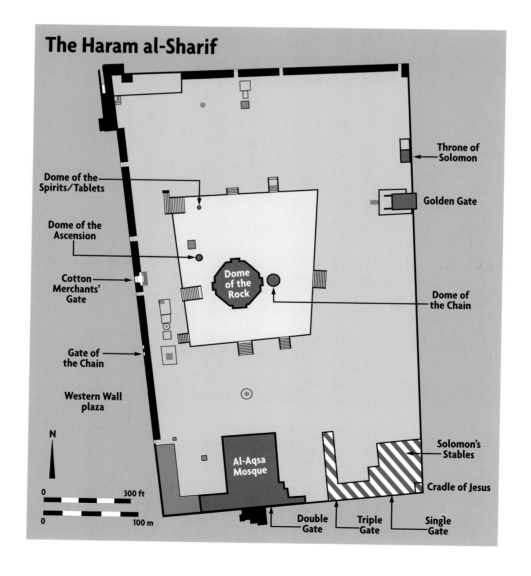

The Haram al-Sharif

Throne of Solomon

Golden Gate

Dome of the Spirits/Tablets

Dome of the Ascension

Cotton Merchants' Gate

Dome of the Rock

Dome of the Chain

Gate of the Chain

Western Wall plaza

N

0   300 ft

0   100 m

Al-Aqsa Mosque

Solomon's Stables

Cradle of Jesus

Double Gate   Triple Gate   Single Gate

The Church of the Holy Sepulchre stands over the traditional site of Jesus' burial and resurrection.

was made when Jesus was brought to the Temple as a baby and a man named Simeon held him in his arms (Luke 2:25–28). As Egeria tells it, "[T]he Lord Jesus Christ placed his foot, on the occasion when Simeon took him in his arms, and his footprint remains there exactly as if it had been made in wax."[21] (Impressions in stone were not uncommon: An anonymous Christian pilgrim account from the sixth century reports that the column to which Jesus was tied when scourged bore "a mark where his hands grasped it, like an impression on wax.")[22]

The tradition that Muhammed ascended to heaven, whether on his horse or otherwise, from al-Sakhra was probably not part of the original conception of the Dome of the Rock, however. Oleg Grabar at the Institute for Advanced Study in Princeton says the tradition developed only in the 12th century, long after the Dome of the Rock was built.[23] Many commentators regard the Qur'an's

The other monumental Muslim structure on the Haram al-Sharif is Al-Aqsa mosque, which anchors the southern end of the platform also known as the Temple Mount.

description of the night flight as a dream episode rather than an actual journey.[24] Gradually, however, it was interpreted as an actual journey. Still later, Jerusalem—specifically the Temple Mount—was identified as the way station on Muhammed's subsequent ascension to heaven, where he received divine revelations.

Further, another structure on the Haram, a small dome supported by columns, is called the Dome of the Ascension (*Qubbat al-Mi'raj*). It was built outside the Dome of the Rock on the same platform to the northwest of the Dome of the Rock (see photo, p. 27). We cannot be sure when it was built, but an earlier Dome of the Ascension is documented in Islamic records before the Crusaders arrived, so it must have been built very early, probably near the time the Dome of the Rock itself was built. If so, this would indicate that the tradition that Buraq ascended from al-Sakhra under the Dome of the Rock had not yet crystallized when the Dome of the Rock was constructed.[25] As Oleg Grabar has remarked, "Had the first and largest of all buildings on the Haram (outside of the congregational mosque on its southern end called al-Aqsa) been built as a *martyrium* to the Ascension of Muhammad, there would certainly not have been any need for a second *martyrium*."[26] On the other hand, the Dome of the Ascension is also associated with Gabriel.[27]

Further evidence that the building was not originally associated with Muhammed's flight comes from the lengthy mosaic inscription that runs above

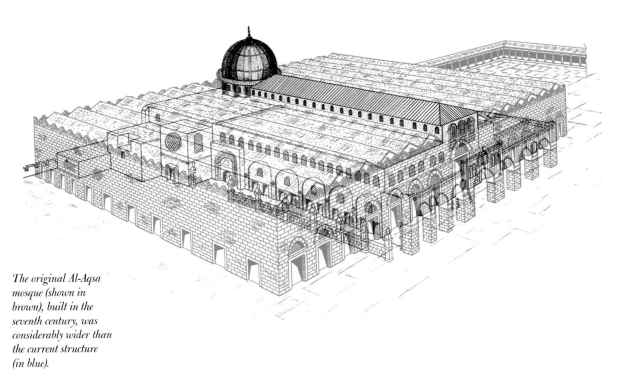

The original Al-Aqsa mosque (shown in brown), built in the seventh century, was considerably wider than the current structure (in blue).

the columns inside the Dome of the Rock. The text makes no mention of Muhammed ascending from the rock beneath. Nor does it mention the enigmatic night journey referred to in the Qur'an (*Sura* 17:1).

What else, then, might the Dome of the Rock memorialize? Another possibility suggested by scholars is Abraham's near-sacrifice of his son on Mt. Moriah, as recounted in Genesis 22—except that in Muslim tradition, the son who climbs Mt. Moriah is not Isaac, but Ishmael, Abraham's first son (by his concubine Hagar), the ancestor of the Arabs. Only when the hand of God intervened, saying "Do not raise your hand against the boy" (Genesis 22:12), did the patriarch desist from lowering the knife on his son's neck. According to this tradition, the mysterious footprint impressed into al-Sakhra belongs to Ishmael.[28] The horns of the ram that Abraham sacrificed on Mt. Moriah in place of his son are said to be kept in the Dome of the Rock.[29]

In both Jewish and Muslim tradition, the near-sacrifice of Abraham's son occurred on the very spot where King Solomon would later construct his Temple. The Jewish tradition is already preserved in the Bible—in the post-Exilic Book of Chronicles: "Solomon began to build the House of the Lord in Jerusalem on Mount Moriah" (2 Chronicles 3:1; cf. Genesis 22:14). The name *Moriah* means "Yahweh is seen [here],"[30] prefiguring his home in the Temple that Solomon would build. In Muslim tradition, Abraham put his foot on the rock, making it

The octagonal plan of the Dome of the Rock echoes the shape of Christian martyria such as the house of St. Peter in Capernaum, pictured here. Martyria were constructed to enshrine the site of an important religious event. The building of the Dome of the Rock may have been influenced by the shape of the traditional Christian martyria.

the *qibla*, the focus of prayer, for all mankind.[31]

In short, the Temple Mount *is* Mt. Moriah.

Why was the Dome of the Rock built where it was—on the site venerated as the spot where the Holy Temple of the Jews once stood? Obviously, this belief must have been incorporated into Islam. As one distinguished commentator recently argued, the construction of the Dome of the Rock was an attempt, in conception, to rebuild the destroyed Jewish Temple.[32] Islamic sources themselves give reason to conclude that the Dome of the Rock was intended "to renew the Solomonic Temple."[33]

In Jewish and Muslim tradition, Mt. Moriah is not merely the site of Solomon's Temple, however. It is Eden.

The book of Jubilees will serve as an example of Jewish tradition. Written in the second century B.C., Jubilees was regarded as authoritative scripture in the Dead Sea Scroll community (it still is in the Abyssynian church). According to Jubilees, "The Garden of Eden was the Holy of Holies and the dwelling of the Lord" (Jubilees 8:19).

Muslim tradition tells us that a black stone embedded in the floor beneath the Dome of the Rock is supposed to be the entrance to Paradise. The elaborate mosaics that fill the interior of the shrine feature repetitive trees, luxuriant foliage, bushes, jewels and floral motifs reminiscent of the Garden of Eden (see photo, p. 28). A tree on the platform of the Haram is associated with God's original work in the world.[34] In Jewish and Muslim tradition, the rivers of Eden flow below the Temple Mount. Creation originated here, an idea reflected in the designation *omphalos mundi* ("navel of the world"), referring to the notion that God created the world in the same way that a human being was created, beginning with the navel. Jubilees, too, set the navel of the world on Mount Zion, by that time identified as the Temple Mount. At the end of time, the Last Judgment will take place here[35] and access to Paradise will be available here. Although Jerusalem is not mentioned by name in the Qur'an, the phrase "from a nearby place" (*Sura* 50:41) was interpreted early on to refer to the Holy City. The passage, literally "the day whereon the crier shall call from a nearby place," was interpreted to refer to the archangel who, on the day of the Resurrection, will call from Jerusalem.[36]

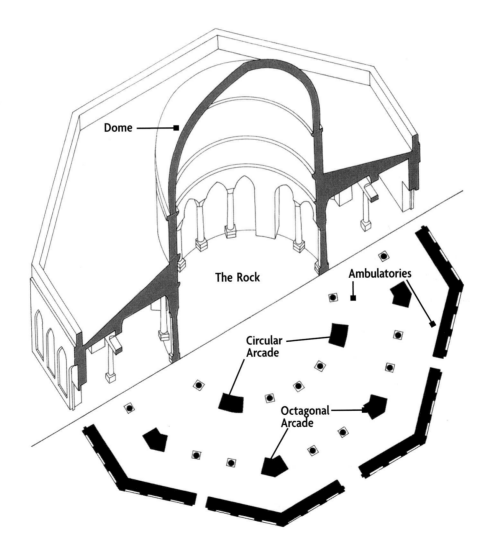

Dome

The Rock

Ambulatories

Circular Arcade

Octagonal Arcade

The Dome of the Rock is an octagon. Inside, an octagonal arcade and a circular arcade enclose the rock mass in the center.

In the Byzantine period, Christians transferred many of the events associated in Jewish tradition with the site of the Temple,[37] including the near-sacrifice of Isaac, to the Church of the Holy Sepulchre.[38] One interesting transference involves the burial of Adam. The Church of the Holy Sepulchre marks the place of Jesus' crucifixion, called Calvary or Golgotha. Golgotha means "skull" in Aramaic. Why is the place of Jesus' crucifixion called "skull"? According to Christian tradition, Adam was buried here—beneath Jesus' cross.[39] In many paintings of the crucifixion, the skull of Adam is depicted at the base of the cross (see photo, p. 29). In Jewish tradition, Adam and Eve were buried under the Temple. (Another tradition holds that the skull of Araunah the Jebusite, from whom King David purchased what was then a threshing floor [2 Samuel 24:18–25], was found buried under Solomon's Temple when the Jewish exiles returned from Babylon and rebuilt the Temple.[40] The Christians did the Jews one better in the matter of skulls.) As archaeologist Rivka Gonen puts it, "The act of creation of the world and of humanity, represented by Adam, was transferred to Golgotha, and the detail that Adam was also buried there was added."[41]

The Dome of the Rock brought all of these traditions back to the Temple Mount, or rather to the Haram al-Sharif, and they have remained there. Despite recent Palestinian assertions that the Temple never existed, there is every reason to believe that since the construction of the Dome of the Rock, Islam has understood the site to have been where the Jewish Temple once stood.[42]

The interior of the Dome of the Rock, showing the rock mass below and the dome above.

Some of the columns in the present Church of the Holy Sepulchre contain elements of the original columns of the rotunda that was built over the tomb of Christ. The small structure in the center is the Aedicule of the Holy Sepulchre, which was built to enshrine and protect the area around the cave in which Jesus is believed to have been buried.

As recently as 2004, a leading primer on Islam asserted:

> The Temple Mount is also the site where the Hebrew king Solomon
> constructed his famous temple, which was later destroyed by the
> Babylonians ... Muslims later built the Dome of the Rock, a shrine
> at the center of the Temple Mount, to mark the location from which
> Muhammad ascended to heaven, as well as the site of Abraham's
> sacrifice and Solomon's temple.[43]

Accounts of the Arab conquest of Jerusalem differ considerably. According
to historians Eliyahu Ashtor and Haim Hirschberg, the most probable version
is that the caliph, Omar (or Umar), sent a subaltern officer to accept the surrender of the city.[44] (Since the Christians surrendered peacefully, the city was
not destroyed and the residents were not murdered, in contrast to Saladin's
reconquest of the city from the Crusaders; the Crusaders mounted a defense,
and a Christian slaughter followed.[45]) According to other accounts, however,
Omar himself led the victorious Arabs. In any event, not long afterward, Omar
was given a tour of the city by the patriarch of Jerusalem, a Christian monk
named Sophronius. More than anything, Omar wanted to see the precise spot
where the Jewish Temple had stood. A converted Jew pointed it out to him.
The Temple, he reported, lay in total ruins covered with debris.[46] "The Christians had desired to fulfill the prophecy of Jesus that this site would remain
desolate forever."[47] (According to the Gospels, "Jesus left the Temple and was
going away, when his disciples came to point out to him the buildings of the
Temple. But he answered them, 'You see all these, do you not? Truly, I say to
you, there will not be left here one stone upon another, that will not be thrown
down'" [Matthew 24:1–2; cf. Mark 13:1–2; Luke 21:5–6].) The Muslims were
in effect restoring the Temple. In several Islamic sources, the buildings on the
Haram "are defined as the restituted Temple of the Jews."[48] The Dome of the
Rock was the Temple restored.[49]

However, "What the Muslims declared to be the rebuilding of the Temple
was, in the eyes of the Christians, the devil's work."[50]

Heribert Busse notes that even "The liturgy celebrated in the Dome of the
Rock is one argument in favor of our thesis that it was 'Adb al-Malik's intention to
restore the Temple."[51] The use of incense in the Church of the Holy Sepulchre,
for example, was adopted in explicit imitation of the ritual in the Temple. 'Abd
al-Malik then adopted the use of incense in the Dome of the Rock.[52]

Soon after the Muslim conquest, a modest wooden Muslim sanctuary was
built south of the site of the Jewish Temple, a later text tells us.[53] Shortly after
660, Mu'awiya, the first Omayyad caliph, built a house of prayer on the Temple
Mount, "at the blessed site where the Temple stood."[54] There "the Saracens

gather to pray." The Christian pilgrim Arculf, who, between 679 and 688, visited "that famous place where once there stood the magnificent Temple," reported that the Muslims had "built an oblong house of prayer, which they pieced together with upright planks and large beams over some ruins."[55] It is clear that "the Muslims took over the Haram area with a definite knowledge and consciousness of its implication in the Jewish tradition as the site of the Temple."[56]

The humble structure erected by Mu'awiya was adequate for the first generations of Muslim conquerors, but not thereafter. In 692 the Dome of the Rock was completed by 'Abd al-Malik.

In general, Islam took over the *topographia sacra* that underlies the Jewish and Christian scriptures. As a leading scholar has observed, "Islam conceives itself as a new rendering of those older Book religions—Judaism and Christianity—whose bedrock is the Rock of Jerusalem."[57]

Visitors to the Dome of the Rock are told of the *miḥrab* (the focus of prayer, the niche toward which prayer is directed) of David and of Solomon.[58] At one point in Muslim tradition, it was thought that King David himself had built the Dome of the Ascension.[59] When Solomon offered his prayer at the dedication of his Temple and stood before the Lord and all the people, spreading his arms to heaven (2 Chronicles 6:12ff), he was facing the rock at the center of the dome, the *miḥrab*.[60]

The Dome of the Ascension (Qubbat al-Mi'raj, in Arabic) is located on the Haram al-Sharif, northwest of the Dome of the Rock. It, too, bears a claim to being the spot from which Muhammed ascended to heaven. If so, the Dome of the Rock may not have been recognized in early Islamic tradition as the spot of Muhammed's ascension.

A cupola on the Haram is called the *Kursi Sulaiman*, the throne of Solomon.[61] The eastern entrance of the Dome of the Rock was called *Bab al-Nabi Daud*, the Gate of the Prophet David.[62]

Muslims were specifically admonished to pray in a spot where the Israelites had prayed to have their prayers of repentance accepted: "Position yourself at the door of the Qubbat al-Sakhra which is called Bab Israfil [the eastern door] and pray there. It is the place at which the Israelites used to pray. If one of them had committed a sin, he went there and prayed to God until his sin was forgiven."[63]

During the Byzantine period, when the site was desolate, Jews would cover the central rock mass, considered the foundation stone of the destroyed Temple, with spices and incense. After the Dome of the Rock was built, Muslims adopted this Jewish custom.

In Islamic tradition the Dome of the Rock is the successor to Solomon's Temple, which is often described in extraordinary terms: Solomon's Temple was so high that Emmaus, about 15 miles from Jerusalem, was in its shadow when the sun rose. When it set, the shadow extended to the Jordan River.

Trees and bushes fill the elaborate mosaics inside the Dome of the Rock. Reminiscent of the Garden of Eden, the lush foliage recalls the Jewish and Muslim traditions that the Garden of Eden was located on the Temple Mount and that the rivers of the garden flow beneath it.

Even before the Dome of the Rock was constructed, the rock was known as the *qibla* (prayer direction) of Moses.[64] 'Abd al-Malik wanted Jerusalem to be the religious center of Islam.[65] According to the earliest Arab historian (Ya'qûbi, 874 A.D.), "'Abd al-Malik forbade the people of Syria to make the pilgrimage [to Mecca]."[66] The most recent scholarship holds that 'Abd al-Malik built this magnificent structure in Jerusalem because he wanted to redirect the *hajj* (annual pilgrimage) from Mecca to Jerusalem.[67] In the early years of Islam, Muslims faced Jerusalem rather than Mecca in prayer. This was a time when political and religious struggles were engulfing nascent Islam. Although 'Abd al-Malik wanted to make Jerusalem into a political and religious center equal to, if not surpassing, Mecca, "this in no way conflicts with what appears to have been two other important considerations in 'Abd al-Malik's development of the Haram: the association of the spot with the Last Days and with the Temple of Solomon."[68]

Having considered the architectural links between the buildings on the Haram and the Church of the Holy Sepulchre, we may also consider the architectural links between these same Muslim structures and Jewish buildings. The Muslim-Christian link related architecture from two parts of the city—across geography, as it were. The Muslim-Jewish link does the same thing over time—with Jewish structures more than 1,500 years earlier than the Islamic structures on the Haram.

In many paintings of the crucifixion, such as this 15th-century example by Italian painter Fra Angelico, the skull of Adam sits at the base of the cross. According to the New Testament, Jesus was crucified at Golgotha ("skull," in Aramaic). In Christian tradition, Adam himself was buried here. While Jewish tradition tells us that Adam was buried under the Temple, Christian tradition transferred this and other significant events associated with the destroyed Jewish Temple to the Christian site of the Holy Sepulchre.

The Dome of the Rock sits in the center of the platform and is anchored at the southern end by Al-Aqsa mosque. This same architectural arrangement is true of the Herodian and the Solomonic periods. In the Herodian period, the Temple was located where the Dome of the Rock now sits, and on the southern end of the platform was the Royal Stoa, which we will examine in more detail later in this book. Similarly, during the period of the Israelite monarchy, Solomon's Temple stood in the center of the platform and his palaces were located on the southern part of the holy precinct surrounding the Temple.

As Miriam Rosen-Ayalon, an expert in Islamic art and archaeology, has remarked, "The concept of an axial relationship between two elements of a religious compound had existed in Jerusalem before Islamic times ... The two major monuments [of the Islamic period] [the Dome of the Rock and al-Aqsa mosque] clearly reflect an established architectural formula which had dominated the Temple Mount for more than a millennium and a half prior to their construction."[69]

While it is possible to debate the significance of one or two matters reflecting Muslim consciousness that the site of the Dome of the Rock was the site of the Solomonic Temple, it is difficult to deny that the Muslims themselves confidently believed that Solomon had built a Temple for the Jews and that it was located where the Muslims built the Dome of the Rock. This was the Muslim view at the time the Dome of the Rock was constructed, and it continued to be the Muslim view until the recent attack on this proposition by some Palestinian authorities.

The Dome of the Rock is shown crowned with a large gilt cross on this seal of the Knights Templar. When the Crusader knights conquered Jerusalem, they erected the cross atop the building, which they believed to be the Israelite Temple. However, when the Muslims recaptured the city, they pulled down the cross and replaced it with the crescent, which is still there today.

When the Crusaders conquered Jerusalem on July 15, 1099, the Temple Mount became a killing field. The Muslims fled to Al-Aqsa mosque, where they surrendered. The next day the Crusaders slaughtered their Muslim prisoners and proceeded to kill thousands more (as well as some Jews).[70] One observer wrote: "[In] the Temple and porch of Solomon, men rode in blood up to their knees and bridle reins."[71]

Under Crusader rule, the Dome of the Rock became a place of Christian veneration and worship.[72] (In a way this was tit for tat: The Muslims had erected a small mosque in the Church of the Holy Sepulchre.)[73] The Crusaders affixed a huge gilt cross atop the Muslim dome. (When the Muslims drove out the Christians at the end of the 12th century, they dragged the cross through the streets of Jerusalem and placed on the dome the crescent, the symbol of Islam, that is still there.) On each face of the octagonal structure, the Crusaders added a Latin mosaic inscription commonly used for the dedication of a church:

> The Temple of the Lord is holy, God's labor and sanctification.
> This is the House of the Lord, firmly built ...
> Blessed be the glory of the Lord from this Holy Place.[74]

When the Byzantine Christians dominated Jerusalem, beginning in the fourth century, they wanted to maintain the desolation of the Temple Mount as proof of Jesus' prediction that the Temple would be destroyed. Christian Crusaders, *au contraire*, revered the Dome of the Rock as the restored Jewish Temple. The Crusaders called the Dome of the Rock *Templum Domini* (the Lord's Temple).[75] Al-Aqsa mosque on the southern end of the Temple Mount initially served as

the palace of the Latin kings of Jerusalem. Later it was given to the Order of the Knights Templar to serve as their headquarters. The Crusaders believed it to be the remains of Solomon's palace (called *Templum Solomonis* or *Palatium Solomonis*) that was once located on the southern part of the Temple Mount.

The last Jewish Temple to grace the Temple Mount, the Herodian Temple, had been destroyed by the Romans in 70 A.D. What happened in the next half millennium—between the Roman destruction and the construction of the Dome of the Rock—will be the subject of the next chapter.

Located under the dome that bears its name, the large rock formation in the Dome of the Rock is called al-Sakhra in Arabic. Thought to be the site of Mt. Moriah (where Abraham nearly sacrificed Isaac), the Israelite Temple and the rock from which Muhammed ascended to heaven, this rock mass is holy in the traditions of Judaism, Christianity and Islam.

III

The Interregnum

WHEN THE ARABS CONQUERED JERUSALEM IN 638 A.D., THEY WERE ABLE to build on the Temple Mount without destroying existing structures from prior periods because there was nothing there.[1] By some accounts, the Temple Mount was simply a garbage dump. I like to call the period from the Roman destruction of Herod's Temple until the Arab conquest—a period of more than half a millennium—the Interregnum.

In this chapter, we will trace the sometimes-mysterious and often-uncertain history of the Temple Mount during this Interregnum. The starting point is clear: In 70 A.D., the Romans captured Jerusalem and burned the Temple. What happened next is less certain. The Jews may have started to rebuild the Temple in the second century during the few years in which they possibly controlled the city during the Second Jewish Revolt (132–135 A.D.). After the Jews were again defeated by the Romans, Emperor Hadrian is said to have erected a temple to Jupiter on the Temple Mount; an equestrian statue of a Roman emperor or two may also have graced the site. We don't know what happened to these Roman monuments. Another attempt by the Jews to rebuild the Temple occurred in the fourth century, when the Roman emperor Julian the Apostate authorized the Jews to do so; the project was soon aborted, however, when Julian was killed in the Persian war and a Christian again became Roman emperor. From then until the Arab conquest in the seventh century, the Temple Mount lay barren, a stark confirmation of Jesus' prediction that not a stone of the Temple would be left standing on another.

Publius Aelius Traianus Hadrianus (better known as Hadrian) was the Roman emperor from 117 to 138 A.D. In 135 he crushed the Second Jewish Revolt and, with it, all hope of restoring the Temple. He rebuilt Jerusalem as a Roman colony named Aelia Capitolina and barred Jews from entering. This larger-than-life bronze statue was unearthed by an American tourist in 1975 in a second-century A.D. Roman fort at Tel Shalem in the Jordan River Valley.

33

The future emperor Titus led the Roman forces in the assault on Jerusalem in which the Temple was destroyed, thus bringing about the end of the First Jewish Revolt.

When we read about the Roman destruction of the Temple in 70 A.D., we assume that the Temple was completely demolished in the battle. Not quite true. It was not so easy for the Romans to demolish the Temple and its appurtenances, especially the massive stone wall enclosing the Temple Mount. The soldiers of the Tenth Roman Legion (*Legio X Fretensis*, in Latin), which was stationed in

Jerusalem for over two centuries after the conquest, would have needed considerable time and strength to pry the huge Herodian ashlars from the walls one by one.[2] In a later chapter we will describe these building blocks in more detail. Here, however, we are concerned only with their dismantlement—a more apt term than destruction—for that is how the soldiers of the Tenth Legion kept busy after conquering the city. Recent excavations of an ancient street that ran along the southern end of the western wall of the Temple Mount have uncovered piles of these huge stones, lying in the road just as the Roman soldiers left them.[3]

Most Herodian ashlars, to use the more technical name archaeologists use for these worked rectangular blocks of stone, can be readily recognized even by educated amateurs. The most-widespread are large, handsome blocks with easily visible, narrow margins and smooth, slightly raised bosses in the center. But there are other kinds of Herodian ashlars as well—for example, perfectly plain, perfectly smooth, rectangular blocks. Some of the stones found lying on the street in recent excavations are of this type.[4] Examples of such plain, smooth blocks can be seen in the Herodian arch above the lintel of the Double Gate on the southern wall of the Temple Mount (see photos, pp. 50–51). Other examples are visible in the photograph of the now-inaccessible Herodian gate below the Golden Gate on the eastern wall of the Temple Mount (see photo, p. 85).

After suppressing the First Jewish Revolt, the Roman soldiers camped in Jerusalem and busied themselves by dismantling the Temple and much of the Temple Mount walls. This floor tile stamped with the impression of the Tenth Roman Legion (Legio X Fretensis) is evidence of this presence.

Many Herodian ashlars appear to have been scavenged for reuse in other Jerusalem buildings.[5] Some were used to construct the Omayyad palaces south of the Temple Mount. Some may be in the bowels of the Holy Sepulchre Church (more on this later). Others might have been reused in what is perhaps an early Judeo-Christian synagogue on Mt. Zion, the western ridge of ancient Jerusalem.

Ancient Jerusalem was built on two ridges. The original settlement rested on the eastern ridge, which stretches south of the Temple Mount for about 10 acres. This ridge is now called the City of David, for it was the city of Jerusalem as King David knew it (see photo, p. 178). It was also the original location of the stronghold of Zion (*metsudat Tsion*), as the Bible calls it (2 Samuel 5:7), which David captured from the Jebusites. Over the centuries, however, the name Zion migrated to the west, to the larger, higher western ridge south of what is today called the Old City. Until the 19th century, when modern archaeology uncovered the City of David, it was thought that the earliest settlement, the original City of David, must have been on this higher

In the photo at left, Herodian ashlars are easily recognizable in secondary use in the wall of this Omayyad palace (right foreground) built adjacent to the southwest corner of the Temple Mount after the Arab conquest of Jerusalem in the seventh century.

These large Herodian ashlars (right) lie in piles along the western wall of the Temple Mount, just where they were thrown down by soldiers of the Tenth Roman Legion after the suppression of the First Jewish Revolt. They were recently uncovered by Israeli archaeologist Ronny Reich.

The most common type of Herodian ashlar (left) consists of a large, handsome block with a narrow margin and a smooth, slightly raised boss in the center. This easily recognizable style has made it possible for scholars to identify Herodian ashlars in secondary use, which were scavenged and used in other buildings. Other Herodian ashlars, however, have a simple, beautifully smooth surface.

The cenotaph of David sits in a building on the southwestern ridge of Jerusalem, known today as Mt. Zion. The Bible says that King David was buried in the City of David, but, as archaeologists have shown, the western ridge was not a part of the city in David's time. In the late 1940s the structure in which the empty tomb sits was found to have been an early synagogue, as well as a mosque.

ridge, still called Mt. Zion. That is why we find the traditional site of the tomb of King David on the western ridge.

The identification (or rather, misidentification) of the tomb goes back at least to the 12th century, when a Jew known as Benjamin of Tudela visited the place and reported that two workmen had accidentally discovered a secret passage leading to a palace of marble columns. There they saw a golden scepter and a golden crown resting on a table. They believed they had discovered the tombs of King David and King Solomon. Suddenly they were struck by a fierce whirlwind, however, and voices told them to leave immediately. After three days, the workmen fell ill and could not be persuaded to return to the site, saying, "God does not want this place to be seen by any human being." This story, as reported by Benjamin, became the basis for erecting a cenotaph of King David, visited today by hordes of tourists, in an ancient building on Mt. Zion.

In the 12th century, the Crusaders rebuilt the building, adding an upper floor with Gothic rib vaulting that came to be identified as the cenacle, the room where Jesus shared his Last Supper with his disciples.

The real story of the building's early years was discovered as a result of war. During Israel's War of Independence in 1948, a shell landed on the building and exploded. While the building was being restored, Israeli architect Jacob Pinkerfeld had the opportunity to study the history of its construction. Pinkerfeld found a niche in the wall about 6 feet above the ancient floor, similar to the Torah niches found in other ancient synagogues, and he identified the building as having been a Roman period synagogue. This identification has been generally accepted. The late archaeologist Bargil Pixner, a Benedictine monk who studied the building intensively, believed that members of the Jesus movement met at this synagogue. In this early period, all members of the Jerusalem Jesus community were Jews; their houses of worship were still called synagogues. Only later were followers of Jesus called Christians and their houses of worship called churches. Pixner believed this was a synagogue of what we might somewhat anachronistically call Judeo-Christians.[6] According to Eusebius there was a flourishing Judeo-Christian community in Jerusalem between the First and Second Jewish Revolts against Rome, that is, between 73 A.D. (the year of the return of the Judeo-Christians who, according to the church historian Eusebius, had fled to Pella, across the Jordan, during the First Revolt) and 132 A.D. (when the Second Jewish Revolt began). These Judeo-Christians enjoyed a certain amount of freedom—they were *religio licita*, a legal religion—because they were considered Jews, rather than converts to a new religion. It was probably they who built the synagogue. Soon, according to Pixner, they identified the site as the location of the Last Supper, which, according to Acts 1–2, was also the place where the apostles prayed after Jesus' post-resurrection appearance and where the first post-resurrection Pentecost was observed. During this festival the apostle Peter delivered the sermon, and people of many lands spoke in tongues and nevertheless understood each other. This Judeo-Christian synagogue ultimately became known as the Church of the Apostles.

The original synagogue building can be "virtually" reconstructed, according to Pixner, as a small rectangular structure, approximately 60 by 30 feet. The surviving walls of the structure are made up of the small building blocks one would expect to find in such a structure, as well as some very impressive ashlars, more than 3 feet high and 3.5 feet long. That they were not hewn for this building is clear. They were laid in a course of stones of different heights. Even more telling, the corners of the stones are chipped, indicating that they were dragged here from another site and are in secondary use. Where could these beautifully hewn ashlars have come from? The speculation is that they came from the dismantled Herodian Temple across the valley. Pixner suggested that perhaps by using these stones, some of the sanctity of the Temple was transferred to the Judeo-Christian synagogue.[7]

Still more Herodian ashlars that may have come from the destroyed Temple have been found in the lowest levels of the Church of the Holy Sepulchre. This

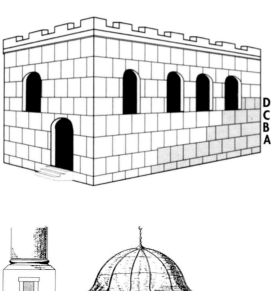

story involves the earliest evidence of Christian pilgrimage to the Holy Land and provides strong confirmation that the church does mark the authentic site of Jesus' burial.

In the 19th century, the so-called Garden Tomb, outside the Old City walls, was proposed as the actual site of Jesus' tomb. But it has been conclusively shown that the Garden Tomb was not used for burials at the time of Jesus' crucifixion. The case for the site of the Holy Sepulchre church, on the other hand, is not only plausible but quite convincing.

The present church reflects a number of rebuildings. The original complex was built by Constantine the Great in the fourth century A.D. on the site where his mother, Helena, supposedly found the cross on which Jesus was crucified. There Constantine built a rotunda around an aedicule (a shrine supported by columns) over the tomb itself. A porticoed courtyard lay in front of the rotunda, and a basilical church stood in front of that, facing the main street of Byzantine Jerusalem. As noted earlier, Constantine's original complex is depicted in considerable detail in a famous sixth-century church mosaic in Madaba, Jordan (see photo, p. 10).

The lower courses of this building on Mount Zion (labeled A–D in the drawings at far left and A–B in the old excavation photo at left) consist of some impressive ashlars more than 3 feet high. The scale of these blocks is shown in the photo at right, where the woman serves as the "meter stick." The fact that the ashlars are laid in a course of stones of different heights also suggests that they were not originally intended for this building. The chipped corners and dinged surfaces of these otherwise beautiful stones indicate that they were dragged from another site—perhaps the dismantled Herodian Temple. The building may originally have been the Church of the Apostles referred to in Acts 2. The reconstruction drawing (upper left) shows the building as it may have looked at that time. The shaded area represents the part of the building that has survived.

A principal reason for accepting the claim that the Holy Sepulchre church marks the authentic tomb of Jesus is that when it was pointed out to Helena, the site was well *inside* the city, amidst the urban hurly-burly. This might seem to refute the authenticity of the site; Jews traditionally buried their dead, with few exceptions, outside the city, and the Gospel of John (19:41) says Jesus was buried in a garden. But, in truth, the fact that people pointed out such an unlikely spot inside the city as Jesus' burial site actually supports the identification. If, in the fourth century, they were going to fabricate a site, it would surely have been outside the walls. They would point out a site inside the walls only if it was genuinely supposed to be authentic.

Only in the 20th century did archaeologists discover that, although in Constantine's time the site was inside the city, in Jesus' time it was outside!

First proposed in the 19th century as the site of Jesus' tomb, the Garden Tomb lies outside the Old City walls, thereby gaining plausibility; the Gospel of John says that Jesus was buried in a garden. It has become a popular pilgrimage site for Christians, but the Garden Tomb was not used for burials in the first century.

Archaeologists have also discovered tombs from the time of Jesus under the church. In other words, the Church of the Holy Sepulchre stands on the site of a first-century burial ground.

Finally, further evidence that the Holy Sepulchre marks Jesus' actual tomb comes from an even earlier building on the same site. Eusebius of Caesarea reports in the fourth century that Hadrian had built a temple to Venus/Aphrodite (he calls her "the impure demon called Aphrodite") on the site where Constantine later built the Church of the Holy Sepulchre. Did Hadrian want to obliterate the cave in which Jesus had been laid to rest?[8]

Eusebius seems to think so. He tells us that Hadrian built his temple to obliterate an early memorial over the tomb of Jesus: "Godless people ... had gone to great pains to cover up this divine memorial of immortality [Jesus' tomb] so that it should be forgotten ... They concealed the divine cave under a heap of earth."[9]

Parts of this Hadrianic temple were reused by the Crusaders when they built the façade of the present Church of the Holy Sepulchre and can still be seen if you know where to look. One researcher lists eight sites within the current church where remains of the Hadrianic temple have been found. [10]

The Church of the Holy Sepulchre stands inside the city of Jerusalem, crowded by buildings on all sides. This would seem to refute the site's authenticity since Jews buried their dead outside the city and John's gospel says that Jesus was buried in a garden. However, 20th-century archaeologists have discovered that the site actually lay outside the city in Jesus' time.

In recent excavations some of the original foundation walls from Hadrian's temple have been uncovered. It is here that we find Herodian ashlars in reuse. Some of these ashlars have the narrow margins and flat, low bosses of so many Herodian ashlars. One of the Herodian ashlars in this wall, however, is a very smooth stone bearing a dipinto (painting) of a ship and a Latin inscription: *DOMINE IVIMUS* ("Lord, we came").[11] Of the many interpretations of this ship and the accompanying inscription, the most likely is that it was drawn by a Christian pilgrim who was invoking Psalm 122, the traditional psalm of pilgrimage: "I was glad when they said to me, 'Let us go to the House of the Lord' [*Domini ibimus*, in Latin]; now we are standing in thy gates, O Jerusalem." Perhaps fulfilling a vow, this Christian traveled to Jerusalem and is saying, "*Domine* (referring to Jesus), we have come." There are other interpretations: He was a Jew. He was a pagan. He was not a pilgrim, but a merchant giving thanks that he had survived a dangerous voyage (the mast of the ship appears broken in the drawing, or is it only lowered?) and arrived safely.[12] There is even disagreement as to the date of the drawing. It might be fourth century, or it might be second. The characteristics of the vessel, however, best fit the second century. And the wall on which it was written was visible only in the second century, when Hadrian built his temple to Venus.

Tombs from the time of Jesus have been discovered beneath the Church of the Holy Sepulchre. The fact that the site was a first-century burial ground lends credibility to the claim that the church stands over the tomb of Jesus.

If, as seems likely, this still-existing ship painting was drawn by a Christian pilgrim on a foundation wall of a Hadrianic temple, as a kind of protest against this Christian-hater, it is the earliest evidence we have of Christian pilgrimage. It also tends to confirm Eusebius's statement that Jesus' tomb was there. But for our purposes here, we need only call attention to the fact that the smooth stone on which the vessel and the inscription were drawn was one of the Herodian stones reused in the wall by Hadrian—a stone that was perhaps scavenged from the destroyed Jewish Temple.

For some time after 70 A.D., the Temple Mount simply lay in ruins, like much of the rest of the city. But the Roman destruction of Jerusalem and the Jewish Temple did not completely smother Jewish nationalism. It flared up again in the mid-second century. The Jews, including those who continued to live in Jerusalem, again revolted against their Roman masters. Known as the Second Jewish Revolt or the Bar-Kokhba Revolt, the struggle lasted from 132 A.D. until it was crushed by the emperor Hadrian in 135 A.D. The losses were enormous on both sides. The Roman historian Dio Cassius (or, often, Cassius Dio) reports that the Romans burned 985 Jewish villages to the ground. The Romans, too, suffered severe losses. The Jewish rebels were led by Simon Bar-Kosiba, renamed Bar-Kokhba (meaning "son of a star") by the rabbinic sage Akiva, in the hope, even expectation, that he might be the Messiah who would restore Israel's glory. Bar-Kokhba may have forced the Roman garrison out of Jerusalem. An entire Roman legion, *Legio XXII Deiotariana*, disappeared in the course of the war. At the end of the war, Hadrian's report of victory to the Roman Senate omitted the customary salutation: "I and the army are well."

This smooth Herodian ashlar, found in secondary use in the Church of the Holy Sepulchre, bears a drawing of a ship and a Latin inscription, DOMINE IVIMUS ("Lord, we came"). This block was part of the foundations for the Roman temple that Hadrian purposefully built over the supposed tomb of Jesus in the second century A.D. The inscription is evidence that, despite the pagan presence, early Christians were making pilgrimages to the holy site.

When Hadrian rebuilt Jerusalem as Aelia Capitolina, he minted coins like this. The obverse (front) bears a portrait of the emperor Hadrian, while the reverse seems to depict a temple and the three Capitoline gods: Jupiter (center), Juno and Minerva. This may be a representation of the temple Hadrian built on the Temple Mount—or at the site of Jesus' tomb.

No local historian was around to record the Bar-Kokhba Revolt, unlike the case with the First Jewish Revolt of 66–70 A.D., which was witnessed by the Jewish soldier and writer Flavius Josephus (discussed in the next chapter). As a result, much less is known about it. The *casus belli* of the revolt is not entirely clear from the ancient historians who do refer to it. In the fourth century, Epiphanius of Salamis seemed to suggest that it was Hadrian's decision in 130 (although Epiphanius dated the decision to 117) to rebuild Jerusalem as a Roman city that led to the revolt.[13] According to Dio Cassius, the spark was ignited by Hadrian erecting a temple to Jupiter (Zeus) on the Temple Mount,[14] although Dio, too, indicates that Hadrian founded the new Roman city before the revolt.[15]

Other accounts indicate that Hadrian's decision to build a new Roman city on the site of Jerusalem was a result of the revolt, rather than its cause. Perhaps Hadrian made his decision in 130 but actually carried it out after suppressing the revolt.[16] Some say, however, that it was Hadrian's prohibition of circumcision that eventually led to the Second Jewish Revolt.

In any event, Hadrian did rebuild the city after the revolt was suppressed. To purge any reference to its previous existence as a Jewish city, Hadrian gave it a new name—Aelia Capitolina—and conferred on it the status of a Roman colony.[17] Aelia was from his own name: Publius Aelius Traianus Hadrianus. Capitolina refers to the three Capitoline gods: Jupiter, Juno and Minerva. (Hadrian also changed the name of the country from Judaea to Palaestina.) Jews were barred by imperial edict from entering Aelia, except once a year, when they were allowed to mourn the loss of their Temple on the Temple Mount on the traditional date of its destruction (Tisha b'Av) both by the Babylonians and later by the Romans.[18]

But that is getting a little ahead of the story. For a time the Bar-Kokhba Revolt was successful. The rebels may even have controlled Jerusalem.[19] It is possible that at this time the Jews began to rebuild their Temple, although the evidence for this is both obscure and late. There are references in rabbinic literature to *Hadrian* destroying the Temple. The same reference appears in an incomplete Christian manuscript known as the *Chronicon Paschale*. Do these references really mean to refer to *Titus's* destruction 70 years earlier? Or do they refer to a Temple that the Jews had begun to build while they controlled Jerusalem near the beginning of the Second Jewish Revolt and that Hadrian really did destroy? Further, the apostate emperor Julian (fourth century), about whom we shall hear more later, refers to *three* destructions of the Temple.[20] It was of course destroyed by the Babylonians in the sixth century B.C. and again by the Romans in 70 A.D. But what is the third destruction? Perhaps it was the Temple the Jews tried to build during the Second Jewish Revolt against Rome.

Some early sources refer to three destructions of the Jewish Temple. This coin minted by the rebels in the third year of the Second Revolt depicts the façade of a temple and what appears to be the Ark of the Covenant inside. Is this only the destroyed Temple the rebels hoped to rebuild, or did they actually begin construction of a third Temple, which was then destroyed by Hadrian?

Another bit of evidence that is often cited in this regard is a coin minted by the rebels that pictures the entrance to the Temple. Was this a depiction of the Temple that had been there? Or the Temple that the rebels had started to build at the beginning of the Second Jewish Revolt? Or the Temple they hoped to build?[21] Whether or not the beginning of a Jewish Temple was on the Temple Mount during the Second Jewish Revolt, it is clear that it was not there at the end of the revolt.

What did Hadrian construct on the Temple Mount as part of Aelia Capitolina? Scholars are not of one mind. And again the ancient sources are obscure and sometimes in conflict.[22] According to Dio Cassius, Hadrian built a temple to Jupiter on what had been the Temple Mount. Most scholars tend to rely on this report; as one scholar has observed, Hadrian built this temple to Jupiter as "a visible symbol of the termination of all Jewish hopes for the restoration of their sanctuary."[23] A coin Hadrian minted in 131 A.D. is said to depict "the façade of the temple of Jupiter that was planned for erection on the Temple Mount."[24] But a plausible case can also be made for locating this temple at the site of the Holy Sepulchre, based on the report of Jerome in the fourth century.[25]

In any event, Hadrian erected an equestrian statue of himself on the Temple Mount. The anonymous fourth-century pilgrim known only as the Bordeaux Pilgrim reports that he saw two statues of Hadrian on the Temple Mount when he visited the site.[26] The Bordeaux Pilgrim probably mistakenly identified the second statue; Hadrian's successor, Antoninus Pius (138–161 A.D.), probably added an equestrian statue of himself, which the Bordeaux Pilgrim saw.[27]

An inscription, probably from the base of this statue, has been discovered in secondary use in the southern wall of the Temple Mount. This stone—engraved with an inscription—can be located in the southern wall of the Temple Mount by the Double Gate near a medieval wall that juts out at a right angle. Just to the right of this medieval wall on the southern wall is an applied ornate lintel from the Omayyad period and above that is a decoration of the same artistic quality forming a straight line. Just above and to the right of this straight-line Omayyad decoration is a stone bearing an upside-down Latin inscription. It is clearly legible:

IMP[ERATORI] CAES[ARI]
TITO AEL[IO] HADRIANO
ANTONINO AUG[USTO] PIO
P[ATRI] P[ATRIAE] PONTIF[ICI] AUGUR[I]
D[ECRETO] D[ECURIONUM][28]

To the Emperor Caesar
Titus Aelius Hadrianus
Antoninus Augustus Pius
Father of the Fatherland, Pontifex Augur
By Decree of the Decurions

It is quite possible that the Bordeaux Pilgrim saw this inscription when it was part of a statue on the Temple Mount.[29] But he misread it. That is why he thought there were two statues of Hadrian on the Temple Mount. Antoninus had been adopted by Hadrian and named as his successor in 138 A.D. Thus, Antoninus's name included the name of Hadrian. The Bordeaux Pilgrim apparently looked only at the first two lines and concluded that it was a second statue of Hadrian. Both had a thick beard and looked much alike when they were older.

Hadrian adopted Antoninus Pius (pictured here) and named him his successor as Roman emperor in 138 A.D. Like Hadrian, Antoninus may have erected an equestrian statue of himself on the Temple Mount. That statue was seen (though incorrectly identified) by the Bordeaux Pilgrim in the fourth century.

If the Bordeaux Pilgrim had looked more carefully at the third line, he would have realized that the statue portrayed Antoninus. Some modern scholars have made the same mistake and read the inscription in secondary use as referring to Hadrian instead of Antoninus.[30] They apparently focused on the name Hadrianus, ignoring the following name, Antoninus.

Between 1948 and 1967 the Old City of Jerusalem, including the Temple Mount, was controlled by Jordan. Soon after the Six-Day War of 1967, which gave Israel control over the West Bank and all of Jerusalem, Hebrew University archaeologist Benjamin Mazar opened excavations in the area south and southwest of the Temple Mount. The dig lasted for ten years. Among his many discoveries were fragments of statues from Aelia Capitolina.[31]

One fragment came from a statue of a goddess. It bears a dedicatory inscription to a Roman citizen named Valeria Emiliana. Although the fragments clearly do not come from the imperial statues seen by the Bordeaux Pilgrim, they do suggest the presence of a nearby Roman temple.[32]

Hadrian may also have transferred the camp of the Tenth Legion from Jerusalem's southwestern hill, where they had billeted since 70 A.D.,[33] to the Temple Mount—at least that is the argument of archaeologist Eilat Mazar, who is completing the report on her now-deceased grandfather Benjamin Mazar's excavation at the southern wall of the Temple Mount. According to Eilat Mazar, Hadrian would not leave the Temple Mount abandoned for long considering its strategic importance. He did not want to take any chance of a resurgence of

Only a small portion of the Double Gate on the southern wall of the Temple Mount is still visible from the outside (far left). Just above and to the right of an applied ornate lintel (left) from the Omayyad period (the rest is hidden by a perpendicular wall built by Crusaders) is a stone with an upside-down Latin inscription (above). This block bears the full name of the emperor Antoninus Pius and has been identified as probably the base of the statue that Antoninus erected on the Temple Mount. Since Antoninus was adopted by Hadrian, his name includes the family name Aelius Hadrianus, which has led many (including some scholars) mistakenly to believe that the inscription refers to Hadrian.

Jewish nationalism. Even a temple to Jupiter and a statue of the emperor would not have been enough to protect the Temple Mount. Mazar locates a wall south of the Temple Mount that she believes enclosed an extension of the Roman camp in that area. Inside the camp, archaeologists found a military bathhouse and a bakery. (Excavation on the Temple Mount itself, of course, is impossible.) The two units of the camp—that on the Temple Mount and the extension south of the Temple Mount—functioned as a single unit. Mazar finds archaeological support for her position in the discovery of 192 coins from Hadrian's Aelia Capitolina during the excavations at the foot of the Temple Mount. Only six such coins were found on the southwestern hill, the site of the earlier Roman encampment. Many Roman dice were also found south of the Temple Mount,

Archaeologist Eilat Mazar believes that when Hadrian rebuilt the city as Aelia Capitolina, he moved the camp of the Tenth Roman Legion from the western end of the city to the Temple Mount. Excavations south and southwest of the Temple Mount revealed several finds to support Mazar's claim, including numerous Aelia Capitolina coins (see p. 46), brick fragments impressed with the Tenth Legion's stamp (see p. 35), a bronze soldier figurine, a gemstone depicting Mars, the Roman god of war, and Roman dice probably used by the Roman soldiers in their games.

presumably used by soldiers in their games. Finally, the excavators also found 240 fragments of broken bricks impressed with the stamp of the Tenth Roman Legion (see photo, p. 35). Eilat Mazar regards this move to the Temple Mount as a central feature of Hadrian's redesign of the city and a direct response to the threat of another Jewish takeover.[34]

Whatever the Romans built on the Temple Mount—whether a temple, statues of the emperor or barracks—we never hear of them again. This is a puzzle. We have no idea what happened to the temple of Jupiter (if it was once there on the

Temple Mount) or to the statues of Hadrian and Antoninus (with the exception of the inscription in the southern wall of the Temple Mount), or who destroyed them. This is just one of the many mysteries with which Jerusalem abounds.

One possibility is that the Jews destroyed them when, for a brief moment in the early fourth century, they received permission to rebuild their Temple—from the new emperor, no less.

In 312 A.D., Constantine, soon to become emperor of the western Roman empire, defeated his rival at the battle of Milvian Bridge, near Rome. Before the battle, according to tradition, he saw a vision of a flaming cross (or the *chi-rho*, the first two Greek letters in the word "Christ") in the sky inscribed, "In this sign shall you conquer." Pursuant thereto, Constantine placed the Christian monogram on his soldiers' shields, thus ensuring his victory. Constantine soon became a Christian devotee, although he was not formally baptized until he lay on his death bed in 337.

In 324, Constantine defeated his rival in the east and thus became sole emperor of the Roman empire. Christianity was declared a licit religion, and Christians became Roman citizens. Within a generation Christianity would become the leading religion of the Roman empire.

From Constantine's time until the Muslim conquest in 638, Christians dominated Jerusalem, except for two brief interludes. The first came in 361, when Constantine's nephew Julian, known as the Apostate, was proclaimed emperor. As much as Constantine had favored Christianity, so much did Julian hate it. Greatly influenced by Greek philosophy, Julian regarded Christianity's worship of Jesus as unacceptable. (He called Christianity a "disease" and Christians "demented.") Judaism, like other religions of the time, had involved the offering of sacrifices when its Temple stood; thus, Julian regarded Judaism as similar to pagan religions, except that the Jews believed in only one God. As one scholar put it, "Julian, as other Hellenic statesmen and writers, held that the Jews were entitled as a nation to an 'ethnic' god of their own. Him they should serve and worship just as other nations should serve and worship their national gods."[35]

Shortly before he embarked on a campaign against the Persians, Julian annulled the anti-Jewish decrees of his predecessors and announced that he would allow the Jews to rebuild their Temple, where they could again offer sacrifices and where he himself would join them in worship. In one of his surviving letters, he writes that "even now the Temple is being raised again." According to the Latin historian Ammianus Marcellinus, Julian even arranged for the money and the building materials for the Temple. Jews from the diaspora also contributed to the effort. One Christian author wrote that the Jews felt as if the Messiah had come.[36] For generations Jews had firmly believed that the Temple would be restored and Jerusalem rebuilt when the Messiah came to place a descendant of David on the throne.

The first phase of the project, according to several Christian authors who later described it, required digging up the foundations of the previous Jewish Temple, which the new project was designed to replace. Apparently, these foundations still existed at the time. The Christian writers who described this work took glee in telling of the Jews who were destroying the remnants of their own Temple.[37]

The entire project foundered, however, when Julian was killed in a skirmish with the Persians, ending his short reign in 363. One tradition holds that the spear that mortally wounded him was flung by one of his own soldiers—a Christian.[38]

A somewhat different account of this Jewish effort at rebuilding the Temple is provided by a church historian from Gaza, Salaman Hermias Sozomen, who wrote in the fifth century:

> The Jews entered upon the undertaking without reflecting that, according to the prediction of the holy prophets, it could not be accomplished. They sought out the most skillful artisans, collected materials, cleared the ground, and entered so earnestly upon the task that even the women carried heaps of earth and brought their necklaces and female ornaments toward defraying the expense.[39]

Sozomen describes the clearing of the site: "When they removed the remains of the former building, they dug up the ground and cleared away its foundation." (This seemingly indicates what was on the Temple Mount at the time—and what was *not* there: no Roman buildings or statues. What happened to them?)

The Jewish project ceased, however, Sozomen tells us, "when fire burst suddenly from the foundations of the Temple and consumed several of the workmen."[40] This was not the worst of it. Repeated earthquakes also impeded and destroyed the work. And everything that was built during the day collapsed at night.

> A more tangible and still more extraordinary prodigy ensued: suddenly the sign of the cross appeared spontaneously on the garments of the persons engaged in the undertaking ... Many were hence led to confess that Christ is God and that the rebuilding of the Temple was not pleasing to Him ... If one does not feel disposed to believe my narrative, let him go and be convinced by those who heard the facts I have related from the eyewitnesses, for they are still alive. Let him inquire also of the Jews and pagans who left the work in an incomplete state.[41]

So the project was aborted, either for the reason Sozomen suggests or due to Julian's death at the hands of the Persians and his replacement by a pro-Christian emperor. The reader can choose between these explanations.

Christianity became the religion of the Roman empire in the fourth century A.D., during the reign of the emperor Constantine. Constantine's nephew Julian (pictured here) became emperor in 361 A.D. Known as the Apostate, Julian despised Christianity and revoked the anti-Jewish decrees of his predecessors. He even authorized the Jews to rebuild their Temple.

During his excavations following the 1967 Six-Day War, Benjamin Mazar also excavated part of the surviving western wall of the Temple Mount, where he discovered a Hebrew inscription he believed to be from the time of Julian carved on the wall, a paraphrase of a line from the prophet Isaiah that may refer to this rebuilding effort during his reign as emperor. The inscription reads: "You shall see and your heart shall rejoice. Their bones shall flourish like grass" (see Isaiah 66:14). In the Bible, this prophetic verse appears in the context of an apocalyptic vision of restoration: "The power of the Lord shall be revealed ... All flesh shall come to worship, sayeth the Lord." Was this inscription engraved by the Jewish builders in the time of Julian to commemorate their effort to rebuild the Temple? Mazar suggested that it was.

A nice story. But the most recent excavators of this area, Ronny Reich and Ya'acov Billig, disagree. Reich points out that instead of "your" bones, as Isaiah

has it, the inscription refers to "their" bones. Nearly 4 feet below the inscription, Reich and Billig discovered between 30 and 40 burials. Reich believes the inscription refers to the bones in these burials, which he dates to approximately the tenth century A.D. If this is true and the inscription does refer to these burials, it can be no earlier than the tenth century.[42]

In any event, Julian died a widower and childless. His successor, Jovian, annulled Julian's anti-Christian decrees and restored Christianity as the religion of the Roman empire. Who knows what the course of history would have been had Julian not been killed?

Was a Roman temple of Jupiter still on the Temple Mount when the Jews started to rebuild their Temple? What about the statues of Hadrian and Antoninus? The ancient sources provide no answer, even though this period, the Byzantine period, saw the flowering of Christian pilgrimage to the Holy Land and many of these travelers' accounts have been preserved. As we noted, the Bordeaux Pilgrim observed that two statues of Hadrian were still there on his visit to the

During excavations along the western wall of the Temple Mount, archaeologist Benjamin Mazar discovered an inscription that he believed was inspired by the brief effort to rebuild the Temple during the reign of Julian the Apostate. The inscription (a paraphrase of Isaiah 66:14) reads: "You shall see and your heart shall rejoice. Their limbs shall flourish like grass." The project was cut short when Julian died in 363 A.D. and was succeeded by a pro-Christian emperor.

Temple Mount, but that was in 333. We have no idea whether they survived the attempt to rebuild the Temple during Julian's short reign in 363. One commentator suggests that Byzantine Christians would long ago have removed the pagan structure and statues on the Temple Mount and that the foundations the Jews were rooting out in preparation for their new Temple were those of the pagan Roman temple of Jupiter, not the Jewish Temple destroyed by the Romans in 70 A.D.[43]

Strangely, although pilgrims flocked to the Holy Land and especially Jerusalem during the Byzantine period, the Temple Mount does not seem to have been on the standard itinerary. The many surviving pilgrim travelogues barely mention the Temple Mount. The Bordeaux Pilgrim reports having seen a stone thought to be the *Even Shetiyah*, the "Foundation Stone" marking the spot where the Holy of Holies, the innermost chamber of the Temple, had stood.[44] But he tells us little else about what was—or was not—there.

The church father Eusebius (c. 265–340) reports that he saw remains of the sanctuary on the Temple Mount. Otherwise, it was bare. "After the pollution caused by the murder of the Lord, [the Temple Mount] experienced the last extremity of desolation and paid the penalty for the crime of its impious inhabitants."[45]

John Chrysostom (c. 347–407), perhaps speaking of the Jewish attempt to rebuild the Temple during Julian's reign, relates that the Jews were uncovering "the foundations [of the sanctuary] by removing masses of earth ... You can see the bared foundations if you visit Jerusalem now."

Jerome (c. 375–420), who lived in Bethlehem and translated the Bible (both the Old and New Testaments) into Latin (the Vulgate), visited the site of the Temple Mount and refers only to the "ruins" of the Temple:

> Right to this present day those faithless people who killed the servant of God and even, most terribly, the Son of God himself, are banned from entering Jerusalem except for weeping, to let them attempt to buy back at the price of their tears the city they once sold for the blood of Christ and that not even their tears be free. You can see with your own eyes on [the anniversary of] the day that Jerusalem was captured and destroyed by the Romans, a piteous crowd that comes together, woebegone women and old men weighted down with rags and years, all of them showing forth in their clothes and their bodies the wrath of God. That mob of wretches congregates, and while the manger of the Lord sparkles, the Church of His Resurrection glows, and the banner of His Cross shines forth from the Mount of Olives, those miserable people groan over the ruins of their Temple ... They groan over the ashes of the sanctuary, the destroyed altar.[46]

The Pilgrim of Piacenza (sixth century) also mentions the ruins of the Temple of Solomon on the Temple Mount.

In the sixth-century Madaba Map, the Church of the Holy Sepulchre is located in the center of the city of Jerusalem. By contrast, only a line of brown tesserae perhaps indicates the empty area on the Temple Mount.[47] Other interpreters say that the Temple Mount has been omitted from the Madaba Map.[48] In either event, the treatment of the Temple Mount on the Madaba Map tellingly reflects the attitude of the Christian world toward the site in the Byzantine period.

The anonymous sixth-century Christian pilgrim whose work is preserved in two fragments known as the *Brevarius* tells us, "There is nothing left there [where Solomon built the Temple] apart from a single cave."[49] This is probably the cave, still to be visited, under the rock of the Dome of the Rock.

That Christian pilgrims would pay but scant attention to the Temple Mount seems odd since the Gospels place Jesus there on more than one occasion and the purpose of the pilgrimage visits was to stand where the events in the Gospels occurred. What accounts for this anomaly? Two related reasons: First, for Christians, that nothing was to be seen on the Temple Mount was a fulfillment of Jesus' prophecy, nearly identical in the Gospels of Matthew, Mark and Luke, that the Temple would be destroyed and "not one stone shall be left here standing upon another that will not be thrown down."[50] As Meir Ben-Dov has observed: "It was important to the Byzantines that the [Temple Mount] remain in ruins as tangible evidence that Jesus' prophecy of the Temple's destruction had been borne out."[51] According to an Islamic account, the Temple Mount area was covered by rubble so high during the Byzantine period that the exact spot where the Temple stood could not be identified. In order to build the Dome of the Rock on the same spot, a certain Jewish convert named Ka'b al-Ahbar was asked to locate where the Temple would have stood based on Jewish tradition.[52] According to another Islamic account, the Christians lost Jerusalem to the Muslims because of the unspeakable sin committed against the Temple site by the Christians: They disgraced it by collecting menstrual napkins of the women of Constantinople and throwing them on the site of the Jewish Temple.[53]

Perhaps another reason Christians were not much concerned with the Temple Mount was because, as recounted in the last chapter, they transferred numerous traditions that Jews had previously associated with their Temple to the Church of the Holy Sepulchre.

Moreover, as Christianity separated from Judaism it replaced the function of the Temple with the Holy Spirit. In these terms, "The problem with the Temple is not only that it is obsolete but also that it was an act of rebellion and even idolatry ... Heaven and earth have [now] met in the moment of the death of a crucified man and not in tabernacle or Temple ... The Temple had become superfluous as a locus of the divine presence."[54]

As noted earlier, from Constantine's time until the Muslim conquest in 638, Christians dominated Jerusalem, except for two brief interludes. The first came in 363 when Julian gave the Jews permission to rebuild their Temple. The second came less than a quarter century before the Muslim conquest put an end to Byzantine Jerusalem. In 614, the Byzantines' traditional enemy, the Persians, conquered Jerusalem. The Christians defended themselves bravely for 20 days, but, in the words of Antiochus Strategius, a Jerusalem monk who was an eyewitness, the Persians "shot from their ballistas with such violence that on the twenty-first day they broke down the city wall. Thereupon the evil foemen entered the city in great fury, like infuriated wild beasts and irritated serpents ... [They] slew all whom they found. Like mad dogs they tore with their teeth the flesh of the faithful."[55]

The Jews, who had been banned from the city since Hadrian's decree nearly 400 years earlier, were allied with the Persians, which is hardly surprising since, during the period of Christian domination, the Jews had been, in the words of one scholar, "repressed ... with increasing ferocity."[56] In gratitude for their support, the Persians handed over the city to the Jews.[57]

According to the monk Strategius, the Jews purchased Christian captives and then sacrificed them:

> The Jews, enemies of the truth and haters of Christ, when they perceived that the Christians were given over into the hands of the enemy, rejoiced exceedingly because they detested the Christians ... when the unclean Jews saw the steadfast uprightness of the [imprisoned] Christians and their immovable faith, they were agitated with lively ire, like evil beasts, and thereupon imagined another plot. As of old, they bought the Lord from the Jews with silver, so they purchased Christians out of the reservoir; for they gave the Persians silver and they bought a Christian and slew him like a sheep.[58]

A popular apocalyptic vision known as the Book of Zerubbabel written at this time claims that the Jewish leader "made sacrifices." This is consistent with the implication of the account of Strategius: If true, Jews were not making human sacrifices, but perhaps they were restoring animal sacrifice. And if animal sacrifices were offered, as one modern scholar has observed, "we can only assume that that occurred in the only place possible, atop the Temple Mount."[59] According to archaeologist and historian Michael Avi-Yonah, "Apparently Temple services

The Persians ruled Jerusalem for a short time at the beginning of the seventh century. The Christian emperor Heraclius re-took the city in 629, bringing back with him the "True Cross" that had been captured by the Persians. This coin, minted in 641 includes a portrait of Heraclius with his son Constantine. The reverse probably depicts the True Cross that Heraclius returned to Jerusalem.

were resumed for the third time after the destruction of the Temple, following previous efforts under Bar Kokhba and Julian."[60]

Jewish revival in Jerusalem lasted only for a brief three-year period, from 614 to 617. At that point, for complicated political reasons, the Persians had a change of heart. The many contemporary Christian authors attribute the reversal simply to divine Providence. The best overall explanation that I have seen is that when the Persians needed the Jews during the war, they supported their cause and rewarded them at the end of the war; but the Persians also needed to keep the peace in their vast empire afterward—and this involved dealing with the Christian majority. So the Persians betrayed the Jews, expelled them from Jerusalem[61] and returned the city to Christian rule. Avi-Yonah, an Israeli writing in modern Jerusalem, calls this "one of the most tragic moments in the history of our nation." The Persian betrayal put an end to the national hope of the Jews for centuries—until modern Zionism relit it.[62]

Whether the Jews made any effort to rebuild their Temple during this three-year period, we will probably never know for sure, although if they offered sacrifices on the Temple Mount, they surely had plans to rebuild the Temple. To say anything further would be sheer speculation.

Persian rule did not last long. Internal disputes soon weakened the Persians, and the Christian Byzantine emperor Heraclius easily negotiated the Persian evacuation of Byzantine provinces. In 629 at the head of a triumphal procession, Heraclius made his entry into Jerusalem, bringing back with him the "True Cross," which had been captured by the Persians. He placed it, along with other relics, in the Church of the Holy Sepulchre.

It is clear that throughout the Roman and Byzantine periods, the Temple Mount was considered to be the site of the destroyed Jewish Temple. Even when Jews were permitted to enter the city only to mourn the destruction of the Temple, it was there that they did so.

Five years after Heraclius's triumphal entry into the Holy City, a new enemy appeared. In 634, the Arab invasion of the Byzantine empire began. One Byzantine city after another submitted to the invaders. By 637 the Arabs were at the gates of Jerusalem. After a nine-month siege, the city surrendered in 638. Jerusalem was now a Muslim city.

IV

Herod's Temple

N OT A STONE FROM THE MAGNIFICENT TEMPLE BUILT BY KING HEROD—known in Jewish tradition as the Second Temple—has been positively identified. Nevertheless, there can be no doubt whatever that it once stood in all its splendor on Jerusalem's Temple Mount. We know it from the first-century A.D. historian Josephus, who saw it with his own eyes. We know it from the detailed references in tractates of the Mishnah, an early rabbinic compilation, and from other rabbinic texts. We know it from the New Testament. We know it from Roman texts—they destroyed it. And, perhaps most indubitably, we know it from archaeological evidence.

As one modern scholar has remarked, "There can be no reasonable doubt that Herod's Temple occupied exactly the same holy site as its predecessors."[1]

In the words of a rabbinic sage: "He who has not seen the Temple of Herod has never seen a beautiful building."[2] Made of gleaming limestone, the entire façade was plated with gold. According to Josephus, when the sun shone upon it at sunrise, people had to avert their eyes lest they be blinded. The lower sections of the other walls were also plated with gold, above which was white limestone. Looking at it from a distance, it was said to look like a snow-clad mountain, "for all that was not overlaid with gold was of purist white."[3]

Josephus—or Flavius Josephus, as he was later known in Rome—was one of the most colorful figures on the ancient stage. For many years, modern Israelis held a debate as to whether or not Josephus was a traitor to the Jewish cause. Born in Jerusalem to a priestly family that was related to the ruling dynasty in Judea, Josephus was appointed by the Sanhedrin (the Jewish judicial authority)

Although not a single stone of Herod's Temple—known as the Second Temple—has been conclusively identified, it certainly stood atop the Temple Mount. This model, created under the supervision of Israeli scholar Michael Avi-Yonah and formerly located on the grounds of the Holy Land Hotel, is based on detailed accounts of the Temple's appearance in the writings of Josephus and the Mishnah.

as commander of the Jewish forces in Galilee during the First Jewish Revolt against Rome (66–70 A.D.). The decisive battle in the region occurred at the beginning of the revolt, at Jotapata, with Josephus in command. For 40 days, Josephus defended the city from the Roman general Vespasian. When the city finally fell, Josephus and 40 of his men fled to a cave, as he relates the story. There, each man resolved to slay his companion rather than be taken captive. When all but two of the men had, in effect, committed suicide, Josephus and the other man decided to surrender. So Josephus.

When he was brought before the Roman commander, Josephus foretold that Vespasian would become the future emperor, a prediction that would soon prove true. When it did, Josephus was released from his chains and taken to Rome. Ultimately he went back to Judea with the new Roman commander, Vespasian's son Titus, who led the attack on Jerusalem. There Josephus tried on several occasions to convince the Jewish rebels to lay down their arms, but he was unsuccessful. He was with Titus when he captured the city and burned the Temple.

After Jerusalem fell, Josephus returned to Rome, where he was granted citizenship and a pension. The emperor even allowed Josephus to live in the urban palace compound. There, under the emperor's patronage, he composed his most famous work, *The Jewish War*, an account of the First Jewish Revolt against Rome. In some respects the work is apologetic. Most Jews, according to Josephus, did not support the revolt. The Romans are often portrayed as pure and unsullied. Titus and Vespasian refrain from unnecessary cruelty and are even anxious to save the Jews. According to Josephus, Titus opposed the Roman destruction of the Temple.[4] Modern scholars say this is probably not true. Josephus was writing with "an apologetic purpose of glorifying his hero for his humanity."[5] On the other hand, Josephus does mourn over the destruction of Jerusalem and describes the soul-gripping bravery of the rebel holdouts on Masada.

As a native Jerusalemite who accompanied the Roman forces when they besieged the city and burned the Temple, Josephus was in an excellent position to know the details of the Temple as it existed at the time. And there is no reason to doubt the accuracy of his references to the Temple, even though he was admittedly writing under the patronage of the Roman emperor. There would be

Vespasian (pictured here) was a Roman general in Judea when the First Jewish Revolt broke out in 66 A.D. In 69 A.D. he returned to Rome and became emperor. He then appointed his son Titus as the new Roman commander against the rebel forces.

no reason for him to falsify his description of the most holy site in Judaism.

Those who regard Josephus as a traitor recall that he deserted his people in its hour of need, defected to the Romans and then became an apologist for their enemy. In his defense, however, it is argued that he fought against the Romans as long as resistance was a viable alternative and then sought to assure the future of his people in the only way possible—by submission to Rome.

Somewhat paradoxically, Josephus's works were not preserved by the Jewish community; we must thank the Christian church for their survival. In the world of late antiquity, Josephus was often compared to the Roman author Livy, and *The Jewish War* was translated into Latin as early as the fourth century. (There is some debate as to whether Josephus wrote two versions of *The Jewish War*, one in his native Aramaic and the other in Greek. If so, the Aramaic version has not survived.)

The classic *Encyclopaedia Judaica* describes *The Jewish War* in this way: "Josephus ranks among the leading writers in world literature. His style is epic, his portrayals plastic, his gift of description captivates the readers alike by its fidelity and its colorful presentation."[6]

In *The Jewish War*, Josephus does not actually describe the Temple, but only refers to it in relating how the Romans burned and destroyed it. (He describes the Temple in detail in a later work, which we will come to in a moment.) But the passing references to the Temple are all the more reliable simply because these details are not at all significant to, or required by, his narrative.

Moreover, he was in an excellent position to know these details, for he describes the Roman progress day by day and, sometimes, hour by hour. He was there.

Regarding the strength of the Temple walls, Josephus tells us that Roman battering rams pounded it for six days "without ceasing," but the battering rams made no impression on the wall. When the Romans set the gates to the Temple compound ablaze, the silver with which they were covered carried the fire to the wood beneath. Josephus also describes what a difficult time the Roman soldiers had in burning the cloisters that enclosed the Temple building; they ended up burning them piece by piece. Finally, the defending Jews shut themselves up in the inner court of the Temple. In the end, flames burst out of the holy Temple itself.

Josephus concludes:

> Anyone would justly lament the destruction of such a work as this was, since it was the most admirable of all the works that we have seen or heard of, both for its curious structure and its magnitude, and also for the vast wealth bestowed upon it, as well as for the glorious reputation it had for its holiness.[7]

The inner enclosure wall (called the soreg) of the Herodian Temple complex separated the outer courts from the inner precincts into which only Jews were allowed. Signs such as this one were posted, in Greek, at regular intervals along the soreg, warning non-Jews not to enter, on penalty of death. The part of the sign that has been recovered is shaded in the reconstruction of the entire inscription below.

L. RITMEYER
© RAD 2001

Josephus was a little over 40 years old in 79 or 80 A.D., when he wrote *The Jewish War*. He wrote another major opus, completed when he was 56, called *Antiquities of the Jews*, a history of his people addressed to the non-Jewish world. *Antiquities* has little of the literary quality of *The Jewish War*, but it does recite Jewish history as Josephus understood it at the time. And it does contain a detailed description of Herod's Temple and Temple Mount.[8]

Here, too, Josephus calls Herod's Temple "a very great work ... a work of the greatest piety and excellence." Josephus tells us that Herod began work on the Temple in the 18th year of his reign and that the building was completed in less than a year and a half; the entire Temple Mount complex, however, was not completed until after Herod's death in 4 B.C. Josephus describes the gates to the Temple compound, the entrance doors to the Temple "adorned with embroidered veils" and a secret passageway that led from the inner Temple to the Antonia fortress, which protected the northwestern corner of the Temple Mount, the only approach to the Temple Mount not protected by a steep valley. He also describes the cloisters or porticoes outside the Temple. According to Josephus, when the Temple was under construction, it never rained during the day, but only at night, so as not to interfere with the work.

One detail especially supports the reliability of Josephus's description: Josephus tells us that an inner enclosure wall, or balustrade (*soreg*, in Hebrew), 4.5 feet high enclosed the Temple and its courts on all four sides, separating the area where Gentiles were permitted (the Court of the Gentiles) from the inner areas where only Jews were permitted. Signs were posted on the *soreg* warning non-Jews from going farther on pain of death.[9] These signs were posted at

A reconstruction by architect Leen Ritmeyer of Herod's Temple Mount, as it probably looked in the mid-first century A.D. The major features include: (1) the Temple, (2) the Royal Stoa, (3) the southern monumental staircase, (4) the Triple Gate, (5) the Double Gate, (6) Barclay's Gate, (7) Robinson's arch supporting a monumental staircase, (8) Wilson's Arch, (9) the Western Wall, (10) the place of the trumpeting and (11) the Antonia fortress.

regular intervals on the stone-lattice balustrade. In 1870, one of these signs—inscribed in Greek—was discovered by the French scholar Charles Clermont-Ganneau approximately 160 feet north of the Temple compound.[10] It is now in the Archaeological Museum in Istanbul. Fragments of another one of these signs—also in Greek—was found in 1935 just outside the wall of the Old City near Lions (St. Stephen's) Gate, a mere hundred yards or so from where it was originally posted.[11] The inscription, now in the Rockefeller Museum in Jerusalem, is engraved on limestone; the missing parts have now been reconstructed on the basis of the one in the Istanbul museum. It reads: "No foreigner may enter within the balustrade and enclosure that surround the Temple. Anyone apprehended shall have himself to blame for his consequent death."

Rabbinic works also supply information about the Temple. The most important is the Mishnah, the earliest collection of rabbinic law. It was compiled (redacted) by Rabbi Judah ha-Nasi (Judah the Prince, known in Jewish parlance simply as "Rabbi") in about 200 A.D. The Mishnah forms the core of the Talmud, a compilation produced several hundred years later that comments on the Mishnah passage by passage. Both Josephus and the Mishnah are sometimes vague and ambiguous, and they are not always in agreement, but it is clear that they are describing the same complex, although perhaps from a different time.[12]

The two Mishnah tractates relevant to our discussion, *Middot* and *Tamid*, are thought to be among the oldest portions of the Mishnah. This fact is of course important because it places them closer to the time when Herod's Temple still stood on the Temple Mount.

Moreover, the literary form of these tractates is different from most of the Mishnah: *Middot* and *Tamid* consist primarily of descriptions, rather than rabbinic discussions, observations and debates (although there is no denying that they also contain legendary exaggerations; for example, the odor from the burning incense at the Temple could supposedly be smelled as far from Jerusalem as Jericho—that's 15 miles away!).[13]

Middot, which means "dimensions" or "measurements," is devoted to a description of the Temple, perhaps as an illustration of measurements, and reflects detailed familiarity with the structure. It is attributed to Rabbi Eliezer ben Jacob, a sage (*tanna*) who lived when the Temple still stood.

The subject of *Tamid* is the daily whole-offering in the Temple, consisting of a lamb in the morning and in the afternoon. It was made every day of every year. The tractate *Tamid* gives detailed and extensive rules for every aspect of the offering. The name *Tamid* means "continuous" or "always."

It seems to me unlikely that these tractates were preserved by oral means. Rather it would appear that the author of these tractates had preexisting manuals containing all the rules and regulations, quite likely from the days when the

Temple still stood.[14] For example, *Tamid* explains how the Temple priests cast lots to determine which ones would perform the myriad sacrificial tasks: slaughtering the animal, sprinkling the blood on the altar, clearing the inner altar of ashes, trimming the candlestick, taking the animal up the ramp, holding up the head or the foreleg or the hind legs, etc.

Middot describes not only the main Temple building but the dozens of flanking rooms and courtyards and balustrades. For example: "There were five gates to the Temple Mount ... There were seven gates to the Temple Court ... There were four rooms in the Chamber of the Hearth."

All the gates had lintels, except the Tadi Gate, over which two stones leaned against one another, forming a pediment.

These details indicate that *Middot* is based on a preexisting manual written by someone very familiar with the day-to-day activities in the Temple when it stood.

In *Middot* the Temple Mount is said to be a square—500 cubits on each side.* In fact, however, the Herodian Temple Mount is much larger and is trapezoidal in shape, not square. One scholar's suggestion is that the measurement in *Middot* represents the original Solomonic platform; he claims to have found archaeological evidence for this position.[15] Another explanation is that these measurements designate the inner sanctified area on the Temple Mount; that is, the Temple itself and the enclosed courts around it.[16] Another suggestion is that it represents the Hellenistic, pre-Herodian Temple Mount.[17]

One statement in *Middot* especially figures in the debate over precisely where on the Temple Mount the Temple itself was located. According to *Middot*, the largest open space was south of the Temple, the next on the east, third on the north and the smallest on the west. Many scholars have come up with different solutions as to where exactly the Temple stood. The most common proposal is that it was located at the present site of the Dome of the Rock.

All the walls of the Temple Mount were high, except the eastern wall, beyond which can be seen the Kidron Valley and the Mount of Olives. The eastern wall was lower so that the high priest who slaughtered the cow on the Mount of Olives during the ceremony of the burning of the red heifer (its ashes, according to Numbers 19, had a purifying quality) could look directly into the Temple.[18]

Other rabbinic texts refer to the existence of the Temple in different contexts. They are especially reliable because they deal with the Temple only indirectly,

*The cubit (Hebrew, 'amah) was the standard unit of length in biblical times. The name derives from the Latin (and Hebrew) for "elbow" and refers to a measurement based on the distance between the elbow and the fingertips. Scholars disagree about its length, suggesting it measured anywhere between 16 and 26 inches, although most agree the cubit likely equaled about 21 or 22 inches.

The southeast corner of the Temple Mount, from which the drop is the greatest, is most likely the "pinnacle of the Temple" referred to in the Gospels of Matthew and Luke.

there being no reason to prevaricate. For example, in the Tosephta, an early rabbinic text that parallels and supplements the Mishnah, we are told that a group of famous rabbis were sitting "at the top of the stairs at the Temple Mount."

Although there are some discrepancies between the rabbinic texts and Josephus (there are even some discrepancies between Josephus in *War* and *Antiquities*), taken as a whole, all agree on the basic structure of the Temple and its elements.[19]

The New Testament—including all four Gospels—is also filled with reliable references to the Temple. For example, in Matthew 4:5 and Luke 4:9, the devil takes Jesus to "the pinnacle of the Temple," probably a reference to the southeast corner of the Temple Mount platform, from which the drop is the greatest. In Mark 11:15, Matthew 21:12 and Luke 19:45, Jesus himself goes to the Temple and drives out the money-changers and

those who are selling pigeons for sacrifices. He does the same thing at Passover in John 2:13–16. Jesus often goes to the Temple and teaches there (John 18:20; see also John 7:14, 8:2,20). On another occasion, when his disciples point out the huge stones and wonderful buildings of the Temple, Jesus responds, "Do you see these great buildings? There will not be left here one stone upon another that will not be thrown down" (Mark 13:1–2; cf. Matthew 24:1–2; Luke 21:5–6). Whether this is an actual foretelling of the destruction of the Temple or a prediction after the fact is not the point and need not be addressed here. Either way, the reference substantiates the existence of the Temple.

Similarly in the Acts of the Apostles, references to the Temple abound. The apostles attend the Temple together (Acts 2:46) and teach there (Acts 5:21). Peter and John see a beggar asking for alms at the gate of the Temple (Acts 3:1–3). Paul, too, goes to the Temple (Acts 21:26); indeed, he was arrested there (Acts 21:27–30).

Those who deny the existence of the Jewish Temple rely on the fact that not a stone of the Temple itself has survived, but the archaeological evidence from the enclosure wall, gates, staircases and even inscriptions is overwhelming.

The massive retaining wall of the Temple Mount encloses the largest platform of its kind in the ancient world. The area enclosed is nearly 36 acres, large enough to hold about 24 football fields. This is twice as large as the monumental

A view of the Temple Mount from the Mount of Olives. According to Mishnah Parah, a high priest would sacrifice the red heifer (whose ashes are purifying) on the Mount of Olives, where he could look directly into the Temple and the Holy of Holies.

forum in Rome. As *The New Encyclopedia of Archaeological Excavations in the Holy Land* observes, "Something of [the] magnificence [of the Temple Mount complex] is still conveyed by the outer walls."[20] The wall was not simply an enclosure wall to hold the platform or esplanade in place. The walls continued impressively skyward, high above the inner surface level, presumably with towers at the corners.

We can get some idea of what the Temple Mount looked like, but on a much smaller scale, from a Herodian enclosure that has survived almost completely intact in Hebron—at the traditional site of Machpelah, where Abraham, Isaac and Jacob are buried with their respective wives Sarah, Rebecca and Leah. (Rachel, Jacob's other wife, whom he loved, died in childbirth on a journey at "Ephrath—now Bethlehem" [Genesis 35:19] and was buried there.)

The beautifully carved Herodian ashlars (rectangular stones) at Machpelah in Hebron create a perfectly flat surface until about halfway up the side of the enclosure. On the upper half of the wall, broad but shallow pilasters (engaged pillars) interrupt the level surface at regular intervals. All this is easy to see at Machpelah. Not so at the Temple Mount enclosure in Jerusalem: The upper part of the Herodian Temple Mount wall has

This drawing by Count Melchior de Vogüé in the 1860s clearly shows the beginning of a pilaster halfway up the wall in Herod's Temple Mount. Israeli archaeologist Ronny Reich has recently discovered fragments of these architectural elements during excavations at the foot of the Temple Mount enclosure wall.

been destroyed and replaced. However, the Herodian Temple Mount wall was similarly designed: Part of the slanted ashlars (at the point where the pilasters begin above the flat surface) and part of the pilasters themselves are still *in situ* in an inaccessible house adjacent to the wall. They have also been recorded in drawings by the early explorers Claude Conder and Count Melchior de Vogüé in the 1860s. Actual fragments of these elements have been found in Israeli archaeologist Ronny Reich's recent excavations at the foot of the enclosure wall.

The Temple Mount walls are built of easily recognized Herodian ashlars with narrow margins and slightly raised, carefully dressed, flat bosses in the center. The play of light and shade created by the handsomely dressed margins and flat bosses of the ashlars and the pilasters must have created an extraordinarily

This Herodian structure in Hebron marks the traditional site of Machpelah, where the patriarchs and their wives (except Rachel) were buried. It still stands much as it did in Herod's time. Its large, beautifully dressed ashlars and elegant pilasters on the upper half of the walls give us some idea of what the enclosure wall to Herod's Temple Mount looked like with similar ashlars and interspersed pilasters.

beautiful and dramatic picture of the massive walls as the setting sun bathed the scene in a warm umber hue.

The usual stone used for these walls weighs between 2 and 5 tons. Some weigh as much as 100 tons. (The depth of the ashlars has been measured by geoelectric survey.) The largest of the stones—in the so-called Master Course of the western wall—has been calculated to weigh 570 tons![21] It is 42 feet long and nearly 11 feet high (see photo, p. 94). It is at least as thick as it is high.[22]

How these stones were raised into place is a puzzle. Ehud Netzer, Israel's most eminent archaeological architect specializing in this period, confesses he cannot find a reasonable explanation as to how such stones were quarried and transported.[23] The smaller ones could have been transported on wooden rollers;

The remains of a stone quarry in Jerusalem. The drawing at right illustrates the process for quarrying the huge blocks that were then formed into Herodian ashlars. First, channels were carved into the rock, so that the stone remained attached only at the bottom; then, timbers were wedged tightly between the blocks on two sides; finally, water was poured over the timbers, causing them to expand, until the increasing pressure split the blocks off from the rock face below.

from quarries north and west of the city, it's all down hill. But the larger stones would have crushed the wooden rollers. Architectural historian Leen Ritmeyer suggests that a ramp led up to the level of each new course of stones.[24] Another suggestion is that the very large stones were quarried in the round and rolled in that condition to the site where chords were cut off to make a square-shaped stone[25]—but the height and depth of these huge ashlars is not the same, so this solution is questionable. The famous Roman architect Vitruvius describes a crane for lifting stones, but these would hardly work for the larger stones in the Herodian wall of the Temple enclosure.

Before Herod could begin to reconstruct the Temple on a much grander scale, he had to demolish the existing Temple. In Herod's day, the Temple built by the exiles returning from Babylon in the late sixth century B.C. may still have stood.

Josephus tells us that when he was growing up in Jerusalem, people still alive could remember the Temple that Herod demolished. In fact, Josephus tells us, the people were fearful that Herod would not be able to realize his grand design for the Temple Mount. What would happen if he were to demolish the existing Temple and then fail to rebuild it? To allay these fears, Herod promised the people that he would not begin demolition until he had assembled everything needed for the rebuild. And indeed that is what he did: He readied a thousand carts to carry the needed stones; he retained 10,000 of the most skillful workmen; he taught many workmen from priestly families to be stonecutters and others to be carpenters. He even bought ahead of time a thousand priestly garments. In short, he did not begin work until everything was well prepared.

Incidentally, archaeological evidence of one of the proud workmen who built the Temple has been recovered. At this time, the more prominent Jerusalem families were buried in caves; after about a year, when the flesh had desiccated and fallen away, the bones were placed in a limestone box called an ossu-

ary, which was placed back in the cave. Some of these ossuaries are inscribed. One, recovered by Israeli archaeologist Vasilios Tzaferis, is inscribed "Simon, the Temple builder."[26]

Before beginning work on the Temple, Herod needed to create a level surface—and, in its original natural condition, that's just what the area was not. Creating a level surface required building an enclosure wall that could be filled in to make a podium. Herod was not the first to build such a retaining wall in Jerusalem in order to create a Temple Mount. He simply enlarged what had been there before, doubling its size. The old Temple Mount was, for the most part, buried. Herod built new expanded enclosure walls on the west, north and south. The walls on these three sides are Herodian at the base. (The higher parts represent later reconstructions.) He could not extend the eastern border because the eastern wall stood on the edge of the steep western slope of the Kidron Valley. However, he had to extend the eastern wall to the north and south to accommodate (and connect to) the new north and south walls. These extensions of the eastern wall would be marked by what is called a straight joint or seam. Courses of masonry normally overlap each other, substantially strengthening the wall. But when an addition is made to a wall, this creates a straight vertical joint. And such extensions were created on the earlier eastern wall when Herod enlarged the Temple Mount with new walls on the north and south.

The straight joint on the southern part of the eastern wall is easy to see. On the east face of the Temple Mount wall, 106 feet from the southeastern corner is a straight joint at the bottom (original) part of the wall. (The upper masonry

features later reconstructions through which the straight joint no longer extends.) To the left of the straight joint—the addition to the eastern wall—we see pure Herodian masonry. It is easy to recognize the ashlars with narrow margins and slightly raised flat bosses. Each block is snugly aligned with its neighbor so that even a knife blade cannot be inserted in between. No mortar is needed in a Herodian wall like this. To the right of the straight joint is very different masonry.

Herod had another problem in extending the earlier Temple Mount in the southeast corner. There, the land drops off precipitously. To fill that area with soil would be an enormous task, and the walls might not be able to bear the weight of all this fill. So instead, Herod built some immense vaulting, now known as Solomon's Stables. Eighty-eight pillars of characteristic Herodian masonry (although all rebuilt in the Omayyad period) divide this huge area into 12 long, vaulted aisles. In the 12th century, Crusader knights actually stabled their horses among these pillars. They had already given the name *Templum Solomonis* and *Palatium Solomonis* to Al-Aqsa mosque, which stood above their "stables." The stables were officially the stables of the knights of the Temple of Solomon. From this evolved the current designation as Solomon's Stables.

In recent years Solomon's Stables have been in the news. The story is part of the larger story of the recent Islamization of the Temple Mount. As mentioned in a previous chapter, Israel gained control over the Old City of Jerusalem, including the Temple Mount, in 1967, during the Six-Day War. However, a decision was quickly made to allow the Temple Mount to be administered by the Waqf, the Muslim religious trust. In effect, the Waqf has controlled the Temple Mount

since then, even to the exclusion of Israeli authorities. As part of Israel, the Temple Mount is supposedly subject to the state's antiquities laws. The Waqf has consistently violated them with impunity, however. On one occasion, unauthorized excavations for a utility pipe uncovered a wall 6 feet wide that extended for more than 15 feet, built of large Herodian ashlars. It may have been the eastern wall of the Herodian Temple complex. Some of the wall was dismantled and the remainder covered up—all without archaeological supervision. An archaeologist from the Israel Antiquities Authority made some notes and a drawing on a quick, unauthorized visit, but that is the only record we will ever have.

At one point a fringe group brought a lawsuit against the government of Israel and the Waqf to stop the archaeological depredation on the Temple Mount. Israel's Supreme Court found that over the years the Waqf had committed 35 violations of the antiquities laws, destroying important archaeological remains. The Waqf impudently continued its violations even during the pendency of the lawsuit. The court, however, declined to issue an injunction in this politically sensitive area. Although acknowledging that the government had disregarded the Waqf's violations more than was desirable, the court simply expressed its confidence that the Israeli authorities would correct this in the future.[27]

Of course, the Waqf simply ignored the court's decision (the Waqf had refused even to appear in the lawsuit).

All this was simply a prelude to the most egregious violation. In 1999 the Waqf began a major excavation on the Temple Mount to create a new entrance to Solomon's Stables—now named the Marwani Mosque, which occupies the entire area of the stables. One scholar in the *Catholic Biblical Quarterly* referred to "illegal excavations by the Waqf on a massive scale."[28] He noted the "penchant of some Muslim officials for destroying it [archaeological evidence] and covering it up." Thousands of tons of archaeologically rich dirt were excavated. Hundreds of truckloads were dumped into the adjacent Kidron Valley or the municipal dump—all

Herod built an immense vaulting, which was rebuilt with original ashlars during the Arab period, to support his southeastern extension of the Temple Mount. This area was named Solomon's Stables by 12th-century Crusader knights who used the area to stable their horses.

without archaeological supervision and under the eyes of the Israeli authorities. Large areas on the Temple Mount were simply paved over (see photos, pp. 4–5). When Israeli archaeology student Zachi Zweig attempted to recover archaeological remains from the Muslim dump in the Kidron Valley, he was arrested by the order of the Israel Antiquities Authority.

All this may be hard to believe, but it is uncontested. The Israeli authorities have been ordered at the highest levels of government to keep hands off. *The Jerusalem Post* referred to the Israel Antiquities Authority as the "archaeological body nominally charged with supervision at Judaism's holiest site."[29] The article went on to explain that "Israeli archaeologists from the Antiquities Authority have not been carrying out supervision for five years now at the bitterly contested site due to their concern about renewed Palestinian violence at the compound." The Israeli newspaper *Ha'aretz* called the overall Muslim effort "the de-Judaizing of the Temple Mount."[30]

In 2004 Bar-Ilan University archaeologist Gabriel Barkay obtained a permit to sift the dirt excavated by the Waqf and, together with his former student Zachi Zweig and volunteers from around the world, they have been doing that for two years as I write. "The project should have been a government-sponsored initiative in coordination with the Antiquities Authority, but neither wanted to do it," Barkay said.

Thus far Barkay has found pottery from the Bronze Age to modern times, as well as a 3-foot marble column, more than 100 ancient coins as early as the Hellenistic period, arrowheads, several ivory combs, oil lamps and fragments of figurines.[31] Some of the pottery dates to First Temple times, as well as later. The prize find thus far is a bulla (a seal impression) engraved with two lines of Hebrew letters from the First Temple period (see photo, p. 3). Archaeological architect Leen Ritmeyer believes a careful professional excavation of the area might have revealed evidence of the eastern part of the southern wall of the original Temple Mount from the First Temple period.[32]

This broad monumental staircase leading to the southern entrance to the Temple Mount would have accommodated crowds of people during Jewish pilgrimage festivals. The alternating depths of the stair treads forced pilgrims to slow their pace while approaching the holy area.

Recently, Arabs have engraved "Allah" on the eastern wall of the Temple Mount, about 30 feet above the ground.[33] The Arabs got that high by climbing up the scaffolding erected by an Egyptian team adjacent to the eastern wall for the purpose of repairing the wall. (An earlier bulge—on the southern wall—was apparently a result of the illegal excavations on the Temple Mount. Jordan was authorized to repair that bulge.) "They are supposed to be fixing and bolstering the wall, not carving names into the ancient structure," Hebrew University archaeologist Eilat Mazar told the Israeli news service *Arutz Sheva*.

As noted earlier, from 1968 to 1978 Benjamin Mazar of Hebrew University (along with field director Meir Ben-Dov) excavated the area south and southwest of the Temple Mount. One of Mazar's most dramatic finds was a broad monumental staircase of 30 steps leading up to gates in the southern wall of the Temple Mount. One can easily imagine thousands of Jews at the turn of the era crowding up these 30 steps on the three pilgrimage festivals: Passover (Pesach), Weeks or Pentecost (Shavuot) and Tabernacles (Sukkot).

The risers on the steps are quite low, between 7 and 10 inches. The treads on the stairs vary between 12 and 35 inches, alternating between narrow and broad. This variation in the size of the treads forces a person ascending the steps to walk with a slow, measured gait, as if participating in a processional.

Two gateways on the southern wall provided access to the Temple Mount through ascending tunnels that opened onto the Temple Mount. One is known as the Double Gate (with two doorways) and the other as the Triple Gate (with three doorways). Together they are now known as the Huldah Gates (although the name originally applied to gates in an earlier construction of the Temple Mount), in memory of the prophetess who proclaimed the authority of the Scroll of the Law found in the Temple during King Josiah's repair work in the seventh century B.C. (see 2 Kings 22). As suggested by the wide expanse of steps leading to the Double Gate, this gate was for ordinary people—the right (eastern) side for going in and the other side for coming out. The narower staircase leading to the Triple Gate indicates that this gateway was for the priests. As reconstructed by Ritmeyer, the Triple Gate consisted of a high central gateway flanked by two small lower gateways.[34]

A third gate, called the Single Gate, was opened later to give direct access to the stables. It was blocked up after the Crusaders were expelled from the Holy Land and has remained blocked up since then.

Three arches mark the location of the Triple Gate, but these are not original. The only original Herodian stone in these openings is a piece of the doorjamb, sitting on the floor at the bottom of the left side of the left-hand arch. In short, the wall has been destroyed and repaired many times, but fortunately the sole Herodian stone is easily identified by its distinctive character.

Blocked-up archways in the southern wall mark the Triple Gate, which served as one of the main gates to the Temple Mount. The only original Herodian element is part of a doorjamb, visible at the bottom left side of the arch on the far left (see detail).

The original Double Gate is even more difficult to see than the original Triple Gate. It is located west of the Triple Gate, but is substantially concealed by a later perpendicular wall (part of a Crusader addition) that juts out at a right angle from the southern wall of the Temple Mount. Only half of the right-hand entry of the Double Gate is still visible on the outside (to the right of the medieval wall).

Above this half-obscured entry is an ornate, decorative half-arch added in the Omayyad period (661–750 A.D.). The stones from the original Herodian gate are visible just above the applied Omayyad arch (see photos, pp. 50–51). They include a rectangular lintel beneath several large, undecorated, trapezoidal stones that form the Herodian relieving arch of the gateway. Just above this reliev-ing arch (which "relieves" the pressure on the lintel by transferring the weight down the jambs) is another piece of applied Omayyad decoration. Interestingly, the Herodian stones in the gate-way were dismantled and re-erected before the Omayyad decoration was added.

In contrast to the exterior of the Double Gate, the interior, with its glorious decorations, is beautifully pre-served. The inside of the gate is, however, even more difficult to see: It is almost impossible to obtain Muslim permission to enter from the Temple Mount compound, which is the only way in. Just inside the Double Gate is a Herodian antechamber with two gorgeously preserved domes carved with geometric and floral motifs. No sur-face has been left unengraved. In conformity with a strict interpretation of the Second Commandment's prohibition against images, however, there is not even a hint of an ani-mal or human image. More than 15 feet in diameter, the decorated domes are among the earliest surviving domes from classical architecture. The kind of detail they exhibit is indicative of the elaborate decoration that must have graced much of the Temple compound before its destruction by the Romans. The predominant floral motif in the decoration is a vine with clusters of grapes, a symbol of blessing, happiness and productivity. According to Josephus and other literary sources, the entrance to the Temple was also decorated with a fruited-vine motif, this one fashioned in gold.

Outside the gates, south of the Temple Mount, Benjamin Mazar excavated dozens of ritual baths (*mikva'ot*), testifying to the holiness of the adjacent area. The leading expert on *mikva'ot*, Ronny Reich, has suggested that two of the 37 subterranean cavities of the Temple Mount are actually *mikva'ot*.[35] In the period of the Hebrew Bible, ritual bathing was required primarily for priests.[36] Only later was ritual bathing required to ensure the purity also of those entering the

Although the outside of the Double Gate has been mostly covered by the addition of a perpendicular Crusader wall (see photos on pp. 50–51), the interior is well preserved. The domed ceilings are beautifully engraved with geometric and floral motifs, avoiding any human or animal image in strict accordance with the Second Commandment.

This mikveh, *or ritual bath, was excavated just south of the Temple Mount. Pilgrims would ritually cleanse themselves before entering the sacred precinct.*

sacred precinct. Indeed, entry into the Court of the Women required *mikveh* bathing the previous day.[37]

One of the excavated *mikva'ot* is especially large and has an unusual square shape and steps on all four sides, not unlike the recently discovered Siloam Pool to the south.[38] Both of these *mikva'ot* were apparently intended for public use, especially during festivals.

A number of weights, as well as a large quantity of coins, were also excavated—testimony to commercial activity in the area.

On the Temple Mount itself, columned porticoes provided a walkway around the west, north and east side of the Temple Mount. Jesus himself walked under one of these porticoes, the Portico of Solomon, according to the Gospel of John (10:23). This is probably the eastern portico, overlooking the Kidron Valley.[39]

When Jesus entered Jerusalem for the last time, he came down the Mount of Olives, crossed the Kidron Valley and entered the city through a gate that led directly to the Temple. The gate in the eastern Temple Mount wall that is closest to where the Temple stood is the Golden Gate, an Omayyad gate that was blocked after the Muslims expelled the Crusaders from Jerusalem. However, a much earlier gate—probably the gate Jesus walked through—lies beneath it.

In the spring of 1969, James Fleming, a young Bible student from the American Institute of Holy Land Studies in Jerusalem, was exploring outside the Golden Gate after a heavy rain. As he knelt down to take a photo, the ground beneath him suddenly gave way. Disoriented but uninjured, he found himself in an 8-foot hole, knee-deep in human bones. He had fallen into a mass grave.

As Fleming examined the face of the wall beneath the Golden Gate, he was astonished to find five wedge-shaped stones set neatly in an arch. These were the remains of a hitherto-unknown gate to Jerusalem.[40] Fleming and his school's director snapped a few photographs, but Muslim religious authorities promptly cemented over and fenced off the area. The gate Jesus probably walked through remains inaccessible today.

On the southern end of the Temple Mount stood the Royal Stoa (or Royal Portico), which Josephus describes in great detail: "It was a structure more noteworthy than any under the sun," he says.[41] Two rows of columns created three aisles—a Roman basilica. A third row of columns, on the northern side, provided direct access to the Temple courtyards. A fourth row of engaged columns decorated the southern wall of the Royal Stoa, which was 600 Roman feet long (a Roman stade, or stadium), the largest known in the east at the time. The side aisles were 30 Roman feet wide; the central nave was one and a half times as wide—45 Roman feet. The side aisles were over 50 Roman feet high and the center nave twice as high—over 100 Roman feet. There were 162 columns, so thick that "it would take three men with outstretched arms touching one another to envelop it." The columns were in the Corinthian order. The result "caused amazement by the magnificence of its whole effect." I mention these details (there are many more) because, even without

The Golden Gate, an eastern entrance to the Temple Mount, was blocked up after the Muslims expelled the Crusaders from Jerusalem. Beneath this gate, archaeology student James Fleming found the arch of an earlier gate when he fell into a Muslim grave adjacent to the gate after a heavy rain. The large, smooth ashlars indicate that this was the gate in the Herodian period, when Jesus may have walked through it as he entered Jerusalem.

archaeological confirmation, the description clearly seems to be written by someone who has seen the building with his own eyes.

It is sometimes said that a prospective column for the Royal Stoa can still be seen in the area of Jerusalem known as the Russian Compound, which is located in the rocky terrain north of the Temple Mount—an area that once served as a quarry. An almost-detached column cracked while being quarried, so the ancient quarryman simply stopped work and left the column attached to the rock on the underside. It is approximately the same height that literary sources give for the height of the columns in the Royal Stoa (27–30 feet).

Some have speculated that this was intended for the Royal Stoa, but the more recent view is that this column was probably intended for a Byzantine church.[42] The Herodian columns were composed of drums, not monoliths. The column in the Russian Compound was probably intended for the Byzantine church known as the Nea that was excavated by Nahman Avigad at the Old City's southern wall.

According to Josephus, the Royal Stoa "was a structure more noteworthy than any under the sun." Though Herod was constrained by the biblically prescribed dimensions when constructing the Temple, the Royal Stoa expressed the architectural scale and grandeur of which he was capable. Based on Josephus's detailed descriptions, this model (looking southwest inside the Temple Mount) and drawing (looking east through the entrance) give us an idea of what the Stoa looked like. The model and drawing were made by architect Leen Ritmeyer.

This column in the Russian Compound (right) is approximately the same height as those used in the Royal Stoa (27–30 feet), whose columns, however, consisted of drums. The pictured stone cracked while it was being quarried, so the workmen simply left it in place, attached to the bedrock underneath.

Hundreds of heavily decorated fragments from Herod's Royal Stoa, however, were found in Benjamin Mazar's excavation at the southern Temple Mount wall. They were apparently thrown down there when the stoa was destroyed. Orit Peleg, a student at The Hebrew University, is writing her doctoral dissertation on these fragments. She hopes to be able to fit some of the pieces back together.

Ad hoc meetings of citizens, settlements of disputes, negotiations of all kinds, banking transactions where Jews from the diaspora exchanged foreign currencies

This stump of an arch (called Robinson's Arch after the man who first noticed it in the 19th century) protrudes from the Temple Mount wall near the southwest corner of the Temple Mount. As shown in the illustration below (areas in blue were found in Benjamin Mazar's excavation), the arch supported a monumental flight of stairs that led up to the Temple Mount from the valley below.

for local ones, payment of the annual half-shekel contributions to the Temple, religious harangues, sales of animals for sacrifice and grain for meal-offerings—all, no doubt, occurred in the Royal Stoa and the neighboring courts. It was probably here that Jesus overturned the tables of the money-changers (Mark 11:15; Matthew 21:12; Luke 19:45). And here both Jesus and some of the apostles preached (Luke 2:46–47, 21:37; Acts 2–3). In many ways Herod's Temple Mount functioned as a Roman forum or Greek agora.

The central function of the Temple Mount was religious. Each year people would bring their first fruits to the Temple as an offering. During the three

This fragment of a stone vessel, inscribed korban *("offering" or "sacrifice"), was found in excavations at the Temple Mount wall. It was probably intended for a Temple offering. It bears the image of two small birds—the customary offering to celebrate the birth of a child.*

pilgrimage festivals—Passover (Pesach), Weeks (Shavuot) and Tabernacles (Sukkot)—people from all over the then-known world thronged to Jerusalem and the Temple Mount. Tithes were given to the priests and Levites and to the poor. Vows were made at the Temple, including the vows of a Nazirite, someone consecrated to God, who is required to abstain from wine and to leave hair uncut (Numbers 6:2–21). Those seeking absolution brought guilt and sin offerings to the Temple. Lepers whose

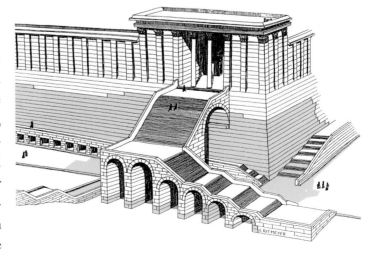

infirmity had ended came here to give thanks. So did grateful mothers after childbirth. In his excavation at the Temple Mount wall, Benjamin Mazar found a fragment of a stone vessel inscribed *korban*, meaning "offering" or "sacrifice." It was engraved with two small birds—doves or pigeons—the customary offering to celebrate the birth of a child.

The Double and Triple Gates provided access to the southern end of the Temple Mount through underground passages. Turning the corner from the southern wall to the western wall of the Temple Mount, we see hints of another entryway. Just north of the southwestern corner of the Temple Mount, a structure juts out from the wall. This was long ago identified as the spring, or stump, of an arch, named Robinson's Arch for the American orientalist Edward Robinson who first noted and identified these protruding stones in 1838. In 1868 the great British explorers Charles Wilson and Charles Warren discovered the pier on which the other side of the arch rested. Until Mazar's excavations a century later, it was thought that Robinson's arch supported a bridge across the Tyropoeon Valley to the Upper City, even though Wilson

This inscribed stone (left) was discovered among the debris thrown down from the southwestern corner of the Temple Mount. It reads, "To the place of the trumpeting ..." The rest is broken off, but it seems clear that it was meant to guide the trumpeter to the spot from which he would herald the beginning and end of the Sabbath. Other fragments with similar rounded tops (photo at right) indicate that the stone was part of the parapet atop the wall

לבית התקיעה להכריז

and Warren failed to find additional piers across the valley.

Mazar, however, located the remains of a series of piers of six vaults of gradually decreasing height running north to south at a right angle to the arch. He also found fragments of steps on top of the collapsed remains of Robinson's Arch. The conclusion is clear: Robinson's Arch supported not a bridge, but a monumental flight of stairs. Here one could ascend from the street at the valley floor up to the Temple Mount—more specifically, to the Royal Stoa on the southern end of the Temple Mount. Mazar noted ruefully, "Perhaps we should have known as much even before our excavations, for Josephus mentions four gates in the western wall [of the Temple Mount], the southernmost of which descends by many steps to the Tyropoeon Valley."[43]

Israeli archaeologist Ehud Netzer believes that this magnificent stairway was reserved for Herod and his retinue when he would visit the Temple Mount. At those times the basilica would be closed off to the public. Netzer notes that Herod was not of a priestly family, so he could not enter the sacred inner areas of the Temple Mount. Because Herod was "forbidden entry (at least publicly) to the crowning glory of his creative genius," he needed a place of his own. The Royal Stoa, "probably the most magnificent secular building ever erected by Herod," was that place. The Royal Stoa, says Netzer, "restored to Herod his rightful status on the Temple Mount."[44]

In the debris from the dismantled walls—near the southwestern corner of the Temple Mount enclosure wall—an extraordinary Hebrew inscription was discovered. It is engraved in a piece of limestone 8 feet long, which has a rounded top indicating it was a kind of parapet or coping on top of the wall or the tower at the southwest corner of Herod's giant Temple Mount. Unfortunately, it is broken off, so we do not have the end of the inscription. But we do have the beginning, and it is clearly legible. It reads "To the place of the trumpeting ..." (*l'bet hatteqi'ah*). Two equally clear Hebrew letters follow: *LH* and a third letter that is only partly there. Scholars have a good time trying to reconstruct the rest of the inscription. There have been at least four different suggestions by leading scholars: "for the priest," "to the Temple," "to herald [the Sabbath]," "to distinguish between the sacred and the profane [periods of time]."[45] What is clear is that a trumpet blast announced the beginning and end of the Sabbath. This sign directed the trumpeter to the high point on the Temple Mount where he would announce the beginning and end of the Sabbath.[46] As one scholar has described it, "It was no doubt an awe-inspiring sight to see the trumpeter on the pinnacle of the Temple Mount as the sun set in the west on the sixth day of the week, blasting the air with his instrument to announce the commencement of the Sabbath."[47]

Further north on the western wall of the Temple Mount is another arch, this time fully preserved (although rebuilt), known as Wilson's Arch, which did support a bridge to the Upper City. It is named for the late-19th-century British explorer Charles Wilson, but he did not discover it. That honor goes to a Swiss physician, Titus Tobler, who saw it in the mid-19th century.

North of the excavations along the western wall is *the* Western Wall, the plaza beside the wall where Jews have gathered for centuries to mourn the destruction of their Temple. (For this reason, it was known as the Wailing Wall until the creation of the State of Israel.) It is the holiest site where Jews gather today. Until modern times, this wall was thought to be the remains of Solomon's Temple. Now it is well understood that it dates instead to Herod's time. And it is not the wall of the Temple but of the enclosure that Herod built to support the level platform on which the Temple could be built, or rather rebuilt. Nevertheless, it retains its holiness.

The northern end of the Jewish prayer area is under cover, its ceiling formed from adjacent structures, including Wilson's Arch. At the northern end of this interior area, a tunnel dug by the Ministry of Religious Affairs with only minimal archaeological supervision extends along the western wall of the Temple enclosure. The tunnel does not go under the Temple Mount, despite frequent press reports that it does, but is adjacent to it. The western wall actually extends many courses lower than the level of the tunnel, so it would be impossible at this level to dig beneath the Temple Mount without blasting through the wall.

This tunnel is of interest here because of some exceptionally large ashlars embedded in the western wall opposite the spot where the Temple presumably stood. It is here that we find the largest stone in the Temple enclosure. As noted earlier, it is 42 feet long, 11 feet high and weighs nearly 600 tons.

The Temple itself was a small building. Herod was limited to the biblically prescribed dimensions of Solomon's Temple.

Fourteen steps led up to a platform on which the Temple and its courts

stood above the rest of the Temple Mount. A wall surrounded the courts. The main entry was in the eastern side, through a gate (perhaps the Beautiful Gate mentioned in Acts 3:2).

Inside this gate was the large square Women's Court. It is not quite clear why it was called the Women's Court since everyone entering the Temple passed through it. Perhaps it was because this court was as far as women could go. Moreover, women were not confined to this court. Those offering sacrifices would proceed to the next court; and this included women after childbirth and on other occasions particular to women.[48]

Fifteen semicircular steps led from the Women's Court to the Nicanor Gate, which opened onto the next court, the Court of the Israelites. On these steps the priests sang the Songs of Ascent (Psalms 120–134). The Nicanor Gate was reputed to be the most magnificent of the Temple gates. Oddly, the Court of the Israelites to which it led was a narrow area only 15 feet deep (but about 220 feet wide). This plan makes sense when we realize the Court of the Israelites was a kind of viewing area—where people offering sacrifices watched as the priests in the next court conducted the sacrificial ritual.

The next court, directly in front of the Temple, was the Court of the Priests, and it contained the great altar. It is not clear what separated the Court of the

Israelites from the Court of the Priests, but whatever barrier was there apparently allowed offerants to view the priests at work.

Around the spacious innermost court was a columned portico. Near the center of this space, a set of 12 steps led up to the Temple.

The Temple itself included three separate spaces: A large open doorway, 70 feet high and 35 feet wide surmounted by an impressive lintel, led into the first room, which was an enclosed porch or portico (in Hebrew, called the *'ulam*).[49] Otherwise the façade was plain. Neither door nor curtain covered the open side of the porch. This porch was wider than the other two rooms.

The next room was the main sanctuary (*heikhal*). Two pairs of gold-paneled doors stood at the entrance to the sanctuary, one on the outside of the sanctuary and one on the inside. On each side of the doorway stood pairs of free-standing columns, magnificently decorated with gold grapevines and flowers.[50] A veil of Babylonian tapestry also hung over the doorway.

Inside the sanctuary stood the incense altar, the showbread table where twelve loaves of bread were placed, and the seven-branched golden candelabrum (*menorah*).

Finally, separated from the main sanctuary by two curtains embroidered with lions and eagles was the shrine (*debir*), or Holy of Holies (*kodesh kodashim*). Gold sheets covered the walls of the square chamber.

In the Holy of Holies stood—nothing. Only the high priest was permitted

Herod's Temple included three separate rooms: a porch or portico, called the 'ulam; the main sanctuary, or heikhal; and the inner shrine, or Holy of Holies (kodesh kodashim). The main sanctuary and Holy of Holies were surrounded by three stories of small chambers, most likely used for storage of ritual objects. This drawing is the work of Leen Ritmeyer.

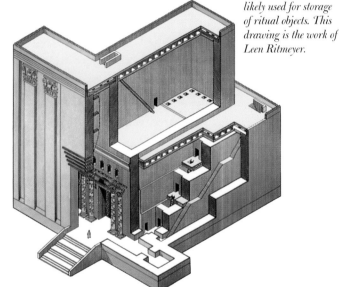

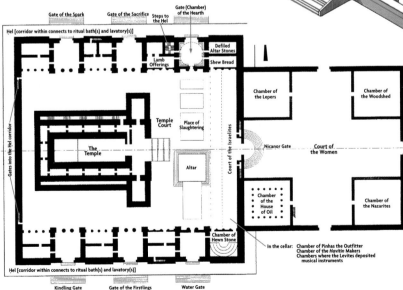

Based on the accounts of Josephus, the descriptions in the Talmud and comparative archaeological materials, modern scholars have been able to reconstruct the major features of Herod's Temple. This recent drawing is the work of Israeli archaeologist/ architect Ehud Netzer.

A triumphal arch (opposite) was erected in Rome to commemorate Titus's victory over the Jews in 70 A.D. The most famous of the bas-reliefs that decorate the Arch of Titus shows the spoils from the Temple held aloft by Roman soldiers (or Jewish prisoners). The Temple menorah has an octagonal base, unique among numerous other ancient menorah depictions. The base also pictures living creatures, which would have been forbidden by the Second Commandment. For this reason, scholars doubt the authenticity of the depiction.

to enter this chamber, and even he could enter only for a specific prayer on the Day of Atonement (Yom Kippur), the holiest day of the Jewish year, when Jews still fast from sunset to sunset. In Solomon's Temple the innermost sanctum had housed the Ark of the Covenant with the two Tablets of the Law, but the Ark disappeared with the Babylonian destruction of the First Temple in 586 B.C. All that remained in the Holy of Holies in Herod's Temple was the *Even Shetiyah*, or Foundation Stone, on which the Ark of the Covenant had rested. Inside the Holy of Holies on Yom Kippur, the high priest would make incense offerings.

Enclosing the main sanctuary and the Holy of Holies were 38 small window-less rooms or cells arranged in three stories. They were probably used to store ritual paraphernalia such as oil, spices and incense. An upper chamber built over the main sanctuary and the Holy of Holies rose above the side chambers, but did not extend over them. At the edge of the roof of the side chambers and on the parapet of the roof of the upper chamber were gold spikes, measuring 1 cubit high, that prevented birds of prey, which were attracted by the smell of the sacrificed flesh, from alighting and soiling the walls with their droppings.

Additional archaeological evidence, as it were, for the Temple accoutrements may be found in Rome. Titus, the general who led the final Roman attack on Jerusalem in 70 A.D., thereafter succeeded his father, Vespasian, as emperor. Shortly after Titus's death, a magnificent triumphal arch was constructed in Rome to commemorate his victory over the Jews. Erected at the eastern end of the Via Sacra, the arch is embellished with a series of bas-reliefs. The most famous of these depicts the Temple vessels held aloft, presumably by Roman soldiers (or Jewish captives), in a triumphal procession. These vessels include the showbread table, trumpets, censers and the Temple menorah.

The menorah raises a problem. It is shown with an octagonal base instead of the usual three-footed base in numerous ancient mosaic depictions. (Actually, the menorahs in the mosaics are four-footed, but the fourth foot is obscured by the one directly in front of it.) It also differs from the triangular base that the menorah appears to have in a drawing scratched into the plastered wall of a Jewish residence hardly a few hundred feet from the Temple. The drawing, discovered by Nahman Avigad in an excavation in the Old City's Jewish Quarter, was made when the Temple still stood. Scholars naturally disagree about whether the Arch of Titus's depiction of the base of the menorah as octagonal is authentic.

The Temple spoils depicted on the Arch of Titus are only a part of the Roman plunder from the Temple. According to Josephus, Vespasian had the golden vessels of the Temple deposited in the Temple of Peace that he established in the Roman Forum.[51]

For centuries, Jews understandably regarded the bas-relief on the underside of the Arch of Titus as a symbol of their defeat. In medieval times Jews were not permitted to pass under the arch. But even when permitted, they would not dignify the depiction by passing under it. Instead they paid a fee to the owner of a neighboring house for permission to pass through his house.

Returning to Jerusalem, we now consider precisely where on the Temple Mount Herod's Temple stood. This, too, is a matter of some dispute. The issues are quite complicated, but most scholars place the Herodian Temple over the rock mass (al-Sakhra) that now lies in the center of the Dome of the Rock. (In this view, the location of the great altar in the Temple Court of the Priests is now marked by the elaborate Islamic cupola to the east of the Dome of the Rock called the Dome of the Chain.) Others say al-Sakhra itself marks the altar in the Court of the Priests in front of the Temple. Still others say the Temple was slightly to the north of al-Sakhra.[52] Wherever it was, Herod's Temple complex was an awesome accomplishment.

Adjacent to the northwestern corner of the Temple Mount, Herod built a fortress that dominated the Temple, allaying any fear he might justifiably have had of a popular disturbance on the Temple Mount. Herod called the fortress the Antonia, after his friend and mentor Marc Antony. (This enables us to date the construction of the Antonia between 37 B.C., when Herod solidified his rule over Judea, and 31 B.C., when Marc Antony was defeated at the Battle of Actium; Herod quickly—and successfully—transferred his allegiance from the former triumvir to the new Roman emperor, Augustus, but, having a certain amount of character and guts, Herod retained the name of the fortress as the Antonia.)

The Antonia is described in detail by Josephus. Inside, it was like a palace, Josephus says, including baths, open courts and all kinds of rooms.[53] Towers rose

Despite all the information we have about Herod's Temple, the question of exactly where it stood on the Temple Mount has been a matter of debate among scholars for more than a hundred years—and remains so to this day. The shaded area marks some of the suggestions for the earlier Temple platform. These drawings mark the Dome of the Rock for locational purposes, and a drawing of the Temple marks the location of the Temple on the mount in the view of the various scholars.

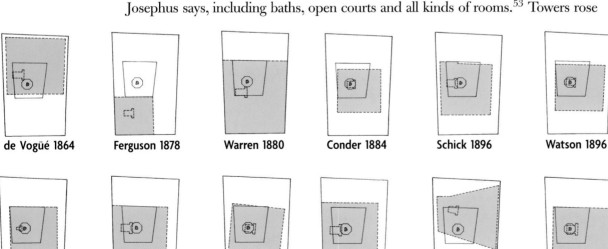

de Vogüé 1864   Ferguson 1878   Warren 1880   Conder 1884   Schick 1896   Watson 1896

Mommert 1903   Dalman 1909   Hollis 1934   Vincent 1954   Kaufman 1983   Ritmeyer 1985

The destruction of the Temple in 70 A.D. is often used to mark the end of the First Jewish Revolt. However, some rebels held out in the Judean desert at the palace/fortress of Masada for a few more years before finally falling to the Romans in 73 or 74 A.D.

from each of the four corners. The tallest—70 cubits high (about 135 feet)—on the southeastern corner looked down on the Temple Mount.[54]

At the point where it joined the Temple Mount were two passageways to the Temple Mount itself. Josephus tells us that a Roman legion would be stationed in the Antonia on Jewish festivals to control the crowds.[55]

The fortress is strategically located.[56] Almost all attacks on Jerusalem have come from the vulnerable north side. On the east and west are steep valleys. On the south is the old City of David that also descends steeply into a valley. The only viable approach for attackers was from the north.

As with the Temple, so with the fortress overlooking it: Herod was not the first to build here.[57] An earlier fortress, known as the Baris ("fortress" in Hebrew is *bira*), was constructed for similar reasons by the Hasmonean ruler John Hyrcanus I (135–105 B.C.). An even earlier tower existed at this point (perhaps the Tower of the Hundred [Nehemiah 3:1, 12:39]), and scholars speculate that even Solomon may have built a protective fortress at this site overlooking the Temple Mount.

The Romans destroyed the Herodian Temple in 70 A.D., less than a century after it was constructed.

The period between Herod's accession in 37 B.C. and the destruction of Jerusalem in 70 A.D. is known as the latest phase of the Second Temple period or the Herodian period (even though Herod himself died in 4 B.C.). If it was a time of turmoil, tension and conflict in Rome, it was also a time of turmoil, tension and conflict among the Jews of Judea. And it was a time of turmoil, tension and conflict between Rome and Jerusalem.

Toward the end of his life, suffering both physically and mentally, Herod foolishly erected a golden eagle over the porch, or portico, of the Temple. Supported by a group of sages, a band of young Jews tore it down and smashed it to pieces.[58] Herod had them executed, but it was a sign of trouble ahead.

From 66 to 70 A.D., the Jews of Judea revolted against Rome. The destruction of the Temple marked the end of what has become known as the First Jewish Revolt against Rome, although some rebels held out at Masada for three or four more years.

The precise causes of the First Jewish Revolt are complex and obscure, but trouble had been brewing since the death of Herod. The Roman emperor Caligula (37–41 A.D.), for example, sought to impose the worship of himself as a deity on the entire population of the empire. In Judea, the gentile population of Javneh (south of Tel Aviv) erected an altar to Caligula that was promptly destroyed by the majority Jewish population. In retaliation, the emperor ordered a golden statue of himself to be set up in the Jerusalem Temple. The Jews appeared *en masse* before Petronius, the Roman governor of Syria, and declared that he would have to kill every one of them before they would allow the Temple to be desecrated in this way.[59] Petronius procrastinated and did not immediately carry through on Caligula's order. In a rage Caligula ordered Petronius to commit suicide. The order reached him, however, after Caligula was assassinated in 41 A.D.,[60] and Jewish unrest subsided—for the moment.

This arm bone tells the touching but gruesome story of a young Jewish woman who fled for her life as the Roman soldiers set fire to her Jerusalem home and began slaughtering the inhabitants. She fell, reaching out for the step of a nearby doorway. She never got up.

The vassal kings that ruled Judea after Herod's time were, beginning in 6 A.D., subservient to Roman prefects (and procurators) like Pontius Pilate (who receives highly critical notices not only by Josephus but also in the Gospels and elsewhere). Jews protested when golden shields inscribed with the name of the emperor were displayed in what had been Herod's palace. They also protested when military standards with images of the Roman emperor were introduced in Jerusalem; these they considered violations of the Second Commandment's prohibition against graven images. Josephus relates a string of riots, assassinations and lootings that, as historian Shaye Cohen describes it, "in retrospect, were forerunners of the Great Revolt."[61]

The same kind of Jewish riots that ignited the revolt in 66 A.D. had thus often occurred earlier in reaction to oppressive and religiously offensive policies, but heretofore they had not resulted in a full-scale revolt.

In 66 A.D. a Roman procurator seized 17 talents from the Temple treasury to pay what he claimed were overdue taxes. In Cohen's words, "[A] particularly violent riot [then] led to the massacre of the Roman garrison in Jerusalem. The governor of Syria intervened, but even he failed to restore the peace. He was forced to withdraw from Jerusalem, suffering a major defeat. The Jews of Judea had rebelled against the Roman empire."[62]

And so the war began.

The Jews themselves were divided and often in conflict. The priestly revolutionaries seemed to have started it. The Sicarii, a party of peasants, attacked the Jewish aristocracy and killed the high priest whose son led the priestly revolutionaries. The priestly revolutionaries, headquartered in the Temple, in turn killed the leader of the Sicarii.

The Roman emperor Nero dispatched Vespasian, one of his most trusted and successful generals, to suppress the Jewish revolt. By 68 A.D. Vespasian (and his son Titus) had quelled the revolt in the north, where Josephus led the Jewish forces in Galilee. Although the Roman forces were poised to attack Jerusalem, the city was temporarily saved by the assassination of the Roman emperor Nero. The death of the emperor automatically terminated Vespasian's commission as a general. In 69, he returned to Rome and had himself proclaimed emperor. He ordered his son Titus, now commander of the Roman forces in Judea, to attack Jerusalem.

It took four Roman legions to conquer Jersusalem. The Roman soldiers were constantly harassed by the Jews. Titus himself was struck on the shoulder by a rock that permanently weakened his arm.[63] Titus first attempted to take the city by storm. However, the siege ramps the Romans built against the city walls were undermined and destroyed by the Jews. After penetrating the outermost of the city's three walls, the Roman forces broke through the second wall only to have the area recaptured by the Jews.

In the spring of 70, Titus decided that he would take the city by starvation. He besieged the city, cutting off all supplies and all means of escape.

Despite a famine in the city (shamefully, mounds of grain had been destroyed in internecine Jewish warfare), Jewish resistance was intense, the defenders scornfully rejecting Roman pleas for surrender. Josephus reports:

> The calamities of the city caused more despondency to the Romans than to the citizens, for they found their opponents in no wise chastened by their severe misfortunes, while their own hopes were continually dashed, their earthworks mastered by the enemy's stratagems, their engines by the solidity of the walls, their close combat by the daring of their antagonists. But worst of all was the discovery that the Jews possessed a fortitude of soul that could surmount faction, famine, war and such a host of calamities.[64]

At the walls of the Temple Mount, the Roman general and his staff considered whether to destroy the Temple. The "rules of war" at the time called for respecting the sanctity of temples. This temple, however, was not simply a temple, but a military fortress. According to Josephus, Titus was opposed to destroying the Temple, arguing that its preservation would be a monument to Roman magnanimity. But a Roman soldier acting against orders flung a firebrand into the sanctuary, and the flames were soon out of control. Other ancient writers, however, say that Titus's destruction of the Temple was a premeditated attack, an assessment most modern scholars agree with.

Whether or not Titus tried to save the burning Temple, as Josephus claims, the historian vividly describes the scene:

> While the Temple blazed, the victors plundered everything that fell in their way and slaughtered wholesale all who were caught. No pity was shown for age, no reverence for rank; children and greybeards, laity and priests, alike were massacred; every class was pursued and encompassed in the grasp of war, whether suppliants for mercy or offering resistance. The roar of the flames streaming far and wide mingled with the groans of the falling victims; and, owing to the height of the hill and the mass of the burning pile, one would have thought that the whole city was ablaze.[65]

The Temple was left a blackened hulk. Titus and his troops spent the next month in a brutal mopping-up operation in the rest of the city:

> Pouring into the alleys, sword in hand, they massacred indiscriminately all whom they met, and burnt the houses with all who had taken refuge within ... [T]hey choked the alleys with corpses and deluged the whole city with blood, insomuch that many of the fires were extinguished by the gory stream. Towards evening they ceased slaughtering, but when night fell the fire gained the mastery.[66]

Judea, personified as a weeping woman, sits under a date palm (a symbol of Judea), mourning defeat at the hands of a Roman soldier (left). Judea Capta coins were minted by the Romans in gold, silver and bronze and were by far the most numerous of the "Capta" style of coins.

Vespasian ordered the Temple and the city razed to the ground.[67] The only construction spared were three towers; parts of one of these can still be seen today in the lower courses of the towers inside the Old City's Jaffa Gate. Herod had named one of the towers for his wife Mariamne (whom he later murdered), another for his friend Hippicus and the third for his brother Phasael. Josephus tells us they were the loftiest towers protecting the city and that "for magnitude, beauty and strength [they were] without their equal in the world."[68] These towers alone the Romans spared "to indicate to posterity the nature of the city and of the strong defenses which had yet yielded to Roman prowess."[69]

Somewhat ironically, the remains of the Tower of Hippicus give us some idea of the strength and beauty of the Temple masonry. Josephus tells us that in the joining and beauty of the stones [they were] in no wise inferior to a temple."[70]

In Jewish tradition the Temple was destroyed on the ninth of the month of Av, although Josephus says it occurred on the tenth.[71] The First Temple, Solomon's Temple, had been destroyed by the Babylonians on the same date in 586 B.C. A similar discrepancy exists, however, regarding the exact date of the destruction of this Temple. According to the narrative in Kings, it occurred on the seventh of the month (2 Kings 25:8); according to the prophet Jeremiah, it occurred on the tenth (Jeremiah 52:12). According to rabbinic tradition, however, both destructions occurred on the same date, the ninth of Av (Tisha b'Av), which is still observed as a day of mourning and fasting.

That the Roman victory did not come easily is perhaps reflected in the fact that neither Vespasian nor Titus took the title *Judaicus* to commemorate their victory in the region, as would have been custom, although they were accorded other honors.[72] Rome, however, was immensely proud of its victory. Over 8 percent of the coins minted by the Flavian dynasty (Vespasian, Titus and Domitian) were Judea Capta coins. They were issued in gold, silver and bronze and were minted at Rome, Antioch and elsewhere in the empire.[73] The emperor was depicted on the front (obverse); on the reverse, various symbolic images were used to represent defeated Judea. The most common was a woman captive, bent, perhaps weeping, looking dejected as in mourning, often beside a palm tree. Occasionally the emperor was shown standing over defeated Judea. The legend was usually in Latin, but sometimes in Greek. And sometimes there was no legend at all; the symbols were so widely understood that no writing was necessary to convey the message.

As a final touch, a special tax was imposed on Jews all over the empire—the *fiscus Judaicus*, a tax of two denarii payable to the imperial Roman treasury in lieu of the half-shekel tax formerly paid to the now-destroyed Temple in Jerusalem.

In Jewish memory, Titus is known as the destroyer of the Temple.

V

The First Second Temple

COMPARED TO SOLOMON'S TEMPLE, WHICH PRECEDED IT, AND HEROD'S, which followed it, the Temple built by the exiles returning from Babylon was a modest affair. Indeed, those who remembered the glorious Temple of Solomon, also called the First Temple, wept when they beheld the first stages of the rebuilding of the Second Temple (Ezra 3:12).

Oddly, the ancient sources reveal almost no details of the Temple built by the exiles. Archaeologist Carol Meyers has observed: "It is perhaps ironic that the temple building that survived the longest—almost exactly five centuries—evoked the least descriptive material in the literary record."[1]

Work on the Second Temple began in the 530s B.C., only a half century after the Babylonians conquered Jerusalem in 586 B.C., destroyed Solomon's Temple and sent the Judahites into exile. As the psalmist says:

> By the waters of Babylon,
> There we sat down and wept
> As we remembered Zion.
> On the willows
> There we hung up our harps ...
> If I forget thee, O Jerusalem,
> Let my right hand wither,
> Let my tongue cleave to my palette.
> (Psalm 137:1–2,5–6)

According to the Bible, the Persian king Cyrus I allowed the exiles to return to Jerusalem in 538 B.C. and begin rebuilding their Temple, which had been destroyed by Nebuchadnezzar and the Babylonians in 586 B.C. A similar proclamation is recorded in the pictured cuneiform text, called the Cyrus Cylinder, in which Cyrus permits a foreign people to resettle its homeland.

A half century later, the Persians had become a world superpower. Babylon was no more. And a beneficent Persian ruler, Cyrus the Great, allowed the exiles to return to their homes.

The fact is that most of them did not. Despite what the psalmist tells us, life was not so bad in Babylon. When push came to shove, most of the exiles stayed—and thrived. As Jeremiah wisely advised, "Seek the welfare of the city to which I have exiled you and pray to the Lord on its behalf; for in its prosperity you shall prosper" (Jeremiah 29:7).

Of post-Exilic Jerusalem, Nehemiah tells us, "the people in it were few" (Nehemiah 7:4). All but the old City of David and the Temple Mount were abandoned, but this was sufficient to accommodate the reduced population. After his famous midnight circumvallation of the old and fallen city wall (Nehemiah 2:13–15), Nehemiah undertook its rebuilding. Assigning different sections to different community groups—families, priests, merchants, artisans—the task was

The tomb of the Persian king Cyrus I (Cyrus the Great) still stands in Pasargadae, Iran. Cyrus conquered the territories of Babylonia and then allowed his new subjects to return to their homelands. To the exiles from Judah, Cyrus returned the Temple treasure confiscated by the Babylonians and allowed them to return to Jerusalem to worship their God and rebuild the Temple.

completed in a mere 52 days. For the most part, the new wall consisted simply of the old wall rebuilt. On the eastern slope, however, which was once densely inhabited, the jumble of stones was so daunting (Nehemiah couldn't even traverse it on his donkey; here, it appears, he dismounted and proceeded on foot) that the returning exiles left the area abandoned and built a new wall at the top of the slope. This, of course, reduced the size of the city even more, but a larger city was no longer needed.[2]

In the 1960s British archaeologist Kathleen Kenyon excavated part of this new city wall—not a very impressive construction compared to walls that had previously protected the city, and a clear sign of the limited resources the returning exiles could muster.[3]

Those who did return were authorized by the Edict of Cyrus to rebuild their Temple. Ezra gives the text of Cyrus's proclamation, issued in 538 B.C.:

> "The Lord God of Heaven has given me all the kingdoms of the earth and has charged me with building Him a house in Jerusalem, which is in Judah. Anyone of you of all His people—may his God be with him, and let him go up to Jerusalem that is in Judah and build the House of the Lord God of Israel, the God that is in Jerusalem; and all who stay behind [in exile], wherever he may be living, let the people of his place assist him with silver, gold, goods and livestock, besides the freewill offering to the House of God that is in Jerusalem."[4]

(Ezra 1:2–4)

Cyrus even released to the returning exiles the Temple treasures that the Babylonian king Nebuchadnezzar had confiscated and taken to Babylon. Ezra lists them: "30 gold basins, 1,000 silver basins, 29 knives, 30 gold bowls, 410 silver double bowls, 1,000 other vessels" (Ezra 1:9–10).

As soon as the exiles were settled in their towns, they rebuilt the altar so that they might begin to offer sacrifices (Ezra 3:1–3).

Then they began reconstructing the Temple itself. Ezra tells us that the work began in the second year of the exiles' return (Ezra 3:8), presumably about 536 B.C. Then, for some reason, work stopped. Perhaps the reason was political foment. The eastern Persian provinces had rebelled. Egypt was in revolt. The people of Yehud (the name of the Persian province that had formerly been Judah) had themselves urged postponing work on the Temple, as Haggai reports: "These people say, 'The time has not yet come for rebuilding the House of the

In the eighth-century A.D. Codex Amiatinus, Ezra is pictured as a scribe in Babylon. He was among the early returnees to Jerusalem. The Book of Ezra records much about the return of the exiles and the effort to rebuild the Temple.

Lord'" (Haggai 1:2). Other possible reasons for the discontinuance of the work may have been drought and the poverty of the returnees (Haggai 1:6–11) or the intervention of the Samaritans.

The work did not resume again until 520 B.C., dated as the second year of the Persian king Darius, at the urging of the prophets Haggai and Zechariah and under the leadership of Zerubbabel, a Babylonian Jew who served as governor of Yehud under Persian rule. (Thus, this Temple is sometimes called Zerubbabel's Temple.) The project was finally completed on the third day of the month of Adar in the sixth year of the reign of Darius (Ezra 6:15): March 12, 515 B.C.

"The Israelites, the priests and the Levites, and all the other exiles celebrated the dedication of the House of God (*Beth Elohim*) with joy" (Ezra 6:16). It was 70 years after the Babylonians had destroyed Solomon's Temple—in 586 B.C.—and more than 20 years since the first wave of exiles returned to the holy city.

After the Temple was rebuilt, Ezra read to the "entire people" the "Teaching of Moses" (Nehemiah 8:1–3), the teaching of Yahweh, the Israelite God, "by the hand of Moses" (Nehemiah 8:14; cf. Nehemiah 10:30, 13:1). Many scholars see this as the first indication that the Pentateuch—Genesis, Exodus, Leviticus, Numbers and Deuteronomy—had been compiled and canonized.

The rebuilt Temple and Herod's Temple are both known in Jewish tradition as the Second Temple. Although the Temple built by the returning exiles would later be demolished and rebuilt by Herod the Great in the years just before the turn of the era, a peaceful alteration or rebuild, such as Herod's, does not constitute the end of that particular Temple era, as would be the case of a violent destruction by an enemy. To avoid confusion, I generally refer to the structures as the first Second Temple and Herod's Temple. Solomon's Temple is the First Temple.

That the first Second Temple was a modest affair is reflected in biblical texts (Haggai 2:3; see also Zechariah 4:10), as well as in Josephus, who tells us that the Temple the exiles rebuilt was 60 cubits smaller and lower than the First Temple that the Babylonians had destroyed. The exiles were not to be faulted

According to the Bible, the rebuilding of the Temple began in earnest during the second year of the reign of the Persian king Darius I (522–486 B.C.). Darius instituted reforms in his empire's political structure by installing local leaders, implementing local laws and encouraging religious practice in the Persian provinces. This led him to install Zerubbabel as governor of Yehud and to lend the support of the Persian court to the rebuilding of the Temple in Jerusalem. Darius sits on his throne in this relief from the Treasury of the Palace at Persepolis (Iran).

for this, Josephus explains, because the measurements were fixed by Cyrus and his Persian successor Darius. The returning exiles did what they could. As in Solomon's Temple, the wood for the first Second Temple was brought from Tyre and Sidon—cedars of Lebanon (Ezra 3:7).

In the second century B.C., a calamity befell the first Second Temple. Its outcome is positive, however. It gives us the story of Hanukkah and, for roughly a century, a renewed Jewish state. It all began when Alexander the Great conquered most of the then-known world, bringing Hellenism to the East. Then, in 323 B.C., he died, as one writer described it, "of exhaustion, war wounds, disease, and drunkenness."[5] His empire in the East was divided among his most powerful generals. To the Ptolemies went Egypt and the south, and to the Seleucids went Syria and the north. Judea, in the middle, often changed hands over the years. In the second century B.C., it was ruled by the Seleucids. Between 175 and 164

After Cyrus the Great defeated the Babylonians, Judah became the Persian province of Yehud. This fourth-century B.C. silver coin inscribed "Yehud" in old Hebrew script was discovered near Jericho and was probably minted in Jerusalem. The three letters are inscribed sideways along the right side of the coin and read YHD from bottom to top.

111

B.C. this was in the personage of Antiochus IV Epiphanes. In an effort to weld his expanding empire together, Antiochus became a great proponent of Hellenization, but the Jews were a problem. Judaism was simply out of place in a predominantly Hellenized empire. By imperial decree, the Jews were compelled on penalty of death "to depart from the laws of their fathers and to cease living under the laws of God" (2 Maccabees 6:1). The Jews were forbidden to circumcise their

sons, to study Torah and to observe the Sabbath (1 Maccabees 1:44–46). Two women who had their sons circumcised were paraded through the streets with their infants hanging from their neck; the children were then hurled headlong from the city wall (1 Maccabees 1:61; 2 Maccabees 6:10).

And, of course, Antiochus desecrated the Temple. Josephus tells us that he forbade the offering of the daily sacrifices and left the Temple bare, seizing the golden candlesticks, the golden incense altar, the showbread table and even the veils "made of fine linen and scarlet."[6] Antiochus cleared out the Temple: He also emptied it of its hidden treasures and left nothing at all behind.[7]

Modern historians differ somewhat as to just why Antiochus acted as he

Alexander the Great (pictured here) defeated the Persians and consolidated most of the known world under his rule. Though he died at the young age of 33, his new empire brought Greek culture (Hellenism) to Judea and much of the Near East. This Classical Greek sculpture is at the Acropolis Museum in Athens, Greece.

did. According to Michael Avi-Yonah, "Antiochus and his advisers seem to have believed the assertions of the radical Jewish Hellenizers, who assured them that the majority of the Jewish nation was ready to abandon the religion of its ancestors and to adopt not only Greek culture, but even Greek religion ... Starting from these mistaken premises, Antiochus IV tried to establish Greek culture and religion in Judaea by force."[8]

Menahem Stern, on the other hand, attributes Antiochus's violation of the Temple not to militant Hellenism, but to financial straits.[9] Josephus agrees and cites numerous classical historians for this proposition.

It was likely some of both. In any event, it is clear that Antiochus desecrated the Temple, stripping it of its treasures, sacrificing a pig on the altar, installing a statue of himself in the Temple courtyard and transforming the building into a temple of Zeus.[10]

According to Apion, the Greek grammarian and sophist from Alexandria (on

The laws and religious beliefs of the Jews set them apart from their Hellenized neighbors. In an attempt to force Greek culture on Jews who resisted Hellenization, the Seleucid king Antiochus IV Epiphanes outlawed many Jewish practices, such as circumcision, and desecrated the Temple, thus inciting the Maccabean revolt in 167 B.C. On the obverse (left) of this silver tetradrachm, is a portrait of Antiochus, and on the reverse (right), he is portrayed as Zeus enthroned, holding the goddess Nike (Victory) in his outstretched hand. The Greek inscription reads "King Antiochus, God Manifest, Bearing Victory."

whom Josephus reports in *Contra Apion*), when Antiochus pillaged the Temple, he found that the Jews had been worshiping the golden head of an ass.[11] Josephus calls this an "incredible lie," adding that, even if it were true, Antiochus should be the last one to talk considering that in his country cats, he-goats and other creatures are worshiped as gods. As for Apion, he would have realized this was a silly story "had he not himself been gifted with the mind of an ass and the impudence of the dog."[12]

But that was not the worst of it. This same Apion reports that when Antiochus broke into the Temple, he found a Greek man being fattened for sacrifice by the Jews, according to an annual custom. The report is worth quoting at length, reflecting, as it does, the stories that were circulating about Jews and Judaism:

> Antiochus found in the temple a couch, on which a man was reclining, with a table before him laden with a banquet of fish of the sea, beasts of the earth, and birds of the air, at which the poor fellow was gazing in stupefaction. [Antiochus's] entry was instantly hailed by him with adoration, as about to procure him profound relief; falling at the king's knees, he stretched out his right hand and implored him to set him free. The king reassured him and bade him tell him who he was, why he was living there, what was the meaning of his abundant fare. Thereupon, with sighs and tears, the man, in a pitiful tone, told the tale of his distress. He said that he was a Greek and

that, while traveling about the province for his livelihood, he was suddenly kidnapped by men of a foreign race and conveyed to the temple; there he was shut up and seen by nobody, but was fattened on feasts of the most lavish description. At first these unlooked for attentions deceived him and caused him pleasure; suspicion followed, then consternation. Finally, on consulting the attendants who waited upon him, he heard of the unutterable law of the Jews for the sake of which he was being fed. The practice was repeated annually at a fixed season. They would kidnap a Greek foreigner, fatten him up for a year, and then convey him to a wood, where they slew him, sacrificed his body with their customary ritual, partook of his flesh, and, while immolating the Greek, swore an oath of hostility to the Greeks. The remains of their victim were then thrown into a pit. The man stated that he had but a few days left to live, and implored the king [Antiochus], out of respect for the gods of Greece, to defeat this Jewish plot upon his life-blood and to deliver him from his miserable predicament.[13]

We are not told what then happened to the man.

After transforming the Jewish Temple into a temple of Zeus (2 Maccabees 6:2), "the Temple was filled with debauchery and reveling by the Gentiles, who dallied with prostitutes and had intercourse with women within the sacred precincts ... The altar was covered with abominable offerings" (2 Maccabees 6:4–5).

Antiochus also built a citadel known as the Acra (or Akra, meaning "high point" in Greek) to control the city and to permit close surveillance of the Temple Mount.[14] Not a trace of it has been found, nor can be; it was destroyed down to its foundation by Simon, one of the Maccabee brothers. We know the Acra only from Josephus,[15] who apparently copied from the Book of Maccabees.[16] Scholars argue about just where the Acra was located—on the southeastern corner of the Temple Mount, south of the Temple Mount as it exists today, south of the Temple Mount as it existed in an earlier period, or on Mt. Zion. I cast my vote with the late Nahman Avigad, one of Israel's most distinguished archaeologists, who located the Acra on a hill overlooking the northwestern corner of the Temple Mount—at the same place where Herod's Antonia Fortress and the Hasmonean Baris were located. This makes sense because, as noted earlier, the only really vulnerable direction from which to attack the Temple Mount was the north.[17] From all other directions it was protected by deep valleys (or, on the south, by the City of David, which descends into a deep valley). Attacks on the Temple Mount traditionally came from the north.

Although we have no clear archaeological evidence of the Acra itself, we do have a fragmentary Greek inscription found by chance near the Old City that records an oath taken by soldiers stationed at the Acra.[18]

Not surprisingly, Antiochus's religious repression and the desecration of the Temple triggered a Jewish revolt. The rebellion, which began in 167 B.C. (and continued for 25 years), was led for a year by a priest from Modi'in (southeast of modern Tel Aviv) named Mattathias. On his deathbed, he appointed Judah Maccabeus, one of his five sons, as military commander of the revolt. Judah was a brilliant military strategist who initially avoided direct confrontation with the Seleucid army, preferring to ambush enemy contingents from the sidelines. Later, he outsmarted the Seleucid army in major battles despite the Syrians' numerical superiority. In 164 B.C. Judah entered Jerusalem and purified the defiled Temple (although that did not end the fighting or the revolt). In celebration, the festival of Hanukkah was instituted—an observance of eight days to commemorate a tradition that when Judah and the Maccabees retook the Temple, the small amount of Temple oil that was available (enough only for one day) miraculously burned for eight days until additional supplies became available.

Eventually, Mattathias's sons established an independent Jewish state for the first time in 450 years. They also started a new dynasty of rulers, known as the Hasmonean dynasty, after Hasmon, an ancestor of Mattathias. Hasmonean territory also expanded dramatically—from the small Persian province of Yehud (formerly Judah) to a nation that embraced most of modern Israel and some land now in Jordan and southern Lebanon.

Paradoxically, the Hasmoneans who began as opponents of Hellenism became, over the years, its proponents. The Temple, however, remained the center of ritual and religious life, especially as the priesthood was synonymous now with the political leadership. In these circumstances, alteration of the Temple and the Temple Mount would be expected. But there appears to be no record of it. However, a young archaeological sleuth might have found a Hasmonean addition to the Temple Mount. He is Leen Ritmeyer, a Dutchman who, in the 1970s, was the architect working on Benjamin Mazar's excavation at the southern wall of the Temple Mount.

To uncover a Hasmonean addition to the Temple Mount, we need to know the dimensions of the pre-Hasmonean Temple mount. Ritmeyer believes he has discovered both.[19]

It all began when Ritmeyer was listening to the speculations of his mentor Benjamin Mazar as to the meaning of the Hebrew word *birah*. The word appears several times in the Bible and is often translated in very different ways. In the New Jewish Publication Society translation, for example, it is translated three different ways, as "gatehouse" (Nehemiah 2:8), "fortress" (Nehemiah 7:2) and "temple" (1 Chronicles 29:1). Mazar speculated to Ritmeyer that *birah* really referred to the Solomonic Temple Mount that the returning exiles wished to

restore. What was the size of the *birah*? The two men agreed that it was a 500-cubit square. That was the size of the Temple Mount as described in Tractate *Middot* of the Mishnah. Although this rabbinic text was redacted more than a century after the destruction of Herod's Temple and the passage does not specify which Temple Mount it is referring to, it could easily mean the Solomonic Temple Mount and thus represent a long tradition.[20]

Ritmeyer's first archaeological clue regarding the Hasmonean addition to the earlier Temple Mount (whether it was Solomonic or simply post-Exilic) came from the bottom step of a stairway leading to the raised podium on which the Dome of the Rock now sits. Eight stairways on the Temple Mount lead up to the Muslim podium that supports the Dome of the Rock. At the top of each

The northwestern stairway leading up to the podium on which the Dome of the Rock sits contains a telltale clue about the location of the pre-Hasmonean Temple Mount. The bottom step is made of large ashlars, unlike the other steps and pavement around it. Until recent paving obscured the front of this step from view, one could make out the margins and bosses on the face of each block, indicating that this "step" may once have been the outer enclosure wall of an earlier Temple Mount.

stairway, an arcade marks the entrance into the sacred area around the Dome of the Rock. In 1972 an Irish architect named Brian Lalor, who preceded Ritmeyer as architect on Mazar's dig, was the first person to notice that the stairway at the northwest corner of the podium is different from all the rest. It has an unusual bottom step, which is made of a single line of large rectangular ashlars; all the other steps are made of much smaller stones. Lalor observed that the side of the step had a margin and boss—as on an ashlar meant to be seen. This indicated the stone was probably once part of a wall on the Temple Mount instead of a step. An early photograph revealed that the stones were different from Herodian ashlars, suggesting that the wall was pre-Herodian. Today, the side of this step is no longer visible; the Waqf has (illegally and without archaeological supervision)

117

paved the area adjoining the step so that the top of the step is now at ground level and the sides are hidden.

Ritmeyer observed another peculiarity: The stairway with this step (or part of a wall)—unlike the other stairways leading to the Muslim podium—is not parallel to the sides of the podium supporting the Dome of the Rock. For this staircase alone, the Muslim builders apparently followed the line of the unusual bottom step, fashioning each higher step at the same angle. Now, while this bottom step is not quite parallel to the podium, it is *exactly* parallel to the east wall of the Temple Mount. Remember that Herod could not change the line of the eastern wall of the Temple Mount when he dramatically expanded the mount. The eastern wall is just where it was previously laid because of the steep decline down into the Kidron Valley.

Ritmeyer pondered the fact that this step was exactly parallel to the eastern wall of the Temple Mount and decided to measure the distance. He wanted to translate the distance into cubits because the royal cubit (equaling 52.5 centimeters or almost 21 inches) is the most likely unit of measurement used in Solomon's Temple. Using this measure, Ritmeyer found that the distance between the lowest step of this stairway and the eastern wall of the Temple Mount is exactly 500 cubits—the very distance prescribed in *Middot* for the Temple Mount![21]

This plan shows the various phases of the Temple Mount, according to architectural archaeologist Leen Ritmeyer. Notice how the northwestern staircase (beginning with the "step"/wall) is not parallel to the podium as are the other staircases. That is because its direction was determined by the pre-existing wall.

Apparently, the step was part of the western wall of the pre-Herodian Temple Mount. If so, Ritmeyer had now fixed the line of both the eastern and western walls of the 500-cubit square Temple Mount described in *Middot*.

From the records of the great 19th-century British engineer Charles Warren, who meticulously examined and recorded almost everything in, on, under and beside the Temple Mount, Ritmeyer found a dry moat or valley 52 feet north of the unusual lowest step of the stairway leading up to the Muslim podium. Ritmeyer concluded that this moat was as far north as the pre-Herodian Temple Mount would have extended. Other clues enabled him to locate the northeastern corner of the pre-Herodian Temple Mount.

From this northeastern corner of the pre-Herodian Temple Mount, Ritmeyer measured 500 cubits south on the eastern Temple Mount wall, and, lo and behold, this point marked the precise point of a bend (outward) in the eastern wall, indicating some sort of ancient change.[22] This bend is about 195 feet from the southern end of the eastern wall.[23] In a previous chapter, we looked at the so-called "straight joint" in this same eastern wall of the Temple Mount 106 feet from its southern end. South of this straight joint is clearly Herodian masonry; the "straight joint" therefore marks the beginning of the Herodian addition to the Temple Mount, as we previously explained (see pp. 75–77). North of this straight joint is entirely different masonry. Ritmeyer argues that this masonry is Hasmonean and that the area between the "straight joint" and the "bend" represents a Hasmonean addition to the Temple Mount.[24]

The Hasmonean dynasty lasted for roughly a century (scholars argue about precisely when it started and when it ended). The last great Hasmonean monarch, Alexander Jannaeus, died in 76 B.C. His wife Salome Alexandra assumed the throne until her death in 67 B.C. Then their two sons, Hyrcanus II and Aristobulus II, in a fratricidal contest, struggled for leadership of the state. The kingdom had been under Rome's thumb for some time, and paradoxically the end of the Hasmonean dynasty came about when Hyrcanus enlisted the Roman general Pompey's assistance against his brother.[25] In 63 B.C. Hyrcanus opened the gates of Jerusalem to Pompey's forces, but Aristobulus and his men shut themselves up in the Temple and refused to surrender. To protect themselves, Aristobulus's forces cut the bridge from the Temple to the upper city, a bridge that perhaps followed the line of what is known today as Wilson's Arch. As mentioned earlier, the Temple Mount is protected by steep natural barriers on the east and west, and by the steep slopes of the original City of David to the south. North of the Temple Mount, the Hasmoneans had previously dug a trench of "immense depth," according to Josephus. However, Pompey's troops were able to fill it. Pompey then brought up siege machines and battered the Temple with *ballistae*. Despite the siege, the priests continued to perform their holy duties, "not omit[ting] any of the sacrifices even when some difficulties arose because of the attacks." After a three-month siege, however, the city surrendered. The Roman soldiers rushed into the Temple and began slaughtering the Jews. Josephus tells us:

> [T]hose who were busied with the sacrifices none the less continued
> to perform the sacred ceremonies; nor were they compelled, either
> by fear for their lives or by the great number of those already slain,
> to run away, but thought it better to endure whatever they might
> have to suffer there beside the altars than to neglect any of the ordi-
> nances. And that this is not merely a story to set forth the praises

In an attempt to gain control of the Hasmonean kingship from his brother, Hyrcanus II enlisted the help of the Roman general Pompey (pictured here). Pompey and his troops laid siege to Jerusalem and eventually conquered it. With the Roman victory, Jewish sovereignty in the region ended for 2,000 years. This first-century B.C. Roman marble bust is located in the Ny Carlsberg Glyptotek in Copenhagen, Denmark.

of a fictitious piety, but the truth, is attested by all those who have narrated the exploits of Pompey.[26]

With Pompey's conquest, Jewish sovereignty of Judea ended.

Surprisingly, however, Pompey left everything inside the Temple as he found it. Although he entered the Holy of Holies with his men, which "before that time," Josephus tells us, "had never been entered or seen before" except by the high priest, Pompey did not plunder the Temple or its treasury. He appointed Hyrcanus II, whose side he had taken in the struggle between the sons of Alexander Jannaeus, as high priest.

Upon Pompey's death, Julius Caesar ascended to sole power of the Roman empire and made Hyrcanus II ethnarch (leader of the Jews) as well as high priest. Among Hyrcanus's advisors and supporters was an Idumean nobleman named Antipater. Antipater was the father of the man who would become known as Herod the Great. In 40 B.C. Hyrcanus was taken prisoner by his brother Aristobulus's son. To disqualify Hyrcanus for a return to the high priesthood, his ears were cut off. Meanwhile, Antipater's line enhanced its pedigree when his son Herod married Hyrcanus's granddaughter. For Antipater's support in Rome's civil wars, Caesar granted him Roman citizenship (and immunity from taxation). In 40 B.C. the Roman Senate appointed Herod king of Judea. A military conflict in Judea ensued. After a two-and-a-half-year struggle for dominance, in 37 B.C. Herod, the son of an Idumean nobleman and a Nabatean mother, mounted a successful siege on Jerusalem and his reign as monarch began.

As Harvard scholar Shaye Cohen describes him: "Herod is an enigmatic figure. A tyrant, a madman, a murderer, a builder of great cities and fortresses, a wily politician, a successful king, a Jew [he converted], a half-Jew, a gentile—Herod was all these and more."[27]

By Herod's time, the modest Temple built by the returning exiles was ready for a thorough overhaul. To embellish his standing among the Jews, Herod decided to rebuild it. And so the first Second Temple built was peacefully dismantled to allow for its reconstruction by that master builder and madman, Herod the Great.

VI

Solomon's Temple

WE ENTER A DIFFERENT WORLD WHEN WE COME TO THE QUESTION of the existence of Solomon's Temple—a far more complicated and hazy world. As with Herod's Temple, not a stone of Solomon's Temple can be positively identified.[1] But unlike Herod's Temple, we do not have for Solomon's Temple indisputable remains of an impressive Temple Mount platform, signs warning non-Jews to stay out or fragments from auxiliary buildings.

We do have, however, a virtual blueprint of Solomon's Temple in the Bible, just as we have a detailed description of Herod's Temple in the works of Josephus. The Bible, in fact, contains two detailed descriptions of Solomon's Temple: one in 1 Kings 6–7 and the other in 2 Chronicles 2–4.* The two accounts are remarkably similar. Chronicles, a post-Exilic account, clearly used the description in Kings as a source. But how reliable is the biblical description? Was it all made up? This raises a very big question, especially in light of the recent attacks on the historicity of the Bible by the so-called biblical minimalists.

Solomon's Temple as described in the Bible is what scholars call a long temple. It measured 20 cubits wide and 70 cubits long. Like Herod's Temple and, doubtless, the Temple the exiles built on their return from Babylon, Solomon's Temple had three parts: a portico or porch (*'ulam*), a main hall (*heikhal*) and an inner shrine (*debir*), later called the Holy of Holies. The Temple was part of

Solomon built the Temple to house the Ark of the Covenant. Two cherubim—hybrid creatures often with a lion's body, large wings and a human face—stood guard over the Ark and may have looked something like this ivory cherub believed to be from ancient Arslan Tash, in Syria.

*Still another description of the Temple may be found in Ezekiel 40–44. It is, however, a visionary, future Temple that the prophet describes from his exile in Babylon, although the design in some respects appears to track that of the Solomonic Temple.

123

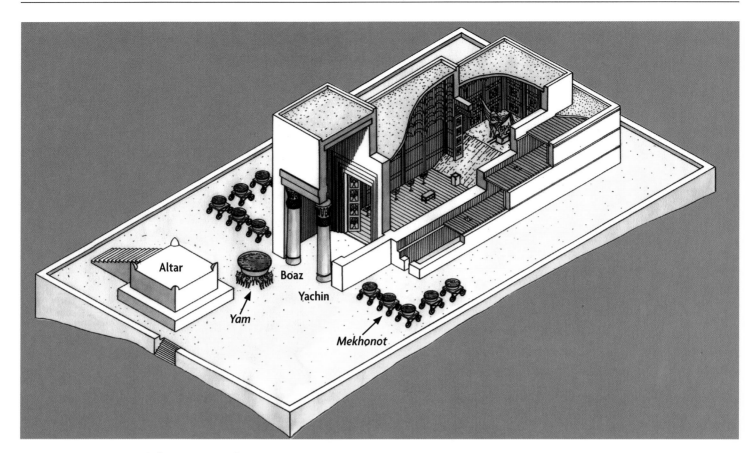

Solomon's royal compound. The wall that surrounded it also enclosed the royal palaces. This arrangement was typical in the ancient Near East.

The Temple took seven years to build and was completed in the eleventh year of Solomon's reign (1 Kings 6:1,38).

The Temple was oriented on an east-west axis. The entrance on the east faced the rising sun and was constructed of stones that had not been reshaped since they were cut at the quarry: "When the House was built, only finished stones cut at the quarry were used, so that no hammer or ax or any iron tool was heard in the House while it was being built" (1 Kings 6:7). Some see significance in both of these facts—one redolent of early sun-worship among the Hebrews and the other related to the divine admonition in Exodus 20:25 (Hebrew verse 22*): "If you make for Me an altar of stones, do not build it of hewn stones; for by wielding your tool upon them you have profaned them." In a sense the entire Temple was an altar to the Lord.

The porch of the Temple was 10 cubits deep and open on the front. There is a question about whether it was roofed or simply had two side walls sticking out from the main building. The biblical text tells us that in (or in front of) the porch stood two bronze pillars named Yachin and Boaz, each of which was crowned

*A handful of books are divided and numbered somewhat differently in the Christian Old Testament and in the Hebrew Bible.

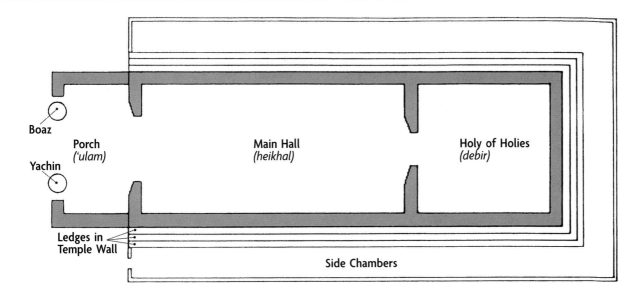

Boaz

Yachin

Porch
('ulam)

Main Hall
(heikhal)

Holy of Holies
(debir)

Ledges in
Temple Wall

Side Chambers

Solomon's Temple was a so-called long temple, composed of a porch ('ulam) entered through two columns named Yachin and Boaz, a sanctuary (heikhal) and a shrine (debir) for the Ark, which was approached in the reconstruction at left by a ramp. More probably it was approached by a stairway (see reconstruction on p. 133). The four-horned altar for animal sacrifice stood just outside in the courtyard, along with a water basin (called yam, or "sea," in Hebrew) and the ten wheeled carts called mekhonot. The plan and reconstruction are by Leen Ritmeyer.

with a capital of lilies and decorated with pomegranates. Why the names Yachin and Boaz were chosen or what they were intended to convey is another puzzle. There aren't even any good theories. Were these columns free-standing or did they hold up the roof of the porch? Many scholars believe that they supported the roof as in analogous temples that have been excavated. Similar porches are seen on a variety of ancient structures, indeed so many that this architectural element has a scholarly name all its own: *distyle in antis*. Other scholars believe these columns were free-standing and that the porch was unroofed—so there was nothing for the columns to hold up.[2]

The porch ('ulam) of the Temple leads into the main hall (*heikhal*), which was 40 cubits long, four times as long as the porch. The two side walls and the front wall of the *heikhal* were decorated with vegetable motifs, buds and blooms, all covered with gold. Whether the *heikhal* had windows is a matter of scholarly dispute,[3] although the text seems to suggest that it did (1 Kings 6:4).

In the main hall stood an incense altar (see photo, p. 128), the showbread table and ten lampstands (*menorot*), five on each side (1 Kings 7:49).

The showbread (or shewbread, in older English translations) is a little mysterious. It is mentioned only briefly in a standard Bible dictionary,[4] apparently because scholars are not quite sure what it is—or rather why it is. It is sometimes referred to as the "Bread of the Presence." In the Jewish Publication Society translation of the Bible, it is called the "Bread of Display." It consisted of 12 loaves baked from the finest flour arranged in two rows on a golden table, perhaps representing the 12 tribes of Israel. (A similar table of bread was in the Tabernacle that preceded the Temple [Exodus 35:13].) The bread was changed weekly, on the Sabbath, and, like other sacrifices, was eaten by the priests.

The lampstands inside the main hall are often thought to have been seven-branched menorahs. It's true that Herod's Temple did have a seven-branched candelabrum. We know this from the contemporaneous drawing of it found in a Jerusalem home only a few hundred feet from the Temple Mount (see photo, p. 98). A seven-branched menorah is also pictured as booty on the Arch of Titus in Rome (see photo, p. 96). However, the description in the Bible of the lampstands in Solomon's Temple says nothing about branches. The many later depictions of the seven-branched menorah are really depictions of the menorah in the Second Temple, Herod's Temple. On the other hand, the Bible is explicit that a seven-branched menorah did stand in the Tabernacle that housed the Tablets of the Law during the Israelites' desert wanderings (Exodus 25:31–40). Some scholars maintain, however, that this description of the Tabernacle is a late composition, maybe even post-Exilic, and therefore not historically reliable.

The archaeological evidence seems to weigh against seven-branched menorahs in Solomon's Temple. No such lampstand from the period of Solomon's Temple or earlier has been recovered archaeologically. What we do have, however, are many lampstands with a single shaft.

One scholar suggests that even though the lampstands in Solomon's Temple may have consisted of a single shaft without branches, the stand may well have held a clay oil lamp with seven spouts.[5] Numerous examples of these seven-spouted bowls or oil

The Bible indicates that Solomon's Temple included ten lampstands (1 Kings 7:49). It is very unlikely, however, that a seven-branched menorah like those in Herod's time would have existed in Solomon's time. Certainly none has been found from the time of Solomon. But it may have been a single-shaft lampstand with a seven-spouted oil bowl on top. Pictured here are an 11th- or 10th-century B.C. clay stand from Shiloh (shown with bowl set on top) and a ninth-century seven-spouted oil lamp from Dan.

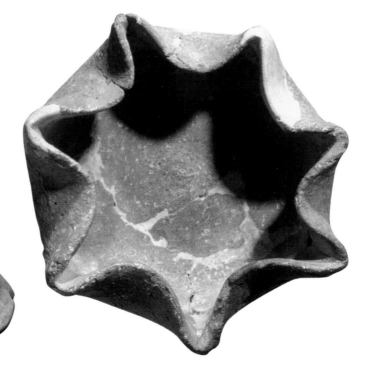

lamps have survived from long before and after Solomon's Temple. Support for this suggestion comes from a vision of the post-Exilic prophet Zechariah that may reflect a memory of the menorah in Solomon's Temple. In his vision he sees "a lampstand all of gold [*menorat zahav*], with a bowl above it. The lamps on it are seven in number" (Zechariah 4:2).

At the end of the main hall, or *heikhal*, was a wall decorated with cherubim and palmettes that separated the main hall from the Holy of Holies.

The *'ulam* and the *heikhal* were 30 cubits high. The Holy of Holies, however, was only 20 cubits high (it was, in fact, a 20-cubit cube). But the whole Temple, according to 1 Kings 7:2, was 30 cubits high. This raises a question: Did a stairway 10 cubits high lead up to the raised floor of the *debir*? Or was there a false ceiling in the *debir*, 10 cubits lower than the Temple roof?

Again scholars are divided,[6] but recent archaeological evidence suggests a stairway. (More about this later.)

In the Holy of Holies stood the Ark of the Covenant containing the Tablets of the Law. Over the ark were two huge gold-plated olive-wood cherubim, their outstretched wings measuring 10 cubits from end to end. The wings of the two cherubim met in the center of the room where the Ark rested.

We have some idea of the appearance of these cherubim from ancient sculptures and reliefs that have survived. They were rather common in the ancient world, in adjacent cultures as well as in Israel. Cherubim are hybrid creatures that vary somewhat. One well-known depiction apparently shows a human face, a lion's body and huge wings. The concept seems to have originated in Egypt. An ivory example from the ninth or eighth century B.C. found at Samaria wears the double-crown of Egyptian pharaohs. This cherub is striding through lotus blossoms, perhaps not unlike the blossoms the Bible tells us decorated the Holy of Holies. Palmettes and palm trees similar to those that decorated the entrance to the Holy of Holies and its back wall are also illustrated in archaeological examples.

Around three sides of the Temple building (the main hall and the Holy of Holies) were side chambers (singular, *yatsia*) three tiers high and entered from outside.

The entrance and back wall of the Holy of Holies (debir) in Solomon's Temple were decorated with palmettes like this ivory example from eighth-century B.C. Samaria.

There are a few strange omissions from the description of the Temple in 1 Kings 6–7. The Temple compound (including the royal palaces) and the restricted Temple area within it undoubtedly had gates, but they are not mentioned. Temple gates are referred to elsewhere in the Bible, however, in connection with events that occurred near them (2 Kings 15:35; Jeremiah 20:2, 38:7; Ezekiel 8:5,14, 9:2, 10:19, 11:1). Some of these references are probably to the Temple compound and others to the Temple area. But no gate is mentioned in the main description of the Temple in 1 Kings 6–7.

The Temple clearly had courts in front of it, but these, too, are not described. We simply have offhand references to them: for example, an "inner

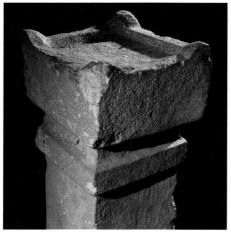

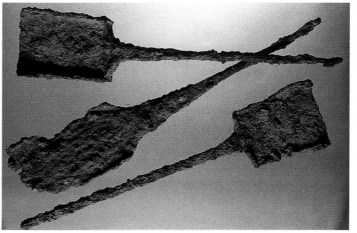

enclosure" (1 Kings 6:36), a "great courtyard" (1 Kings 7:9–12) and "two courts of the House of the Lord" (2 Kings 21:5, 23:12). Prophetic and poetic passages also refer to the "courts of God," "courts of the House of the Lord" and "my courts" (e.g., Psalm 116:19). Some of these courts may have been added after the original construction of the compound. In the mid-ninth century B.C., the people of Judah are said to have prayed in the "new court" (2 Chronicles 20:5). Jeremiah is told to go to the Temple court to speak to those who are coming to "worship in the House of the Lord" (Jeremiah 26:2).

The description in 1 Kings 6–7 also makes no mention of an altar in the courtyard in front of the Temple. It is mentioned later, however: The bronze altar was "too small" to hold all the offerings made at the dedication of the Temple (1 Kings 8:64). About 200 years after Solomon built the Temple, King Ahaz replaced the Temple altar with a large new one fashioned after an altar he had seen in Damascus (2 Kings 16:10–16).[7] The old bronze altar was moved to the side of the new one. Elsewhere are incidental references to the altar of the Temple (Ezekiel 8:5; 9:2).

Also in the Temple courtyard were some of the strangest accoutrements of the Temple: the *mekhonot*, or wheeled stands with large bowls on top. Five *mekhonot* stood along each side of the porch. The description of them is quite detailed but not always easy to understand (1 Kings 7:27–40). Each one had

This four-horned altar from Beersheba (above left), standing 5 feet high and measuring 9 feet on each side, is probably very similar to the altar that stood before Solomon's Temple and that the priests used for performing animal sacrifices. This one was found dismantled with its stones secondarily incorporated into a wall following a religious reform that made Jerusalem the exclusive place for sacrificial offerings. It was excavated by Israeli archaeologist Yohanan Aharoni.

The small horned altar from Megiddo (lower left) and bronze shovels from Tel Dan (lower right) are probably very similar to the incense altar and shovels that were housed in the main sanctuary of Solomon's Temple.

Ten mekhonot, *or wheeled carts, like this one (right) stood in the courtyard of Solomon's Temple. They were elaborately decorated with palms and cherubim, and the priests may have used them for ritual ablutions. This example comes from Cyprus and displays cherubim and palmette designs.*

four wheels with two axles and stood about 5 feet high. The four-sided stands had cut-out pictures of lions, oxen and cherubim on the sides. Palm trees filled in gaps in the design. The entire contraption was made of bronze fashioned by the artisan Hiram the Phoenician, so it is no surprise that our best archaeological exemplar of such a stand comes from Cyprus in the 11th century B.C. It is much easier to get an idea of these lavers, as they are called in the biblical text, from a picture than from a verbal description.

The *mekhonot* held water used in priestly ablutions, but we cannot be more specific. In front of the *mekhonot* (and slightly to the side) was the *yam* (literally, "sea"), a large bronze basin that also held water for priestly use. The *yam* rested on the hind-quarters of 12 bronze oxen, 3 facing each of the four points of the compass. One scholar has suggested that the *yam* in the Temple represented the cosmic sea.[8]

The presence of the *mekhonot* and the *yam* with their water for ritual purposes is another indication that there indeed was a sacrificial altar in the courtyard in front of the Temple, even though 1 Kings 6–7 does not mention one. Indeed, the later description in the Book of Chronicles corrects this omission (2 Chronicles 4:1).

Another odd thing about the biblical description of the building of the Temple: the involvement and assistance of King Hiram of Tyre (not to be confused with the artisan of the same name). (In the parallel account in Chronicles, the king is called Huram [2 Chronicles 2:2ff].) This Phoenician monarch not only supplied the timbers for the Temple—cedars of Lebanon—he also provided workmen from Sidon to shape the timbers (1 Kings 5:6 [Hebrew vs. 20]). He sent masons to help cut the stone blocks for the foundation of the Temple (1 Kings 5:18 [Hebrew vs. 32]). And he sent Solomon an expert in bronze (the artisan Hiram) to fashion Yachin and Boaz, the two bronze pillars for the porch, as well as the *yam*, the *mekhonot* and other bronze pieces. As one commentator has put it, "[T]he Phoenicians are clearly associated with the technical and material aspects of the temple-building project."[9]

One can only wonder at this repeated biblical admission that the Phoenicians were so heavily involved in the building of Solomon's Temple. It has the ring of truth. Even if the biblical text was written much later, the author of the biblical text probably had a contemporaneous record of this assistance when he repeatedly acknowledged that Solomon did not do all the work himself, but required significant Phoenician help. This weighs strongly in favor of the existence of Solomon's Temple. If the story were fictional, it would be very unlikely to include an admission of so much foreign—that is, pagan—assistance.

A thousand years after Solomon built the Temple, Josephus described it in detail from sources then available to him, both the biblical accounts and other sources. Josephus apparently realized the importance of Hiram's contribution to the construction of the Temple. He even quotes from correspondence between

Hiram and Solomon. Apparently aware that his readers might be dubious about this, Josephus adds:

> The copies of these epistles remain at this day, and are preserved not only in our books, but among the Tyrians also; insomuch that if any one would know the certainty about them, he may desire of the keepers of the public records of Tyre to show him them, and he will find what is there set down to agree with what we have said. I have said so much out of a desire that my readers may know that we speak nothing but the truth, and do not compose a history out of some plausible relations.[10]

To claim that Solomon's Temple did not exist would also require an explanation of the many references to it in the histories of later kings of Judah. It

This relief from the palace of the Assyrian king Sargon II in Khorsabad (Iraq) shows cedars of Lebanon being brought by boat for the construction of his palace. The Bible says that the Phoenician king Hiram of Tyre supplied cedar timbers for the building of Solomon's Temple. They may have been floated down the Mediterranean coast, as illustrated in this relief.

When the Assyrian king Sennacherib (shown here watching the battle of Lachish in southern Judah) laid siege to Jerusalem, King Hezekiah cut down the gold-plated doors and doorposts of the Temple and gave them to the Assyrians in order to purchase their withdrawal from the city.

is generally recognized (except by the most extreme biblical minimalists, who question the historicity of much of the biblical record) that the accounts of the reigns of the kings of Judah in the ninth, eighth and seventh century B.C. are generally reliable. While they may be occasionally biased (like all historical narrative), they are not fictional. Many of these historical narratives refer in an almost offhand way to the Temple.

For example, when Athaliah, the only woman to rule Judah, sought to murder heirs to the throne, one of them was hidden in the Temple for six years (2 Kings 11:1–4; see also 2 Kings 11:10–11). Why would the text say that he was hidden in the Temple (an especially unlikely hiding place) if there were no Temple?

We are told that, in the late eighth century B.C., in order to induce Sennacherib to withdraw, Hezekiah paid tribute, giving the Assyrian monarch the treasury of the Temple. Hezekiah even "cut down the doors and the doorposts of the Temple of the Lord, which King Hezekiah had overlaid [with gold] and gave them to the king of Assyria" (2 Kings 18:16). The annals of Sennacherib confirm that Hezekiah paid a heavy annual tribute to the Assyrian monarch.[11]

'AIN DARA TEMPLE

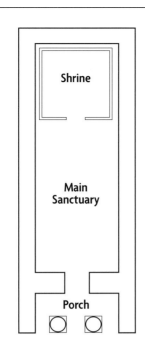

SOLOMON'S TEMPLE

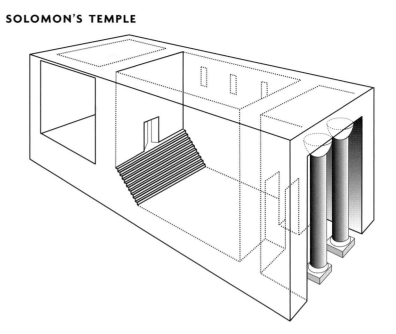

The temple at 'Ain Dara in Syria (left) has a plan similar to Solomon's Temple (right), with a columned porch, a sanctuary and a shrine at the back. The 'Ain Dara temple also had an additional room, called the antechamber, between the porch and the main sanctuary.

Sennacherib mentions, among other things, a tribute of 30 talents of gold. The Bible mentions the exact same figure (2 Kings 18:14).

Ezekiel repeatedly locates events in the Temple that could as easily be located elsewhere if the Temple did not exist (Ezekiel 8:6, where it's called *miqdash*; 8:14–16, where it's called *Beth Yahweh*; and 9:3,6,7, where it's called *ha-bayit* and *miqdash*).

As we will explore later in some detail, several Judahite kings repaired the Temple. Why would they be given credit for repairing a Temple that did not exist? To detect such a fiction, if that is what it was, would not be difficult. Everyone who read these accounts when they were first composed or heard of them at that time would know whether or not a Temple stood on the Temple Mount in Jerusalem.

While we have no direct archaeological evidence of Solomon's Temple, we do have some indirect evidence. Not surprisingly, the closest parallels to Solomon's Temple that have been uncovered are in Syria—under ancient Phoenician influence. The closest one has received almost no publicity (probably because the excavation report is in German.)[12] It is at a site called 'Ain Dara, northwest of Aleppo, near the Turkish border.[13]

The 'Ain Dara temple has the same plan as Solomon's Temple, except that in the 'Ain Dara temple, the main hall has an antechamber. From the porch, the 'Ain Dara priest would enter the antechamber, then the main chamber, behind which was the Holy of Holies or shrine. The temple is roughly contemporaneous with Solomon's Temple (more about this later).

Like most ancient temples, both the 'Ain Dara temple and Solomon's Temple stood on the highest elevation in the city. Like Solomon's Temple, the 'Ain Dara

temple was built on a platform. Both temples were approached by a courtyard. At 'Ain Dara, a large stone basin, undoubtedly used for cultic purposes, stood in the courtyard. As we have already seen, a large basin (the *yam*) also stood in the courtyard of the Jerusalem Temple. The 'Ain Dara temple was heavily decorated in stone reliefs that included lions and mythical animals with wings and human faces (sphinxes and cherubim), as was the case in Solomon's Temple (1 Kings 7:29). The two buildings also shared floral designs, including lilies and palmettes.

Enclosing both temples on three sides were a series of chambers. Although the chambers at 'Ain Dara have not survived to their full height, scholars estimate, based on the thickness of the walls and support piers, that they stood three stories high, as in Solomon's Temple.

One scholar who has studied the two temples found that the 'Ain Dara temple shares *33* of the 65 architectural elements mentioned in the Bible in connection with Solomon's Temple.[14]

Like Solomon's Temple, the 'Ain Dara temple (left) was approached through a courtyard and was decorated with various floral motifs and mythical creatures such as cherubim (below). The cherub here has a lion's body, wings and a human face.

In the shrine at 'Ain Dara was a podium or dais, approached by a ramp. This may help clarify an ambiguity in the biblical description of Solomon's Temple. Was the Holy of Holies in Solomon's Temple raised and approached by a stairway or did it have a false ceiling? The 'Ain Dara temple suggests an answer: The Holy of Holies in Solomon's Temple did *not* have a false ceiling. It was approached either by a ramp, as at 'Ain Dara, or by a stairway 10 cubits high. (In another temple with close parallels to Solomon's Temple, the temple of Tell Ta'yinat, which we will discuss later, the shrine room is reached by means of a stairway.)

The 'Ain Dara temple also suggests a function for the famous columns of Yachin and Boaz, which are sometimes thought to be free-standing pillars at the entrance to Solomon's Temple.[15] The analogous columns in the 'Ain Dara temple supported the roof of the porch.[16] In short, the 'Ain Dara temple tells us that the columns called Yachin and Boaz probably supported the roof of the porch.

The most dramatic finds in the 'Ain Dara temple are gigantic footprints embedded in the floor. In the passage from the porch into the building are two footprints, a right and a left, then slightly further on, a single left footprint, and then, on the threshold of the main hall, a right foot, as if a giant, probably the deity, paused at the entrance before striding into the temple. Each of these footprints is more than 3 feet long. The distance between the two single footprints

Giant footprints in the floor (left and right) of the 'Ain Dara temple were meant to indicate the presence and immense size of the deity. The Israelite Temple, too, was considered the home of the deity, and the Ark of the Covenant was, at least poetically, his footstool. Each of the footprints in the 'Ain Dara temple is more than 3 feet long and would have belonged to someone over 65 feet tall.

is 30 feet. Considering the size of the prints and the length of the stride, these feet would belong to someone about 65 feet tall!

This is probably how the god of 'Ain Dara was envisaged. An echo of this is perhaps found in the description of God's throne in the Temple of Solomon. As we noted earlier, over the Ark of the Covenant in the Holy of Holies rested two giant cherubim with their wings extended. The cherubim in Solomon's Temple measured 10 cubits (about 17 feet) from wingtip to wingtip (1 Kings 6:23–26). They were also 10 cubits high. In short, they were enormous. These cherubim were thought to be the throne of God. As the psalmist says, "You who are enthroned on the cherubim" (Psalm 80:2; see also 2 Kings 19:15; Isaiah 37:16). That Yahweh's throne was formed by two huge cherubim reflects the Israelite vision of God as being of superhuman size. Indeed, the train of his robe would fill the Temple, according to one prophetic vision (Isaiah 6:1). The Ark of the Covenant was his footstool. In short, Yahweh was not unlike the 'Ain Dara god of giant footprints. He neatly fit into an authentic ancient Near Eastern context.

As Lawrence Stager of Harvard University tells us, "The 'Ain Dara temple has important implications for the historicity of Solomon's Temple. The description of Solomon's Temple (1 Kings 6–7) is neither an anachronistic account based on later temple archetypes nor a literary creation. The plan, size, date and architectural details fit squarely into the tradition of sacred architecture known in north Syria (and probably in Phoenicia) from the tenth to eighth century B.C."[17]

The Temple was the *axis mundi*—the cosmic mountain linking heaven and earth. Here order was established, and, by the rituals performed, order was constantly

renewed. Stager points out that the images of the flora and fauna that decorated Solomon's Temple—the palm trees, colocynths (a kind of gourd), calyxes and exotic cherubim—recall the Garden of Eden. This same program is found in the 'Ain Dara temple, where we find palm trees, lilies and mythological beasts.

By evoking the Garden of Eden, the Temple becomes what Stager calls "a mythopoeic realization of heaven on earth ... For the ancient Israelites, as well as for many peoples today, Jerusalem was and is the cosmic center, where heaven meets earth."[18]

The temple at Tell Ta'yinat in Turkey, near the modern border with Syria, is dated to the ninth–eighth century B.C. and is another close contemporary of Solomon's Temple. The two-columned porch at Tell Ta'yinat recalls the biblical description of Yachin and Boaz, the two named columns on the porch of Solomon's Temple, and provides reliable evidence that they, too, may have supported a roof. The Tell Ta'yinat temple also had a raised shrine room, which was approached by stairs, thus providing another possible solution to the question of how the inside of Solomon's Temple looked.

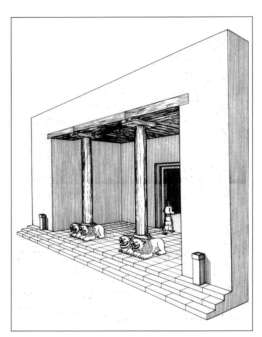

In an earlier chapter, we remarked on the tradition that the six-day creation occurred on the same spot on which the Temple would later stand. According to some Jewish traditions, the dust from which Adam was created was taken from here.[19] Not only Adam, but Cain, Abel and Noah all offered sacrifices here.[20] And Adam and Eve were buried at a spot now under the Temple.[21]

'Ain Dara is not the only excavated temple that provides a comparison with Solomon's Temple. Until the excavation of the 'Ain Dara temple, the temple that was usually cited as a comparison was the Tell Ta'yinat temple, dating to the ninth–eighth century B.C. and excavated in 1936 in Turkey, near the modern Syrian border. The temple at 'Ain Dara is closer in size and architectural details to Solomon's Temple. However, the shrine room at Tell Ta'yinat is approached by stairs rather than a ramp as at 'Ain Dara, thus opening the possibility that the Holy of Holies in Solomon's Temple was approached by a set of stairs rather than by a ramp. A number of other ancient temples similar to Solomon's Temple have also been found at the northern sites of Zinjirli, Alalakh and Hammath, and in Israel at Megiddo and Hazor. Each of these was adjacent to the palace of the ruler, as was the case with King Solomon's Temple.

The 'Ain Dara temple is closer in time to Solomon's Temple than these other temples, but dating ancient temples is often a shaky matter. They were frequently rebuilt and remodeled, so if we were to be precise, we would have to distinguish between the various phases of each of the buildings. The basic elements of the 'Ain Dara temple, however, were there long before Solomon is supposed to have built his Temple. According to the 'Ain Dara excavator, the first phase of that temple was constructed in about 1300 B.C. and lasted to about 1000 B.C., the traditional date for David's conquest of Jerusalem. Solomon's reign was about 40 years later. In phase two of the 'Ain Dara temple, from 1000 B.C. to 900 B.C., which precisely corresponds to the reign of King Solomon, much of the decoration was added. In phase three, from 900 B.C. to 740 B.C., the side chambers were constructed.

Solomon's Temple clearly had its predecessors. Can we say that this form disappears after the time of Solomon? Not really. Some of its features survive in later temples. However, we can say that Solomon's Temple, as described in the Bible, is appropriate for the tenth century B.C. and less appropriate, say, for the seventh century B.C. or even later.

Excavated temples such as the one at 'Ain Dara do not prove the existence of Solomon's Temple, but they do demonstrate that the biblical description is entirely plausible. More than that, the Bible's mention of the involvement of a foreign pagan culture and king—the Phoenicians and King Hiram—strongly supports the historicity of the account, as do more or less casual references to it in the records of later kings of Judah.

Why then do we have no archaeological evidence of Solomon's Temple? As one commentator recently put it:

> Perhaps the greatest irony regarding the archaeology of the Near East
> is that the biblical temple, arguably the most famous sacred structure
> in world history, is entirely absent, in all its phases, in the archaeo-
> logical record. The primary reason for this is that the Temple Mount
> in Jerusalem, the building site of the First and Second Temples, is
> also a Muslim holy site, the location of the Dome of the Rock, and
> is unavailable for archaeological excavation or exploration.[22]

Ancient temples were considered the abode of the deity. There is no techni-cal word in Hebrew for temple. Instead, temples are regularly referred to as the "house" (*beth* or *beit*) of the deity. *Beth Dagon*, for example, is the temple of the Philistine god Dagon. And *Beth Yahweh* is the temple or house of Yahweh (Yahweh being the personal name of the Israelite God).

Throughout the Near East, temples included an anthropomorphic represen-tation—a cult statue—of the deity who "lived" in the temple. But there was no such image or statue in the Israelite temple. This is a major distinction between the Israelite Temple and all other Near Eastern temples.

Even without anthropomorphism, however, the Bible insists upon the presence of the deity in the Temple. At the installation ceremony of the Temple, when the Ark of the Covenant, which had been resting at Kiriath-jearim (modern Abu Ghosh, just outside Jerusalem) was brought into the

Temple, the priests were unable to perform the service inside the Temple because a cloud—*kavod Yahweh* (1 Kings 8:11), which is variously translated as the "Glory of the Lord" or the "Presence of the Lord" (New Jewish Publication Society translation) or the "Honor of the Lord"—filled the whole Temple (note again the super size of the deity). King Solomon then addressed the congregation:

> "The Lord has chosen
> To abide in a thick cloud:
> I have now built for You
> A stately House,
> A place where You
> May dwell forever."
> (1 Kings 8:12–13)

As Baruch Levine has noted, "[I]t is from the Temple that the deity appears and gives strength to the people."[23]

> Awesome is God in his sanctuary,
> the God of Israel.
> He gives power and strength to his people.
> (Psalm 68:35 [Hebrew vs. 36])

> In my distress I called on the Lord,
> Cried out to my God;
> In his Temple, he heard my voice;
> My cry to him reached his ears.
> (Psalm 18:6 [Hebrew vs. 7])

In this respect, the Temple of Israel's God is firmly in the tradition of other ancient Near Eastern temples. As the psalmist declares:

> For the Lord has chosen Zion;
> He has desired it for his habitation:
> "This is my resting place forever; here I will reside."
> (Psalm 132:13–14)

From his Temple, God protects his people:

> Father of orphans and protector of widows
> is God in his holy habitation ...

where the Lord will reside forever.
(Psalm 68:5,16 [Hebrew vs. 6,17])

There the people connect with the Everlasting:

How lovely is your dwelling place,
O Lord of hosts.
My soul longs, indeed it faints,
For the courts of the Lord;
My heart and my flesh sing for joy
to the living God.
(Psalm 84:1–2 [Hebrew vs. 2–3])

A careful look at Solomon's declaration at the Temple dedication ceremony, however, betrays some fascinating developments in Israel's understanding of the God who dwelled in the Temple. The Book of Kings is part of what scholars call the Deuteronomistic History, consisting of Deuteronomy, Joshua, Judges, Samuel and Kings. The Deuteronomistic History was initially edited in the late seventh century B.C. A later edition (what we see in our Bible) comes from the period after the Babylonian Exile of the sixth century B.C. But even the first edition drew on earlier sources that have not been preserved. Solomon's speech in 1 Kings 8:12–61 (about "a place where you may dwell forever") appears to come from one of these early sources. In the New Jewish Publication Society translation of this passage, from which I have quoted, it appears as poetry. The text goes on and on, however, in prose as Solomon expands on his dedicatory prayer. There it is not Yahweh who dwells in the Temple, but rather his "name." The Temple is a "house where my [God's] name might abide." This is repeated several times. "Will God really dwell on earth?" Solomon asks. He answers his own question: "Even the heavens to their uttermost reaches cannot contain you, how much less this house that I have built." God's actual dwelling place is identified several times: "[When we pray to you], O hear in your heavenly abode." This is repeated several times in this remarkable chapter (1 Kings 8:34,36,39,43). If God is in heaven, what of the Temple? "You have said: My name shall abide there" (1 Kings 8:29). "All the peoples of earth ... will recognize that your name is attached to this house that I have built" (1 Kings 8:43). Later Solomon refers to the "House which I have built to Your name" (1 Kings 8:48). The house is no longer the house of the deity, but the house of his name. As the psalmist says:

We ponder your steadfast love, O God,
in the midst of your Temple.

Your name, O God, like your praise,
    reaches to the ends of the earth.
(Psalm 48:9–10 [Hebrew vs. 10–11])

Clearly, in these texts we see a development from the earlier Canaanite conception of the Temple as the deity's actual dwelling place, to a more spiritual, non-anthropomorphic Israelite conception.[24] The shift from the Lord's actual presence to the Presence of his name (*kavod*) is, as Michael Fishbane has observed, "a radical shift of sensibility."[25]

The God whose Presence (*kavod*) is in the Temple is also universalized. "All the peoples of the earth will know Your name and revere You" (1 Kings 8:43). By the time of Second Isaiah[26] (sixth century B.C.E.), he is not only Israel's God, but a universal God: "For my house shall be called a house of prayer for all peoples. Thus declares the Lord God" (Isaiah 56:7–8).

At the end of time, Israel will be redeemed and the Lord will rule from Mount Zion. In the biblical period, Zion had migrated from the Jebusite Fortress of Zion to the Temple Mount.[27]

As the prophet Isaiah foretells:

Then the moon shall be ashamed,
And the sun shall be abashed.
For the Lord of Hosts will reign
On Mount Zion and in Jerusalem,
And the Presence will be revealed to His elders.
(Isaiah 24:23)

In that day, a great ram's horn shall be sounded; and the strayed who are in the land of Assyria and the expelled who are in the land of Egypt shall come and worship the Lord on the holy mount [*har ha-kodesh*] in Jerusalem.

(Isaiah 27:13)

As the Psalmist envisioned:

O that the deliverance of Israel might come from Zion!
When God restores the fortunes of His people,
Jacob will exult, Israel will rejoice.
(Psalm 53:6 [Hebrew vs. 7]; see also Psalm 14:7)

At the end of time, men will live again as they did at the beginning of time—in the Garden of Eden. So the Temple evokes not only images of the end of time, but also of the beginning of time.[28]

Within the Temple precinct, there were areas of varying degrees of holiness, for space in ancient Israel was not homogenous. It could be sacred or profane—and to varying degrees. When the patriarch Jacob awoke from his dream of the stairway (or ladder) to heaven, he exclaimed, "Surely the Lord is present in this place ... How awesome is this place" (Genesis 28:16–17). God called out to Moses at the site of the burning bush, "Remove your sandals from your feet, for the place on which you stand is holy ground" (Exodus 3:5). This same holy character was attached to the site of the Temple.

The Mishnah powerfully expresses this: "There are ten degrees of holiness. The Land of Israel is holier than any other land ... The walled cities [of the Land] are more holy ... Within the wall [of Jerusalem] is more holy ... The Temple Mount is even holier ... The rampart [to the Temple Mount] is more holy ... The Court of Women is even holier ... The Court of the Israelites is more holy ... The Court of the Priests is more holy ... Between the *ulam* and the altar is more holy ... The *heikhal* is yet holier ... The Holy of Holies is more holy than all of them."[29]

* * * * * * * *

In early 2003 the public learned of an inscription that, if authentic, would go far toward demonstrating that the First Temple, the Solomonic Temple, was an actual structure. If authentic, it would be the first royal inscription found of an Israelite king: Yehoash, king of Judah (or Jehoash in English, which uses the Germanic transcription), who ruled toward the end of the ninth century B.C., little more than a hundred years after King Solomon purportedly built the Temple. The Yehoash (or Jehoash) inscription, as it is known, is a 15-line Hebrew inscription on a black stone approximately the size of a piece of typing paper. It describes the collection of money for the repair of the Jerusalem Temple and closely parallels descriptions of the same event in 2 Kings 12:4–16 (Hebrew vs. 5–17) and 2 Chronicles 24:4–14.

Although the inscription is named for King Yehoash, it does not include his name. The top of the stone is broken off and the first line is entirely missing. The first surviving line of the inscription reads: "-hazyahu king of Judah." The first word is only the last part of a name—and it can only be *Ahazyahu*, the Hebrew name of the king we call Ahaziah in English. Obviously the first line of the inscription ended with the first letter of Ahaziah. What did the first part of the inscription say before it said "Ahaziah king of Judah"? Scholars know this form well from the Bible and other sources. Ahaziah is the father of the person who wrote the inscription—namely, Yehoash. So scholars have reconstructed the first and second lines to read, "I am Yehoash son of Ahaziah king of Judah." Hence the attribution of the inscription to Yehoash.

After a century, the Temple that Solomon built needed repairs. (Yehoash would not be the last king of Judah to improve the condition of the Temple. See 2 Kings 18:16 with reference to Hezekiah a century later and 2 Kings 22:3–6 with reference to Josiah almost a century later still.) The Yehoash inscription recites that he collected money (i.e., silver) for the repairs contributed by people all over the land. With it the king could buy "quarry stone and juniper wood and Edomite copper" for the repairs. Yehoash "made repairs to the Temple and the encircling walls ... May Yahweh ordain his people with blessing." The full text is printed in the box below.

Here are some quotations from 2 Kings 12:4–16 (Hebrew vs. 5–17), which seem to refer to the same event:

> Jehoash said to the priests, "All the money, current money, brought into the House of the Lord as sacred donations—any money a man may pay as the money equivalent of persons, or any other money that a man may be minded to bring to the House of the Lord—let the priests receive it, each from his benefactor; they in turn, shall make repairs on the House, wherever damage may be found."

(2 Kings 12:4–5 [Hebrew vs. 5–6])

Jehoash Inscription

HEBREW TRANSCRIPTION	TRANSLITERATION	TRANSLATION
... חזיהו · מ[לכ] .... [י]	Line a. ['nky yhw' š bn ']	[I am Yeho'ash son of A-]
הדה · ואעש · את · ה....	Line 1. ḥzyhw . m[lk . y]	hazyahu king of Judah,
ה · כאשר · נמלאה · נ[ד]	Line 2. hdh . w'ʿs . 't . h'[gr]	and I made the collection (of silver).
בת · לב · אש · בארצ · ובמד	Line 3. h . k'šr nml'h . n[d]	When it (the collection) was fulfilled, the generosity
בר · ובכל · ערי · יהדה · ל	Line 4. bt . lb 'š . b'rṣ . wbmd	of heart of men in the land and in the desert,
תת · כספ · הקדשמ · לרב	Line 5. br . wbkl . ʿry . yhdh . l	and in all the cities of Judah
לקנת · אבנ · מחצב · ובר	Line 6. tt . ksp . hqdšm . lrb	giving consecrated silver abundantly
שמ · ונחשת · אדמ לעשת ·	Line 7. lqnt . 'bn . mḥṣb . wbr	to buy quarry stone and juniper
במלאכה · באמנה · ואעש	Line 8. šm . wnḥšt . 'dm . lʿst	wood and Edomite copper, performing
את · בדק · הבית · והקרת ס	Line 9. bml'kh . b'mnh . w'ʿs	the work in good faith. And I made the
בב · ואת · היצע · והשבכ	Line 10. 't . bdq . hbyt . whqrt [.] s	repair of the Temple, and the encircling walls,
מ · והלולמ · והגרעת · ה	Line 11. bb . w't . hyṣʿ . whšbk	and the storied structure, and the lattice works,
דלתת · והיה · הימ · הזה	Line 12. m . whlwlm. whgrʿt . wh	and the spiral staircases, and the recesses,
לעדת · כי · תצלח · המלאכה ·	Line 13. dltt . whyh . hym . hzh	and the doors. And this day will become
יצו · יהוה · את · עמו · בברכה	Line 14. lʿdt . ky . tṣlḥ . hml'kh	a witness that the work will prosper.
	Line 15. yṣw . yhwh . 't . ʿmw . bbrkh	May Yahweh ordain his people with blessing.

Brackets indicate reconstructed letters. Transcription by Christopher Rollston, Emmanuel School of Religion; transliteration and translation by Frank Moore Cross, professor emeritus, Harvard University.

After some delay on the part of procrastinating priests, the money collected was used to pay "the carpenters and the builders who worked on the house of the Lord, to the masons and the stonecutters, as well as to buy timber and quarried stone for making repairs on the house of the Lord" (2 Kings 12:11–12 [Hebrew vs. 12–13]).

Essentially the same description, although somewhat embellished, is found in a later biblical text (2 Chronicles 24:4–14). In addition to "masons and carpenters," Chronicles mentions "craftsmen in iron and bronze [or copper]."

The parallels between the inscription and the biblical text are, of course, striking. For some, that is enough to pronounce the inscription a forgery, relying on the principle that "It's too good to be true."[30] On the other hand, the first line of the inscription, which contains the name of the king who supposedly repaired the Temple, has not survived. Is this a sign of authenticity? Or was a forger smart enough to omit the name, while allowing its certain reconstruction? Something else that might point to authenticity: It is a very long inscription as these things go; forgers normally forge only short inscriptions, just a few words—fewer chances to make mistakes, more likely to fool the experts.

The Yehoash inscription came to public attention within two months of another startling inscription that had electrified the world: a bone box, or ossuary, inscribed "James, son of Joseph, brother of Jesus." And the Yehoash inscription was uncovered in the home of the owner of the James ossuary. That two such astonishing inscriptions should surface within a couple of months and from the same source soon led to a police investigation and the appointment of a committee by the Israel Antiquities Authority to examine the two artifacts and decide whether they are authentic or fake. The Israel Antiquities Authority committee declared both of the inscriptions fakes, and the police have subsequently indicted the owner and several leading Israeli antiquities dealers with the crime of creating forgeries or knowingly selling or attempting to sell them.

I am not convinced the Yehoash inscription is a forgery. But neither do I believe it is authentic. Since it would be so important if it is authentic, however, it is worthwhile looking at the question in more depth.

One thing is sure: The Yehoash inscription was known to insiders several years before it became public. Oded Golan, the owner of the James ossuary, owns one of the largest antiquities collections in Israel; he frequents Arab antiquities dealers in the Old City almost weekly. That is how, he says, he became aware of the Yehoash inscription: It was shown to him by an Arab antiquities dealer named Abu Yasser. Golan persuaded the owner, he says (there is considerable skepticism about Golan's truthfulness), to allow him to have it examined by the Israel Museum because Golan felt that is where it belonged if it were authentic. The Israel Museum kept it for well over a year before deciding not to acquire the inscription. In all, four years elapsed between the time it came to Golan's attention and the time the Israel Antiquities Authority seized it from him. In the meantime, the alleged owner, Abu Yasser, had died. (The plaque with the inscription is now being held by the Antiquities Authority, pending the trial for forgery.)

There has been speculation that the tablet may have come from the Waqf's illegal excavation to open up a monumental entrance to Solomon's Stables and an underground mosque (see Chapter IV). But this cannot be since the plaque came into Oded Golan's possession before this excavation. It is, of course, possible that the inscription came from the Muslim cemetery outside the eastern wall of the Temple Mount. The Muslims have been using the cemetery for new burials for a number of years.

Several very prominent scholars are convinced that the Yehoash inscription is a forgery on paleographic, orthographic and linguistic grounds. Paleography is the study of the shapes and forms of each letter, which change over time, as car grills do. In this way, each letter can be dated, and a forger's mistakes are sometimes easily discovered. There are also small differences in related Semitic dialects like Hebrew, Moabite, Ammonite and Edomite that can also trip up a forger. Orthography is spelling, which also changes over time. Harvard's Frank

2 Kings 12:4–16

Jehoash said to the priests, "All the money offered as sacred donations that is brought into the house of the Lord, the money for which each person is assessed—the money from the assessment of persons—and the money from the voluntary offerings brought into the house of the Lord, let the priests receive from each of the donors; and let them repair the house wherever any need of repairs is discovered." But by the twenty-third year of King Jehoash the priests had made no repairs to the house. Therefore King Jehoash summoned the priest Jehoiada with the other priests and said to them, "Why are you not repairing the house? Now therefore do not accept any more money from your donors but hand it over for the repair of the house." So the priests agreed that they would neither accept more money from the people nor repair the house.

Then the priest Jehoiada took a chest, made a hole in its lid, and set it beside the altar on the right side as one entered the house of the Lord; the priests who guarded the threshold put in it all the money that was brought into the house of the Lord. Whenever they saw that there was a great deal of money in the chest, the king's secretary and the high priest went up, counted the money that was found in the house of the Lord, and tied it up in bags. They would give the money that was weighed out into the hands of the workers who had the oversight of the house of the Lord; then they paid it out to the carpenters and the builders who worked on the house of the Lord, to the masons and the stonecutters, as well as to buy timber and quarried stone for making repairs on the house of the Lord, as well as for any outlay for repairs of the house. But for the house of the Lord no basins of silver, snuffers, bowls, trumpets, or any vessels of gold, or of silver, were made from the money that was brought into the house of the Lord, for that was given to the workers who were repairing the house of the Lord with it. They did not ask for an account from those into whose hand they delivered the money to pay out to the workers, for they dealt honestly. The money from the guilt-offerings and the money from the sin-offerings was not brought into the house of the Lord; it belonged to the priests.

Cross says the Yehoash inscription is not just a forgery, but "a rather poor forgery." Johns Hopkins professor Kyle McCarter calls one of the errors "a real howler." Other leading scholars agree: Edward Greenstein of Tel Aviv University; Victor (Avigdor) Hurowitz of Ben-Gurion University of the Negev; and Joseph Naveh of Hebrew University.

But just as you're about to declare "Case closed," along comes another set of equally prominent scholars who say the case for a forgery has not been made. These scholars include André Lemaire of the Sorbonne; Ada Yardeni, a leading Israeli paleographer and epigrapher; linguist Chaim Cohen of Ben-Gurion University of the Negev; Bible scholar David Noel Freedman of the University of California at San Diego; and archaeologist Gabriel Barkay, among others.[31]

At the risk of getting somewhat technical, let's look at perhaps the most prominent alleged error. In line 10, the inscription speaks of the "repair of the Temple," or *bedeq ha-bayit* in Hebrew. The alleged forger uses the word *bedeq* to mean repair, and, indeed that is its meaning—but only in modern Hebrew. In ancient Hebrew, *bedeq* refers to something that is damaged or broken. In the biblical account that inspired the forgery, *bedeq* refers to the fissures or cracks

2 Chronicles 24:4-14

Some time afterwards Joash decided to restore the house of the Lord. He assembled the priests and the Levites and said to them, "Go out to the cities of Judah and gather money from all Israel to repair the house of your God, year by year; and see that you act quickly." But the Levites did not act quickly. So the king summoned Jehoiada the chief, and said to him, "Why have you not required the Levites to bring in from Judah and Jerusalem the tax levied by Moses, the servant of the Lord, on the congregation of Israel for the tent of the covenant?" For the children of Athaliah, that wicked woman, had broken into the house of God, and had even used all the dedicated things of the house of the Lord for the Baals.

So the king gave command, and they made a chest, and set it outside the gate of the house of the Lord. A proclamation was made throughout Judah and Jerusalem to bring in for the Lord the tax that Moses the servant of God laid on Israel in the wilderness. All the leaders and all the people rejoiced, and brought their tax and dropped it into the chest until it was full. Whenever the chest was brought to the king's officers by the Levites, when they saw that there was a large amount of money in it, the king's secretary and the officer of the chief priest would come and empty the chest and take it and return it to its place. So they did day after day, and collected money in abundance. The king and

Jehoiada gave it to those who had charge of the work of the house of the Lord, and they hired masons and carpenters to restore the house of the Lord, and also workers in iron and bronze to repair the house of the Lord. So those who were engaged in the work labored, and the repairs went forward at their hands, and they restored the house of God to its proper condition and strengthened it. When they had finished, they brought the rest of the money to the king and Jehoiada, and with it were made utensils for the house of the Lord, utensils for the service and for the burnt-offerings, and ladles, and vessels of gold and silver. They offered burnt-offerings in the house of the Lord regularly all the days of Jehoiada.

in the Temple that are to be repaired. The forger is saying the Temple is to be damaged or broken, instead of repaired, precisely the opposite of what the forger intended. He is obviously a speaker of modern Hebrew who simply assumed the word meant the same thing in ancient Hebrew.

Is the case proven? Well, not quite. Professor Freedman and his colleagues (Shawna Dolansky Overton and David Miano) contend that Professor Cross and his like-minded colleagues are mistranslating *bedeq ha-bayit*.[32] Another word in the inscription (*'asah*) refers to the repairs to the Temple; *bedeq* refers to the crack (or breaches) in the Temple. In short, the supposed forger is using *bedeq* properly when the text is properly understood.

Even a member of the Israel Antiquities Authority committee that declared the inscription a forgery (Ronny Reich) notes that *bedeq ha-bayit* in the inscription "is not the action of repair and maintenance [as in modern Hebrew], but rather the problem that needs to be repaired, i.e., the poor condition of the building with its cracks and defects." Chaim Cohen, a specialist in the usage of ancient Hebrew and other Semitic languages, agrees; he contends that the inscription properly transmits and understands biblical Hebrew. The text is saying that Yehoash claims to have renovated "the breach(es) of the Temple (*bedeq ha-bayit*) and of the surrounding walls, and the (multi-) storied structure, and the meshwork, and the winding stairs, and the recesses, and the doors." Cohen goes on to comment: "Understanding the phrase as deriving from modern Hebrew usage can only be achieved by completely ignoring the phrase's immediate and wider contexts—a flagrant violation of one of the most fundamental rules of Biblical and comparative Semitic philology."[33]

Moreover, one linguistic oddity in the inscription can be understood to sustain authenticity. As noted above, the inscription mentions copper from Edom, south of the Dead Sea. Copper (or bronze—they are the same word in Hebrew) is not mentioned in the account of this episode in Kings, but it is mentioned in Chronicles. For Cross this demonstrates how the forger jumped around, copying here from Kings, there from Chronicles. Cross also notes that the forger was smart enough to know that Edom was a chief source of copper in biblical antiquity. However, Haifa University professor Ronny Reich, perhaps reflecting a change of mind since voting that the inscription was a forgery, now believes that "Edomite copper" is a mistranslation; a correct translation would seem to demonstrate the authenticity of the inscription, although he did not say so explicitly. Reich points out that the Hebrew letters that constitute the name Edom can mean a number of other things, Hebrew spelling being largely consonantal without vowels. Thus these letters can mean not only Edom, but also "red" or "man(kind)" or "earth" or "ground." Admittedly, none of these makes much sense as modifiers of "copper." But there is also another possibility. The word can also mean "Adam"—not the first man mentioned in Genesis, but a city named "Adam" in the Book of

Joshua. Could the Yehoash inscription be saying that the copper came from the city of Adam, rather than from Edom? Reich powerfully demonstrates that it could—and probably does. By putting together various references in the Bible, Reich shows that the city of Adam was a center for fabricating copper objects for the Temple. It is much more likely that the inscription refers to the place where the copper was fabricated (the city of Adam) than where the copper was mined (Edom). In Reich's words, "Would King Jehoash, needing copper fittings for repairs to the Temple, have sent to the distant desert copper mines [of Edom] for ingots extracted from copper ore or would he have gone instead to the quite-close Jordan Valley workshops, like those in the city of Adam, where copper nails, door hinges and the like were available? The answer is obvious. He would have gone to the workshops in the city of Adam."[34] Did the forger know about the copper-casting tradition of the city of Adam in the Jordan Valley, which even the greatest experts like Cross did not know about until pointed out by Reich in his careful dissection of the biblical text? Hard to believe the forger was so smart. And, if not, the inscription would seem to be authentic.

At the very least, we have a clash of experts. The experts who say the case for a forgery has not been made point out that there are very few Hebrew inscriptions from this period with which to compare the inscription. As Professor Freedman put it, "What do we really know about the Hebrew of official royal inscriptions of Judah in the ninth to eighth centuries B.C.? The answer is simple: Not much."

Freedman goes on:

> Authenticated inscriptions frequently challenge our knowledge of biblical Hebrew, containing syntax, vocabulary and orthography that differ from biblical usage. Of the very few inscriptions of any kind from this period, including those of neighboring nations, every one provides something novel and sometimes disturbingly surprising about a language we may think we know but don't always fully grasp. And the surer we are, the more surprised we are likely to be by what comes out of the ground.[35]

If the test applied by those who find the Yehoash inscription to be a forgery were applied to other inscriptions, even the most famous biblically related inscriptions, such as the Siloam inscription documenting King Hezekiah's construction of a water tunnel under Jerusalem in the late eighth century B.C. and the Mesha inscription giving a different slant on a mid-ninth-century B.C. war with the Moabites described in the Bible, would be considered forgeries.[36] (Neither the Siloam inscription nor the Mesha inscription, incidentally, was found by archaeologists or other scholars, but no one today doubts their authenticity.)

We find the same divisions concerning the Yehoash inscription among the so-called hard scientists who have looked at this inscription. The two scientists on the Israel Antiquities Authority committee who found it to be a forgery (Yuval Goren and Avner Ayalon) are opposed by three scientists at the Geological Survey of Israel (Amnon Rosenfeld, Shimon Ilani and Michael Dvorchek) who, before the object came to light publicly, found it authentic and who continue to hold this view even after examining the reasoning of the committee scientists who concluded that the inscription is a forgery. In addition, Joel Kronfeld of Tel Aviv University has joined the increasingly loud chorus criticizing the work of the Israel Antiquities Authority scientists as not supporting their conclusion.[37]

Another factor weighs heavily in my mind. The plaque containing the inscription had a big crack in it that runs diagonally through lines 7–10. The letters of the inscription in lines 7–10 run across this crack. This means that either these letters were engraved before the plaque developed this crack or the forger engraved these letters across the crack. No one, so far as I know, has made this latter argument. Any effort to engrave across the crack would break it. This point is emphasized by what actually happened: When the police confiscated the plaque from Oded Golan's apartment, they took it from Tel Aviv to Jerusalem; on the way, the plaque broke in two along the crack. True, we don't know whether the plaque was so fragile that it broke from bumps in the transportation or whether the police dropped it on the floor. Giving the police the benefit of the doubt, it appears the plaque was in very fragile condition. No forger would even try to engrave letters across this crack; he would be well aware that the plaque might break if he tried.

If the letters were engraved before the plaque developed the crack, either the letters are ancient or the forger somehow managed to crack the plaque (deliberately?) after he engraved it. It is difficult to imagine how the forger could crack the plaque after engraving it or that he would even try, thereby endangering the entire enterprise. Ronny Reich points out to me that his examination revealed patina in the crack, although the patina has not been scientifically examined.[38]

If all this is true, the engraving must be ancient. And if it is ancient, it attests to the existence of Solomon's Temple.

Oded Golan has been indicted and charged with forging the inscription on the plaque, so we may learn more about this as the case progresses. But I, for one, am not yet ready to declare it a slam-dunk forgery.

* * * * * * *

It is time to face the challenge of the so-called "biblical minimalists," a group of scholars centered in Copenhagen, Denmark (Niels Peter Lemche, Thomas Thompson) and Sheffield University in England (Philip Davies, Keith Whitelam), who deny almost all historicity of the biblical narrative and, therefore, of the biblical descriptions of a Temple built by a perhaps-fictional king.

This 15-line Hebrew inscription, known as the Yehoash inscription, describes the repairs to the Israelite temple by King Yehoash in the ninth century B.C. The inscription is currently at the center of a controversy as to whether it is a forgery or authentic. It conforms rather closely to biblical descriptions of repairs Yehoash made to the Temple. Is this evidence of forgery or authenticity—or neither?

Roughly stated, their position is encapsulated in the assertion of Davies that King David "is no more a historical figure than King Arthur."[39] The same goes for King Solomon.

The biblical minimalists paint with a broad brush. They defend their position not so much by an alleged paucity of archaeological evidence, but rather on the nature of the biblical text, suggesting that it is legend and myth, much like stories from other cultures that created a romantic and glorious history that is patently untrue. Thus, Thompson calls one of his minimalist books *The Mythic Past*.

Some of the minimalists' work appears to be ideologically driven; that is, biblical-minimalist articles and books are sometimes fiercely anti-Zionist, some would say even tinged with anti-Semitism. A book by Whitelam, for example, is

This 13th-century B.C. hieroglyphic stele, known as the Merneptah Stele or Israel Stele, describes Pharaoh Merneptah's campaign into Canaan and mentions three cities and a people that he allegedly destroyed. All scholars agree that the people mentioned is "Israel" (see detail at right). At this time Israel was not yet a state, but only a people. The pharaoh clearly exaggerates, however, when he claims to have destroyed Israel.

entitled *The Invention of Ancient Israel—The Silencing of Palestinian History.*

When archaeological finds do seem to contradict some of their basic contentions, the minimalists twist and turn to avoid the implications. For example, the famous Merneptah Stele is a hieroglyphic inscription—found quite accidentally in the 19th century and now displayed in the Cairo Museum—that mentions Israel. There can be no question that the applicable hieroglyphs are to be read "Israel." No one disputes this. And Israel is placed in the northern hill country of Canaan, just where the Bible says the early Israelites settled. This reference to Israel is part of a description of Merneptah's late-13th-century B.C. campaign into Canaan, in which he claims to have destroyed Ashkelon, Gezer, Yanoam and Israel, in that order. The line of text concerning Israel reads: "Israel is laid waste; his seed is not" (proof that even contemporaneous records are not always reliable).

In hieroglyphics, special signs called determinatives are often attached to words to indicate what kind of word it is. Determinatives have no phonetic value themselves. For example, a special determinative is attached to the names of towns and cities to indicate that the word refers to a city. In the Merneptah Stele, Ashkelon, Gezer and Yanoam all have this determinative attached to them. Another determinative indicates a people. That is the determinative attached to Israel. Israel has not yet become a nation; it is still a people.

If you're looking for evidence of early Israel, it would be hard to imagine something better than this—a people living in the area where and when, according to the biblical account, the Israelites were said to be emerging. Moreover, these Israelites were so important that the pharaoh of Egypt knew of them and boasted at defeating them. That must have been worth bragging about.

What do the biblical minimalists do with this? They cannot argue that the hieroglyphic word should be read other than Israel. But "what this entity [Israel] precisely was is, on the other hand, not as easy to ascertain as people may be inclined to believe," writes minimalist Niels Peter Lemche. He contends that Merneptah's Israel may be simply a geographical designation or a political designation instead of an ethnic designation. In any event, the Israel of the Merneptah Stele is a different Israel from the biblical Israel, which represents "a much later interpretation of a tradition of Israel."[40]

Another more recent find has made the biblical minimalists squirm even more. In arguing that David was a mere mythical construct, the minimalists could point to the fact that there was absolutely no archaeological evidence that such a man ever existed. Indeed, not even the name David—any David—appeared in the ancient onomasticon (a list of names). And that was true—until 1993. In that year Israeli archaeologist Avraham Biran discovered a stele at Tel Dan in northern Israel that mentioned "the House [Dynasty] of David." The inscription is in Aramaic and is written by a non-Israelite monarch (so it cannot be attacked as an Israelite fabrication). Dating to the mid-ninth century B.C., little more than a hundred years after David, the inscription affirmatively attests to the long-lasting importance of the Davidic dynasty.

The minimalists' reaction to this has been either (or both) that the reading "David" is incorrect (Aramaic, like Hebrew, is written only with consonants [*DVD*], so it could be read with other vowels, perhaps meaning "uncle" or "beloved") or, as a last resort, that the whole inscription is a forgery, salted by some unidentified forger into Biran's excavation. Suffice it to say that no one professionally involved in archaeology has bought either of these strained and incredulous assertions, and they are generally disregarded, despite the fact that some minimalists continue to trumpet them.

The biblical minimalists have not had much to say specifically about Solomon's Temple, however. Their attack is broad based, on the very existence—or nonexistence—of the United Monarchy. Presumably, if the biblical account of the United Monarchy was as devoid of historicity as the minimalists claim, the glorious Israelite Temple would also be a figment of a later writer's imagination.

A much more serious and sophisticated assault on the historicity of the biblical description of the United Monarchy is made by Israel Finkelstein, a prominent Israeli archaeologist at Tel Aviv University. He is often regarded as a biblical minimalist, but he denies the sobriquet. His view: "[F]rom a purely literary and archaeological standpoint, the minimalists have some points in their favor. A close reading of the biblical description of the days of Solomon clearly suggests that this was a portrayal of an idealized past, a glorious Golden Age."[41]

Unlike some biblical minimalists, however, Finkelstein does not deny the existence of David and Solomon or of the United Monarchy. He also accepts

This stele from Tel Dan in northern Israel, excavated in the 1990s by Israeli archaeologist Avraham Biran, dates to the mid-ninth century B.C. It includes a reference to "the house of David" (BYT DVD), little more than a century after the great king ruled. This reference—by a foreign ruler who writes in Aramaic—is powerful evidence that the Davidic dynasty was not a fictional creation of later biblical writers.

the implications of the Tel Dan inscription. The Tel Dan inscription "is dramatic evidence of the fame of the Davidic dynasty less than a hundred years after the reign of David's son Solomon," Finkelstein writes. "The question we must therefore face is no longer one of David and Solomon's mere existence. We must now see if the Bible's sweeping description of David's great military victories and of Solomon's great building projects is consistent with the archaeological evidence."[42]

Until recently the archaeological evidence for King Solomon's great building prowess was very considerable—especially the monumental fortified gateways at three major ancient Israelite cities: Gezer, Hazor and Megiddo. The gateways were dated to the tenth century B.C., the time of Solomon. Moreover, the Bible itself tells us that Solomon fortified these very places (1 Kings 9:15).

That was the situation until Finkelstein developed his so-called "low chronology." According to his revised chronology, the archaeological strata (or levels) that had been dated to the tenth century B.C. (the time of Solomon) must be redated and lowered to the ninth century B.C. In other words, these monumental fortified gateways were no longer constructed by Solomon, but rather by some unspecified ninth-century B.C. successor.

Under this new chronology, what do we have from the time of Solomon, who, Finkelstein recognizes, did indeed exist? Well, it is the archaeological material previously attributed to the 11th century B.C. and thus usually associated with the time of the biblical Judges. The material evidence of this period reflects an extremely poor and rather simple society. Under Finkelstein's new low chronology, this material now becomes associated with the King Solomon. No wonder Finkelstein is not impressed with Solomon's accomplishments.

The arguments Finkelstein makes are complex and technical. Suffice it to say here that they have won the agreement only of people involved in the current excavations at Megiddo, which Finkelstein co-directs. His low chronology has been resoundingly rejected by a host of leading archaeologists. Among them are Lawrence Stager, excavator of Ashkelon; former director of the Albright Institute in Jerusalem and excavator of Gezer, William Dever; the Albright's current director and the co-director of the excavation of Philistine Ekron, Seymour Gitin; Amnon Ben-Tor of The Hebrew University, excavator of Hazor; Trude Dothan of The Hebrew University, co-director of the Ekron excavation; Ephraim Stern of The Hebrew University, recently retired director of the excavation of Tel Dor; and Amihai Mazar of The Hebrew University, excavator of Tel Rehov in northern Israel, where some of the most damning evidence against Finkelstein has been found.

Perhaps the lone exceptions (other than Finkelstein's supporters at the Megiddo dig) are Ilan Sharon and Ayelet Gilboa, two younger archaeologists who together succeeded Ephraim Stern in leading the excavation at Tel Dor.

Finkelstein has another string to his bow, however, and it is Jerusalem. Jerusalem is probably the most excavated site in the world. The entry for Jerusalem in the standard archaeological encyclopedia of excavations in the Holy Land lists 126 different excavations between 1853 and 1992. There have been numerous Jerusalem excavations since then. The result: Very little has been found from the tenth century B.C. This is the basis for Finkelstein's conclusion that "the most optimistic assessment of this negative evidence is that tenth century Jerusalem was rather limited in extent, perhaps not more than a typical hill country village."[43]

Several things need to be said about this contention. First, be careful of negative evidence. Just when you think it tells you something, the unexpected turns up.[44] The old saw is that the absence of evidence is not evidence of absence. I would modify this somewhat: Negative evidence *is* persuasive only when affirmative evidence would be expected.

The Stepped Stone Structure is located on a ridge south of the Temple Mount, known as the City of David. It probably served as the foundation for a major fortress or administrative building on top of the hill, perhaps King David's palace, as archaeologist Eilat Mazar believes.

What about the negative evidence—or lack of evidence—from Jerusalem? There are two answers: (1) It is there if you know where to look. (2) Whatever paucity of evidence exists (or doesn't exist) is explainable and understandable.

The largest Iron Age monument in Jerusalem from the biblical period (the Iron Age, 1200–586 B.C.) is called the Stepped Stone Structure. It stands in the oldest part of Jerusalem, the ridge known today as the City of David. The Stepped Stone Structure rises to a height of a 12-story building and is generally regarded as the foundations of a major fortress or administrative building. (In a very recent excavation on the ridge, Eilat Mazar of The Hebrew University has uncovered a building that may be related to the Stepped Stone Structure; she believes that the building may well be King David's palace.) The Stepped Stone Structure was either there when David conquered the city or comes from the period of the United Monarchy of David and Solomon, depending on who does the dating. In addition to this structure, tenth-century Jerusalem had available a complex water system (although no pottery sherds from this period have been

found at the Gihon Spring in the recent excavations directed by Ronny Reich and Eli Shukron). Some architecture and pottery from the tenth century B.C. have also been found at various sites in the ancient city. Summing up the evidence of a myriad of excavations, Jane Cahill, a leading expert on Jerusalem (she is publishing the excavation report for the late Israeli archaeologist Yigal Shiloh's major excavation in the City of David), states: "Virtually every archaeologist to have excavated in the City of David has found architecture and artifacts dating to the period of the United Monarchy."[45]

There is a good reason why they haven't found even more. As is the case with the Temple Mount, much of the crest of the City of David is unavailable for excavation because of modern buildings. Further, until recently Jerusalem excavators didn't know enough to keep the small pottery sherds that can be so important for dating purposes, so they may well have thrown away tenth-century B.C. exemplars without realizing their importance. Equally important, because much of ancient Jerusalem was built on the slopes, and Jerusalem builders used stone, rather than mud-brick, each successive builder went down to bedrock, destroying what was previously there, in order to provide a firm foundation for the new structure. Earlier buildings were often simply dismantled for their masonry. All this has prevented the accumulation of superimposed archaeological strata characteristic of Israel's tells. Still, the paucity of pottery from the tenth century B.C., especially at the Gihon Spring, remains a problem.

Several cuneiform tablets found at Tell el-Amarna in Egypt consist of correspondence between the Egyptian pharaoh and Abdi-Heba, a 14th-century B.C. king of Jerusalem. This provides contemporary evidence that Jerusalem was the center of a city-state at that time, even though no archaeological evidence of this city has been found at the site. Similarly, a city of the 10th century B.C. was doubtless there, even though only meager evidence from this period has been excavated.

The period of the United Monarchy is not the only period in Jerusalem's history for which the archaeological evidence is sparse. There is even less from the 14th century B.C., but we know there was an urban center here at the time. We know it from an archive of cuneiform tablets found in Egypt consisting of correspondence between two successive pharaohs and their subservient city-states in Canaan. One of these 14th-century B.C. city-states was Jerusalem. Several letters between the then-king of Jerusalem, Abdi-Heba, and the Egyptian pharaoh have been found at Tell el-Amarna. So there must have been a city here in the 14th century B.C., but no evidence of it has been found *in situ*.

Finkelstein points out, however, that "excavations in the City of David have revealed impressive finds from the Middle Bronze Age [specifically, the 18th century B.C.] ... [but] just not from the tenth century B.C."[46]

He's right: City walls, towers and water systems have indeed survived in Jerusalem from the Middle Bronze Age, but for a very good reason: All of them continued in use for a thousand years before being replaced in the eighth century B.C. That is why they survived. But the rest of the Middle Bronze Age city—the residences, administrative buildings, cult equipment, pottery—has completely disappeared. Nothing has survived. In this sense, the situation in the Middle Bronze Age is much like that in the 14th century B.C. (the period of the Amarna tablets) and the tenth century B.C.

Finkelstein regards Solomon, although he existed, as a mere tribal "chieftain."[47] He ruled over "a marginal, isolated, rural region, with no signs of great wealth."[48] About Jerusalem, Finkelstein writes: "The image of Jerusalem in the time of ... Solomon has for centuries been a subject of mythmaking and romance ... [In the Bible] Solomon's greatest achievements were his building activities. In Jerusalem he constructed a magnificent, richly decorated Temple to YHWH, [and] inaugurated it in great pomp."[49] From all this, I thought Finkelstein would deny that Solomon ever built a Temple. But nowhere, so far as I have been able to read, does he specifically talk about whether Solomon built a Temple. Just to make sure, I decided to call my old friend and ask him directly.

He began by reaffirming his belief in the existence of both David and Solomon. As the Tel Dan inscription corroborates, they founded a dynasty: the House of David. It was customary in the ancient Near East to build a temple at the founding of a dynasty. But there was an even better argument that I had in mind and that I was glad to hear instead from Finkelstein himself:

Finkelstein believes that the Bible was actually composed in the late seventh or early sixth century B.C. Clearly a Temple existed on the site *sometime* in the First Temple period, as indicated by the remains of the pre-Herodian Temple Mount and the long, firmly established tradition of the Temple. The question then is whether, like so much in the description of Solomon's kingdom (as Finkelstein's reads it), the Bible is exaggerating Solomon's accomplishments, attributing to him what was actually built by a later Judahite king. Did the seventh-century B.C. author of the Book of Kings, for his own political purposes, attribute to Solomon the Temple that was really built by some late First Temple-period Israelite king? I thought this would comport with so much else of Finkelstein's view of Solomon's accomplishments. But no, he explained to me, not the Temple. If the Temple were actually built by Hezekiah (for example), it would not be credible to attribute it to Solomon; everybody would know it wasn't true.

These arrowheads from the sixth-century B.C. Babylonian siege of Jerusalem were found among the ashy remains of the sixth-century destruction. The excavation was conducted by Israeli archaeologist Nahman Avigad in the Old City.

The importance of this explanation is not only the intrinsic power of the argument itself, but also the fact that someone so generally skeptical as Finkelstein, someone who denigrates Solomon's accomplishments, someone who is often called a biblical minimalist, someone who claims that almost nothing has been found from the tenth century B.C. in Jerusalem excavations nevertheless recognizes that Solomon did exist and that he did build the Temple.

The First Temple was destroyed by the Babylonians in 586 B.C. after standing continuously for nearly 400 years. Nebuchadnezzar, the Babylonian destroyer of the Temple, had attacked Judah 11 years earlier. He had even laid siege to Jerusalem. The Judahite king Jehoiachin had surrendered, rather than attempt to break the Babylonian siege. Judah became a Babylonian vassal. Jehoiachin himself was carried off to exile in Babylonia, along with his royal court, leading citizens and thousands of ordinary people. (The number ranges from more than 3,000 to 10,000, depending on the source: Jeremiah 52:28; 2 Kings 24:14,16.) The treasures of Jehoiachin's Jerusalem palace as well as the gold from the Temple were paid as tribute to the conqueror. The Babylonian king "carried off from Jerusalem all the treasures of the House of the Lord [*Beth Yahweh*] and the treasures of the royal palace; he stripped off all the golden decorations in the Temple of the Lord [*Heikhal Yahweh*]—which King Solomon of Israel had made" (2 Kings 24:13). But Nebuchadnezzar pointedly did not destroy the city or the Temple (2 Kings 24:10–17). Moreover, after 39 years in prison, Jehoiachin was released and apparently received a royal allowance, even supping at the Babylonian monarch's table, a fact indirectly confirmed in cuneiform records from Babylonia.[50]

But back in Judah, a Babylonian puppet Zedekiah had been placed on the Judahite throne. Nine years later, Zedekiah rebelled (2 Kings 25:1 [Hebrew 24:20]). This time, in what was clearly a deliberate act of retribution and reprisal, Nebuchadnezzar destroyed the city and burned the Temple. Nebuzaradan, the Babylonian chief of the guards, "burned the House of the Lord, the king's palace and all the houses of Jerusalem" (2 Kings 25:9; cf. 2 Chronicles 36:19).

Zedekiah managed to escape and fled toward Jericho. He was soon captured, however, and made to watch as his sons were killed "before his eyes," the text tells us. His eyes were then gouged out so that the last thing he saw was his sons being murdered (2 Kings 25:5–7; Jeremiah 52:9–11). Zedekiah himself was deported in chains to Babylon, where he died.

Thus ended the state of Judah and the Temple of Solomon.

On the ninth day of the month of Av (Tisha b'Av), in commemoration of the destructions of both the First and Second Temples, the Book of Lamentations is read in the synagogue. In many synagogues the congregants sit on the floor listening

Thousands of ordinary Judahites, as well as members of the royal court, were led off to exile in Babylon after Nebuchadnezzar conquered Jerusalem and burned the Temple in the early sixth century B.C. This relief from the palace of Sennacherib depicts the similar deportation of the inhabitants of Lachish after the Assyrian conquest of 701 B.C.

to the wailing cantillation of the *hazzan* (chanter). It is a day of fasting:

> O Fair Maiden Zion.
> For your ruin is vast as the sea.
>
> ...
>
> Lift up your hands to Him
> For the life of your infants,
> Who faint from hunger.
>
> ...
>
> Alas, women eat their own fruit,
> Their new-born babes!
> Alas, priest and prophet are slain
> In the Sanctuary of the Lord!
> Prostrate in the streets lie
> Both young and old.
> My maidens and youths
> Are fallen by the sword
>
> ...
>
> Because of Mount Zion which lies desolate;
> Jackals prowl over it.
> (Lamentations 2:13,19,20–21, 5:18)

But, as we know, that was not the end, only the beginning:

> Your iniquity, Fair Zion, is expiated;
> He will exile you no longer.
>
> ...
>
> But You, O Lord, are enthroned forever.
> (Lamentations 4:22, 5:19)

SITE OF
THE ANTONIA

Excavated Ditch

Gate Tadi
Northern limit of Temple Court

MORIAH

Dome of the Rock

MORIAH

Golden Gate

Present line of Fort Wall

Council House

VII

Before Solomon's Temple

THE CORE ELEMENT IN SOLOMON'S TEMPLE WAS THE ARK OF THE Covenant, which held the Tablets of the Law in the Holy of Holies. Solomon's Temple brought together Israel's holiest possession and its holiest place. Before that, they were separate.

In biblical tradition Moses received the Tablets of the Law inscribed by the finger of God on Mt. Sinai. The tablets contained in the Ark of the Covenant were actually a second set. The first set was flung down and smashed by Moses when he came down from the mountain and found the people worshiping a golden calf.

In popular lore these tablets contained the Ten Commandments. But that's not quite what the biblical text says, even though tablets with the Ten Commandments have been the subject of Supreme Court litigation as to whether, and under what conditions, they may be displayed on public property. Exodus 24:12 says only that the stone tablets contained *torah* and *mitzvah*—law and commandment. Exodus 31:18 tells us that there were *two* tablets. Exodus 32:15 says they were inscribed on *both* sides. None of these passages mentions ten of anything.

That there were ten is derived from notices in Exodus 34:28 and Deuteronomy 4:13 and 10:4. But these passages refer not to ten commandments (*mitzvot*) but to ten words or things or sayings (*aseret ha-devarim*). In the two places where the so-called Ten Commandments appear in the Hebrew Bible (Exodus 20:1–17; Deuteronomy 5:6–21), they are not numbered, and the number ten is not mentioned. Indeed, it is not clear that there are ten; different faith traditions

What was on the Temple Mount before Solomon's Temple? According to archaeologist Rivka Gonen, the site was originally a cemetery. She believes that many of the underground cavities recorded by 19th-century explorer Sir Charles Warren were once Middle Bronze I shaft tombs (2200–2000 B.C.). These cavities, including the cave under al-Sakhra in the Dome of the Rock, are visible as dark shaded areas on this plan of the Temple Mount drawn by Warren in 1867.

Moses smashed the original Tablets of the Law when he came down from Mt. Sinai and found the Israelites worshiping a golden calf. The scene is depicted in this 1659 oil painting by Rembrandt. Moses later received a second set of tablets that was housed in the Ark of the Covenant.

number them differently, sometimes dividing, sometimes combining lines in order to come out with ten. Further, it is not always clear what these "commandments" really are. The first one (or the first part of the first one, depending on the faith tradition) is not a commandment at all, but simply a declaration of faith: "I am the Lord your God, who brought you out of the land of Egypt, out of the house of slavery" (Exodus 20:2; Deuteronomy 5:6).

When the Hebrew Bible was translated into Greek (the Septuagint), the Hebrew for "ten sayings" was translated literally as the "Decalogue" in Greek. This is surely more accurate than Ten *Commandments*, which is simply not biblical. (The *Encyclopaedia Judaica* discusses the Ten Commandments under the heading "Decalogue," not "Ten Commandments.") Traditional rabbinic exegesis derives no fewer than 13 commandments from the lists in Exodus and Deuteronomy.[1]

In any event, Moses was instructed to place the tablets bearing the ten sayings in a wooden box: the Ark of the Covenant (Deuteronomy 10:1). The box, made of acacia wood overlaid with gold, measured 2.5 by 1.5 cubits (4 feet 4 inches by 2 feet 7 inches) and was 1.5 cubits high (Exodus 25:10). It was carried by two poles placed through rings on the sides of the box.

The biblical text is not entirely clear about where the Ark of the Covenant was initially housed. The Book of Exodus describes a tent called the Tent of Meeting that Moses pitched and entered when he talked to the Lord. A pillar of cloud would stand at the entrance to the tent when Moses was inside. The people would then rise, stand at the entrance of the tent and bow low (Exodus 33:7–11). But the text does not specify that the Ark of the Covenant was placed in the Tent of Meeting.

The text does tell us that the Ark of the Covenant was placed in the Tabernacle, which was a separate tent-like structure, although very different from the Tent of Meeting. The Tent of Meeting seems to have been set up and cared for by one person, Joshua son of Nun, who years later would lead the Israelites in the conquest of Canaan. In the desert, however, he was a mere youth (Exodus 33:11). The Tabernacle, in contrast to the Tent of Meeting, was an elaborate complex that is twice described in meticulous detail, once in six chapters (Exodus 25–30) that contain the Lord's directions to Moses and again in six chapters (Exodus 35–40) that describe its actual construction.

The Tabernacle was a tent-like wooden-framed structure with gold and silver fittings covered with linen and goat's hair, and then animal skins, and divided inside by a veil, behind which was the Holy of Holies, the resting place of the Ark of the Covenant. The veil was held up by poles of acacia wood overlaid with gold. Images of cherubim were woven into the veil. In front of the veil was an incense altar overlaid with gold, the showbread table with its 12 loaves and a (probably anachronistic) *seven*-branched gold menorah, or lampstand. This tent-like structure was located in a courtyard enclosed by a wall of curtains held up by poles. In the courtyard was a bronze basin and a sacrificial altar for burnt offerings. (Sound familiar? Reminiscent of Solomon's Temple?)

The Tabernacle was attended by Levites dressed in elaborately described vestments, in contrast to the Tent of Meeting, for which a single attendant—a youth—sufficed.

While the Tabernacle (*mishkan*) and the Tent of Meeting (*ohel mo'ed*) are thus quite distinct, there is nevertheless some confusion—even in the Bible itself (see, for example, Exodus 31, where the Tent of Meeting is described as if it were the Tabernacle). A standard dictionary tells us that another name for *mishkan* (Tabernacle) is *ohel mo'ed* (Tent of Meeting).[2]

Dispelling the confusion requires us to unpack the text a little. The passages describing the Tent of Meeting are earlier texts. The texts relating to the Tabernacle are attributed by scholars to a later source called the Priestly

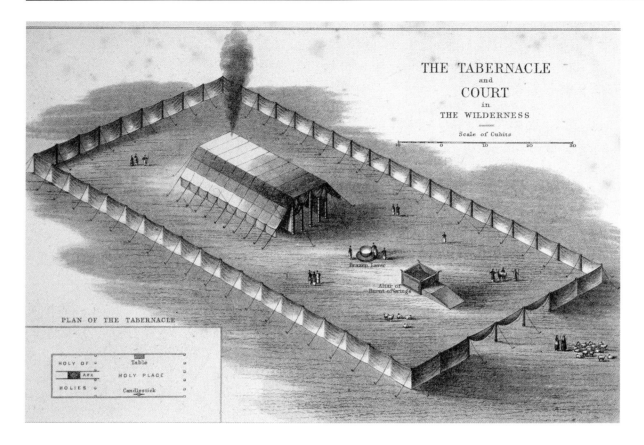

THE TABERNACLE
and
COURT
in
THE WILDERNESS

Scale of Cubits

PLAN OF THE TABERNACLE

HOLY OF   Table
ARK   HOLY PLACE
HOLIES   Candlestick

In the desert, the Ark of the Covenant was housed in a tent-like wooden-framed structure called the Tabernacle. This 19th-century lithograph shows the Tabernacle as it may have looked, with a large bronze basin out front for priestly ablutions and a horned altar for animal sacrifices.

Source (usually abbreviated simply P), which was redacted only in the sixth century B.C.

The biblical portrait of the Tabernacle, in the words of one scholar,

> raises doubts as to what extent the tabernacle can be considered an actual fact during the wilderness period. The constant movement of so large a structure is difficult to envisage in desert conditions, nor is it likely that wilderness Israel had the craftsmen, materials, or wealth to erect it. Above all, the Priestly account records a structure that, in its shape and the cultic objects it contains, resembles Solomon's Temple. What it presents is a description of the Temple under the guise of a portable sanctuary. It is thus a retrojection of the Jerusalem Temple to the wilderness epoch, in accordance with the Priestly view that all Israel's religious institutions originated at that time, but with the knowledge that a permanent building did not exist before the settlement in Canaan.[3]

It may be that the Ark of the Covenant was initially housed in the simpler Tent of Meeting, rather than in the more elaborate Tabernacle. A clue comes from a later episode: When David is considering building a permanent home

168

for the Ark of the Covenant, the prophet Nathan has a night vision telling him that it should be built only by David's successor Solomon. In the meantime, the Lord tells Nathan that he is satisfied to be present in a tent: "From the day that I brought the people of Israel out of Egypt to this day I have not dwelt in a house, but have moved about in Tent (*ohel*) and Tabernacle (*mishkan*)" (2 Samuel 7:6). If the Ark of the Covenant invokes the divine presence, then the Lord may well have resided in the Tent of Meeting.

In many ways, the description of the Tent of Meeting seems more plausible than that of the Tabernacle. As one scholar suggests, the Tent of Meeting is "much more likely to have existed [than the Tabernacle] during the wilderness wanderings."[4] The passages referring to the Tent of Meeting are generally considered part of a far older authorial strand of the Bible than the Priestly passages describing the Tabernacle.[5] It seems clear that the Divine Presence is associated with the Tent of Meeting: "Whoever sought the Lord would go out to the Tent of Meeting" (Exodus 33:7).

Thus, the Tent of Meeting may well be historical—and with it, the Ark of the Covenant. Whether they contained stones inscribed by God is a matter of faith, not history. Inscribed stones were, of course, quite common at the time. Consider, for example, the Merneptah Stele or the Mesha inscription, discussed in the previous chapter.[6]

The Ark of the Covenant traveled a circuitous journey through the wilderness to the Holy of Holies in Solomon's Temple, its final resting place. When the Israelites left Sinai, the Ark preceded them: "The Ark of the Covenant of the Lord traveled in front of them ... to seek out a resting place for them" (Numbers 10:33). Moses would say, "Advance, O Lord" (Numbers 10:35), and the Ark would guide them on their journey, as its laws were to do in their lives.

The Ark itself was a palladium, a protective shield, for the Israelites. It was carried in the priestly procession around the walls of Jericho when the walls collapsed (Joshua 6:1–15).

After the Israelites settled in the land, the Ark of the Covenant was housed in a shrine at Shiloh, about 20 miles north of Jerusalem, for nearly a century. Excavations at ancient Shiloh have led the archaeologist in charge to conclude that Shiloh was an Israelite cult center with a structure on the summit that probably housed the Ark. The summit was not excavated because it was badly eroded and damaged by later building activity. However, just down the slope were "storerooms [that] were in some way connected to the sanctuary ... The amount of effort expended in erecting the pillared buildings on the steep slope ... is astounding ... It is indeed hard to understand the decision to erect the pillared buildings on the slope unless they were planned and constructed as part of a larger complex ... in the direction of the summit."[7] If he is correct, this is where the Ark of the Covenant was housed during its stay in Shiloh.

When a battle with the Philistines near Ebenezer (near Aphek, west of Shiloh) was going badly for the Israelites, the Ark of the Covenant was brought from Shiloh to lead the battle. Alas, it was to no avail; the Philistines captured the Ark. After seven months, however, it gave them so much trouble (it caused a statue of the Philistine god Dagon to collapse repeatedly and gave the Philistines themselves terrible hemorrhoids) that they sent it back on a cart drawn by two cows (the Philistines also included a gift for the Israelites: five golden mice and five golden hemorrhoids). When the cart arrived in Israelite Beth-Shemesh (15 miles west of Jerusalem), some men looked into the Ark of the Covenant and immediately died (1 Samuel 6:19; the part about looking into the Ark of the Covenant is not in all Bible translations. The New Jewish Publication Society translation, where it does appear, admits that the meaning of the Hebrew is uncertain; in any event, the death of the men of Beth-Shemesh is clear).

The surviving men of Beth-Shemesh then sent the Ark to Kiriath-jearim, outside Jerusalem, where it remained for 20 years, in the house of Abinadab (1 Samuel 7:1). Not long after he was anointed as king, David decided to bring the Ark to Jerusalem. It was taken from Abinadab's house in Kiriath-jearim and loaded onto a cart drawn by oxen, with Abinadab's two sons guiding it. The oxen stumbled and Abidadab's son Uzzah reached out to prevent it from falling. He was instantly struck down and died. David became frightened and would not allow the Ark to come into his house in the City of David. So the Ark was put into the house of Obed-edom the Gittite (his name suggests he may have been an Edomite from Philistine Gath). There it remained for three months, during which Obed thrived. When David saw this, he brought the Ark into his own house in the City of David, where it was placed in a tent that David had pitched for it. David offered sacrifices (but no altar is mentioned) and danced, leaping and whirling before the Lord (2 Samuel 6).

David was aware of the discrepancy: He was living in a palace of cedarwood while "the Lord abides in a tent" (2 Samuel 7:2). David was doubtless thinking of building a more permanent home for Israel's God. However, Nathan the prophet had a night vision in which the Lord told him to tell David that he was not the one to build a house for him. Rather, the Lord promised, David's successor "shall build a house for My name" (2 Samuel 7:12–13).

So the Ark of the Covenant remained in a tent until King Solomon built a permanent house for it. It remained in Solomon's Temple until the Babylonian destruction of 586 B.C. What happened to it thereafter remains a mystery. The Bible gives us no hint. The Ark is not mentioned among the spoils of the Temple that Nebuchadnezzar took to Babylon (Jeremiah 52:17–23; 2 Kings 25:13–17). It seems clear that the Ark was not in the Second Temple built by the returning exiles. Indeed, Jeremiah prophesies that when the exiles return and flourish in the Land, they will completely forget about the Ark of the Covenant; instead of

the Ark being the throne of Yahweh, all of Jerusalem will be his throne (Jeremiah 3:16–17). According to 2 Maccabees 2:4–7, Jeremiah took the Ark (and the incense altar) back to Mt. Sinai and hid it so that it would remain unknown until the messianic age. The Holy of Holies in the Second Temple was apparently empty, except for the *Even Shetiyah*, the Foundation Stone, which protruded three fingerbreadths above the floor.[8] One scholar believes this stone still lies north of the Dome of the Rock under a Muslim cupola called the Dome of the Spirits or Dome of the Tablets.[9]

Having traced the Ark from the wilderness to its permanent home in Solomon's Temple, we must now inquire of the place chosen for this permanent home.

The site for the Temple was chosen not by Solomon, not by David, but by an angel of the Lord. According to the Bible, the site was a threshing floor owned by a Jebusite named Araunah (2 Samuel 24:18–25). In a later biblical account, telling essentially the same story, the fellow's name is Ornan instead of Araunah (1 Chronicles 21:18–26). An angel of the Lord was visiting a pestilence

When the Israelites carried the Ark ahead of them into battle, it was captured by the Philistines. However, as depicted in this fresco from the third-century A.D. synagogue at Dura Europos in Syria, the Ark was only a source of trouble for the Philistines; it caused the statue of their god Dagon to collapse, and it gave the Philistines hemorrhoids. They quickly returned the Ark to the Israelites, as shown here.

This cupola on the Haram al-Sharif is called the Dome of the Spirits or the Dome of the Tablets. Located north of the Dome of the Rock, some believe that the flat stone under this dome is the Foundation Stone (Even Shetiyah) from the Second Temple's Holy of Holies, referred to in Mishnah Yoma.

upon the Israelites for a transgression by King David (he had taken a census), killing 70,000 people from Dan to Beersheba. "But when the angel extended his hand against Jerusalem to destroy it, the Lord renounced further punishment and said to the angel who was destroying the people, 'Enough! Stay your hand!' The angel of the Lord was then by the threshing floor of Araunah the Jebusite" (2 Samuel 24:16), or Ornan the Jebusite (1 Chronicles 21:15).[10]

That same day, a prophet named Gad instructed David to set up on the site an altar to the Lord. So David approached Araunah to purchase the site, explaining what he intended to do. Araunah offered to give it to David, along with some oxen to sacrifice to the Lord. David insisted on paying for it, however.

He did not want to make a sacrifice to the Lord on land that cost him nothing. David paid 50 shekels for the land and the oxen. (In the post-Exilic account in Chronicles, the price jumps to 600 shekels of gold, apparently to take account of inflation.) David then built an altar and offered sacrifices to the Lord.

Long before David built an altar on the site, another altar had been built there. According to the Bible, Abraham had built an altar on a mountain in the land of Moriah, where he bound his son to sacrifice him before desisting at God's command and sacrificing a ram instead (Genesis 22). Although the particular mountain in the land of Moriah is not mentioned in Genesis 22, in Jewish tradition it became identified with the Temple Mount. In 2 Chronicles 3:1, we are told that Solomon built the Temple on Mount Moriah, no doubt a reference to the *Akedah*, the binding of Isaac. (Moriah is mentioned in only two books of the Hebrew Bible, the first and the last, as a kind of bookends.) This identification with the near-sacrifice of Isaac lent an extraordinary holiness to the site of the Temple.

Prior to David's conquest of Jerusalem, the city was not possessed by any Israelite tribe (although it was allotted to the tribe of Benjamin in Joshua 18:28). After David's conquest of the city, it became both the religious and political focus of Israel. And the choice of the site for the Temple tied together Abraham, the founder of the people, and David, the founder of the nation.

The connection between David and Abraham is enhanced by another parallel in their tales: David's insistence that he pay for the threshing floor and Abraham's insistence that he pay for the cave of Machpelah in Hebron in which to bury his wife Sarah. Although Ephron the Hittite offered to give him the cave, Abraham insisted on paying full price—400 shekels of silver (Genesis 23). Obviously, entitlement to the land is the issue: Abraham, the founder of the people, and David, the founder of the nation, both acquired good title by purchase.

David intended to build a Temple to the Lord on the site he had purchased. He assembled much of the materials, including cedars of Lebanon from the Phoenicians, and then, on his deathbed, he charged his son Solomon to construct the Temple on the site (1 Chronicles 22:2–6). In Kings, however, we are told that David could not build the Temple because of the wars he was engaged in (1 Kings 5:3 [Hebrew vs. 17]). So Solomon—as the Lord had promised his father David (2 Samuel 7:12–13)—began to construct the Temple in the second month of the 480th year after the Exodus from Egypt (1 Kings 6:1).

There are other versions of what happened on the site prior to the time Solomon built his Temple on it. Archaeologist Rivka Gonen suggests an entirely different history of the site. It was not a threshing floor, but a cemetery, she says.[11] Gonen has studied the cemeteries in ancient Canaan that date from the period archaeologists call Middle Bronze I (2200–2000 B.C.)[12] and that sit on the ridge line on which Jerusalem sits. These cemeteries are filled with so-called shaft tombs, in which a deep shaft is cut into the rock down to a small cave that serves as the tomb. She believes many of the cavities under the Temple Mount, which were meticulously recorded and described in minute detail by the great 19th-century explorer Charles Warren (later Sir Charles Warren), were originally shaft tombs. Several of these cavities have been considerably altered over the years, often turned into cisterns in later times. But Gonen believes she can still see some of the remains and details of the original tombs.

Perhaps the most dramatic vestige of a tomb on the Temple Mount can be found in traditions related to al-Sakhra itself, the rock mass directly under the golden dome, which gives the Muslim structure its name. Under this rock mass is a cave entered today by a stairway with 14 steps. The cave itself is nearly square—about 24 feet on each side. In the floor is a depression about 8 inches deep, now covered by a marble slab. In Muslim tradition this is the Well of Souls. The souls of people heading for hell are stored here. Does this tradition preserve an ancient memory that the site was once a cemetery? The suggestion is also supported by another Muslim tradition that the prophet Zechariah is buried here. In Jewish tradition, the exiles who returned from Babylon found the skull of Araunah the Jebusite under the Temple altar. Another Jewish tradition has Araunah's skull discovered even earlier, by the high priest Hilkiah, in the First Temple period. Such traditions are quite astonishing when one remembers that the Temple is the ultimate source of ritual cleanliness and purity—and nothing defiles more than a corpse.

The rabbis, too, seem to have suspected a burial on the Temple Mount— under the rock mass below the Dome of the Rock, no less. According to the Mishnah (*Parah* 3:2), "There were courtyards in Jerusalem built over the rock, and beneath them the rock was hollowed out [as a protection against defilement] for fear of any grave down in the depths."

An archaeological detail leads Gonen to suggest that the site was indeed once a cemetery: A shaft about 18 inches in diameter perforates the rock ceiling of the cave and connects it to the rock surface. "Could this be a remnant of an Middle Bronze I shaft tomb?" Gonen asks.

The Middle Bronze I settlement of Jerusalem was in the area known later (and today) as the City of David, located on a ridge south of the Temple Mount. The area of the Temple Mount, north of the city, would be a logical place for a cemetery for this settlement.

A third version of the prehistory of the Temple Mount is related by the first-century historian Josephus. It involves the mysterious character known as Melchizedek. In Genesis, Melchizedek is the king of Salem (presumably Jerusalem) and a priest of El-Elyon, which means "God the Most High" (Genesis 14:18). That this is the Hebrew God is indicated by the fact that in the same chapter Abram (as he then was named) swears by El-Elyon, whom he calls the creator of heaven and earth (Genesis 14:22). Melchizedek blesses Abram and

gives him bread and wine after the patriarch defeats four kings who had invaded the lands of his allies. Abram then gives Melchizedek a tenth of everything he owns—a tithe (Genesis 14:20).

Obviously this Melchizedek was a righteous person. Indeed, his name can be understood to mean "king of righteousness" (*malchi zedek*). In Psalm 110 the Lord tells David that he is a priest "after the manner of Melchizedek," so it appears that the mysterious Melchizedek continued to be revered.

In the New Testament Epistle to the Hebrews, Jesus himself is declared a priest. He is designated as such by God, who makes Jesus a high priest "according to the order of Melchizedek" (Hebrews 5:10; see also Hebrews 6:20, 7:17).

Melchizedek also figures in the Dead Sea Scrolls, where he is the head of the army of light. He presides over the final judgment, condemning his demonic counterpart Belial/Satan, the Prince of Darkness.[13]

Josephus tells us much the same thing that the Bible tells us about Melchizedek,[14] but he adds that long before Solomon built the Temple, *Melchizedek* built a temple:

> [Jerusalem's] original founder was a Canaanite chief, called in the
> native tongue "Righteous King" [Melchi-zedek]; for such indeed he

In Muslim tradition a marble slab in this cave below al-Sakhra covers the Well of Souls, where souls headed to hell were temporarily stored. Other traditions and some modern scholars believe that this is a remnant of an ancient burial cave.

was. In virtue thereof he was the first to officiate as priest of God and, being *the first to build the temple*, gave the city, previously called Solyma, the name of Jerusalem.[15]

So far as I have been able to discover, that is the only place this is mentioned in extant ancient literature, but the story must have been circulating around the turn of the era.

Other archaeologists and biblical scholars approach the question of the Temple Mount in pre-Solomonic times from a completely different viewpoint. For example, Swiss biblical historian Ernst Axel Knauf argues that a Canaanite temple preceded the Israelite Temple on the Temple Mount and that Solomon simply made some alterations in the old Canaanite temple but did not build a new temple from scratch.[16]

The standard scholarly view is that, until the time of David and Solomon, the Temple Mount was outside the city; the Canaanite (or Jebusite) city that David conquered in about 1000 B.C. was, well, the City of David, which does not include the Temple Mount. Even today, the City of David designates the ridge south of the Temple Mount. The City of David is separated from the Temple Mount by a small area between the two, known as the Ophel. Knauf contends that the pre-Davidic city was not confined to the ridge known as the City of David, but rather that it included the Temple Mount: "The common assumption that the city did not spread to the north until after Solomon built the Temple is baseless and another case of 'Bible Archaeology,'" he says. "A town covering the southeastern hill [the City of David] must always have included the Temple Mount." Otherwise, Knauf reasons, the city would have been indefensible since the Temple Mount area would look down on the city from the north, its only vulnerable side.

Moreover, Knauf points out, even the Bible hints that there was an earlier temple on the Temple Mount and that David himself (before Solomon) had converted it into the Temple of Yahweh: After David's son born of his adulterous relationship with Bathsheba died, David went to "the Temple of Yahweh" and prostrated himself (2 Samuel 12:20). Solomon had not yet been born. Whatever this "Temple of Yahweh" was, it must have preceded Solomon. In the biblical story of Solomon and the Temple (in 1 Kings 6–7), Knauf argues, nothing is constructed, "just redecorated."[17] In the Bible's description of the Temple, we are being given "a theological construct whose aim is to dissociate Israel's noblest sanctuary from its Canaanite roots."

In short, "It is not just Solomon's Jerusalem that lies basically hidden under the Haram, the same assumption must apply to David's Jerusalem." Knauf recognizes that he has formulated "a hypothesis which cannot be tested or refuted archaeologically." He consoles himself with the thought, however, that even if it were possible to excavate on the Temple Mount, "one should not expect any meaningful structures" from this early period; the Romans undoubtedly destroyed them. But what about stray pottery sherds? They probably washed down the slopes of the Kidron Valley and then in a stream to the east, Knauf says, on their way to the Dead Sea. This dubious proposition is refuted, however, by the sifting of the soil removed from the Temple Mount and dumped into the adjacent Kidron Valley. Gabriel Barkay and his team of sifters have recovered tens of thousands of sherds from the First Temple period.

Israeli archaeologist David Ussishkin contends that the Temple Mount was not included in the city even in King Solomon's time.[18] Although it was not in the city, he tells us, the Temple Mount was "the Royal acropolis ... built as a separate entity by Solomon as described in the biblical text, and it was incorporated in the expanding city in a later period." What about Solomon's Temple? Ussishkin sees four possibilities: (1) A Canaanite temple stood on the site, and Solomon remodeled it; (2) Solomon established a modest Temple;[19] (3) Solomon built the Temple as described in the Bible; (4) the Temple was built hundreds of years later when the city expanded but the construction was attributed to Solomon. "Being an archaeologist," Ussishkin adds, "whose expertise is archaeological evidence, I cannot choose between these possibilities."[20]

We have reached the end of our excavation. As is often the case, the lowest level or stratum is the most obscure.

VIII

Conclusion

J EWISH, CHRISTIAN AND MUSLIM TRADITIONS AGREE THAT KING SOLOMON
built the Temple on the Temple Mount. This has been firmly embedded
in Jewish tradition for nearly 3,000 years. The Christian belief dates from
the time of the Gospels and is a kind of negative affirmation: Jesus predicts that
the Jewish Temple of his time will be destroyed so thoroughly that not one
stone will sit upon another (Matthew 24:1–2; cf. Mark 13:1–2; Luke 21:5–6).
To emphasize the point, when Jerusalem became a Christian city in the fourth
century, the Temple Mount was deliberately desecrated and maintained in that
state during the entire period of Christian rule.

In building the Dome of the Rock, the Muslims wished to remove the focus
of the city from the Church of the Holy Sepulchre and restore it to the site of
the destroyed Jewish Temple. In the Muslim psyche, the Muslims in the seventh
century A.D. were restoring the Solomonic Temple.[1]

When the Crusaders established the Latin Kingdom of Jerusalem, they placed
a golden cross on the Dome of the Rock and called it *Templum Domini.*

In the 20th century, all three religions continued to regard the Temple
Mount as the site of Solomon's, and later Herod's, Temple. As late as 2004, a
popular Muslim primer identified the site as the place where Solomon's Temple
once stood.

Of course, traditions are not facts. And it remains theoretically possible
that none of them is grounded in fact. Still, the traditions are entitled to
some, if not conclusive, weight, especially when they are so consistent and
so firmly embedded.

*According to Jewish,
Christian and Muslim
traditions, the Temple
Mount in Jerusalem
was the location
of the Temple of
Yahweh built by King
Solomon. Although no
archaeological remains
from this Temple have
been found, tradition,
historical texts and
logic all point to its
existence. There can be
no reasonable doubt
that Solomon's Temple
once stood atop the
Temple Mount.*

*This view shows
the archaeological
excavation of Benjamin
Mazar south of the
Temple Mount and,
below that, the ridge
known as the City of
David, where Jerusalem
was located in the tenth
century B.C.E.*

179

Of course that is only the beginning of our analysis. We must also deal with the distinction between myth and reality . Clearly there is both myth and reality in the history of the Temple Mount. In the faith traditions of two religions, the patriarch Abraham almost sacrificed his son on Mt. Moriah, identified with the site of the future Temple; the son was saved only when a divine command ordered the father to desist. Whether that actually happened is not subject to historical proof or disproof. Three different kinds of questions are involved. First, did Abraham go up on a mountain to sacrifice his son? That is a historical question, but one that is not subject to proof or disproof. We simply know too little. Second, did the deity intervene? That too is not subject to proof or disproof. It is a matter of religious faith. Different people understand the story differently. (For many people the story retains its power regardless of whether or not it is historically accurate.) Finally, there is the question of whether the writer of the story had in mind the Temple Mount when he referred to Mt. Moriah. This again is a historical question—but unanswerable. If it is only a tradition, it is already to be found in the Bible, however—in the second Book of Chronicles (3:1). The skeptic may well respond: But why isn't the association between Mt. Moriah and the Temple Mount found in earlier biblical books, like Genesis or Kings? To that there is no definitive answer. There are some historical questions where the only answer is uncertainty.

We must also assess the quality—the historical validity—of our sources. None of our sources announces that it is a fairy tale without historical value. All purport to report accurately what happened, yet we all make distinctions. Why did the effort of the Jews to rebuild the Temple during the fourth-century A.D. reign of Julian the Apostate fail? According to the church historian Salaman Sozomen, everything built by the Jews during the day collapsed at night from repeated earthquakes; fire then burst from the foundations consuming several workmen; finally, the clothes of the Jewish workmen who continued to attempt to construct their Temple suddenly bore the sign of the cross, which led them to abandon the task. Most historians, however, attribute the cessation of work to the fact that Julian was killed in a battle with the Persians and was replaced by a Christian emperor. I think we can say in this case that Sozomen is less reliable than the modern historians, although a person of deep religious faith may have difficulty in explaining precisely why. Can people of faith explain why some alleged miracles are intrinsically less believable than others?

If the question of Sozomen's reliability is easy to assess—he is unreliable—the reliability of other historical sources is more difficult. The great historian Josephus is mostly reliable, but sometimes not—and sometimes it is hard to tell. In many instances there are internal disagreements within Josephus's writings.

The same is true of biblical accounts. Scholars spend their lives trying to determine the historical reliability of various biblical sources. Needless to add, there are some fierce disagreements here as well.

With these considerations in mind, there is nevertheless no reasonable doubt that Herod built his Temple (the Second Temple) on the Temple Mount. No serious scholar disputes this. As to the existence of this Second Temple, Josephus is a powerful witness: He was there. He was with the Roman army that destroyed it. It is inconceivable that he would have made up so detailed a story when there were so many people to contradict a fabrication. Nor had he any reason to do so. Moreover, his testimony, in the main, is confirmed by independent rabbinic sources.

Then there is the archaeological evidence: a monumental staircase on the south leading up to the Temple Mount, a tunnel with elaborate original decoration also leading up to the Temple Mount (inside the Double Gate), remains of another monumental staircase on the southern part of the western wall also leading up to the Temple Mount, remains of a huge monumental platform built of original Herodian stones, and inscriptions warning gentiles to keep out. Dozens of *miqva'ot* (ritual baths) from the Herodian period excavated adjacent to the Temple Mount (and, arguably, others on the Temple Mount itself) testify to the holiness of the giant platform. A fragment of a bowl for the sacrifice of a dove bears an inscription *korban* (sacrifice). Another inscription points to the place where the commencement of the Sabbath was announced by the blast of a trumpet. When all this is combined with Josephus's detailed eyewitness account (as well as descriptions in rabbinic literature and references to the Temple in the New Testament), it is difficult to question the existence of the Second Temple, Herod's Temple, on the Temple Mount.

The denier is left with only one argument: We have nothing from Herod's Temple itself. True, but the site of the Temple itself is not open to archaeological excavation—and never has been. In these circumstances it is especially true that the absence of evidence is not evidence of absence. Besides, we do have some peripheral evidence. Benjamin Mazar excavated at the southern Temple Mount wall and uncovered hundreds of elaborately carved fragments from Herod's royal stoa that Josephus tells us Herod built on the southern end of the Temple Mount—fragments apparently thrown down by Roman soldiers when they destroyed the buildings on the Temple Mount. These fragments confirm the basic reliability of Josephus's account. We may even have found some stones of Herod's Temple that were dragged from the Temple Mount and are in secondary use elsewhere, embedded in the wall of another sacred structure: the Church of the Holy Sepulchre.

But what of Solomon's Temple? Did he build his Temple on the Temple Mount in Jerusalem?

There is a long tradition of erecting religious structures on sites where previous holy structures have been located. The very existence of Herod's Temple suggests that the site was already the location of an earlier holy structure.

As we go back further in time, things admittedly become murkier. On the other hand, there is certainly nothing to suggest Solomon's Temple was *not* there.

Moreover, it defies logic to suppose that an account would be written of the Temple at a time when there was no Temple. No public text would claim there was a Temple on the Temple Mount if anyone could go there and see that there was no Temple. This raises the question of when the earliest biblical text describing the Temple on the Temple Mount was written—a hotly debated issue. For our purposes, however, we may take the latest date proposed by responsible scholars (e.g., Israel Finkelstein of Tel Aviv University, who is often regarded as a biblical minimalist): the seventh century B.C. That means there must have been a Temple on the Temple Mount during the First Temple period, that is, before the Babylonian destruction of 586 B.C. In this scenario, conceivably the Temple may have been built by some later king, after the reign of King Solomon. At the very least, however, it must be recognized that there was a Temple on the Temple Mount in the First Temple period.

By the time of the prophets, however, the Temple was already such an ancient and established institution that it could be criticized. Isaiah, who lived in the eighth century B.C., attacked the Temple rituals as insufficient. For him the Temple is an old and atrophying institution, implying a far older origin:

> "What need have I of all your sacrifices?"
> Says the Lord.
> "I am sated with burnt offerings of rams,
> And suet of fatlings,
> And blood of bulls;
> And I have no delight
> In lambs and he-goats...
> Trample My courts no more
> Bringing oblations is futile,
> Incense is offensive to me...
> Your new moons and fixed seasons
> Fill Me with loathing...
> Though you pray at length,
> I will not listen...
> Cease to do evil;
> Learn to do good.
> Devote yourselves to justice;
> Aid the wronged.
> Uphold the rights of the orphan;
> Defend the cause of the widow."
> (Isaiah 1:11–17)

Isaiah could criticize the Temple this way only if it were already an old, established institution in the eighth century B.C.

Micah, who lived shortly after Isaiah, is similarly critical of the Temple institutions, implying that it is hardly a recent creation:

> Hear this, you rulers of the House of Jacob,
> You chiefs of the House of Israel,
> Who detest justice
> And make crooked all that is straight,
> Who build Zion with crime,
> Jerusalem with iniquity!
> Her rulers judge for gifts,
> Her priests give rulings for a fee,
> And her prophets divine for pay;
> Yet they rely upon the Lord, saying,
> "The Lord is in our midst;
> No calamity shall overtake us."
> Assuredly, because of you
> Zion shall be plowed as a field,
> And Jerusalem shall become heaps of ruins,
> And the Temple Mount [*har ha-bayit*]
> A shrine in the woods.
> (Micah 3:9–12)

Despite his criticism, the prophet sees a new day dawning:

> In the days to come,
> The Mount of the Lord's House shall stand
> Firm above the mountains;
> And it shall tower above the hills.
> The people shall gaze on it with joy,
> And the many nations shall go and shall say:
> "Come,
> Let us go up to the Mount of the Lord,
> To the House of the God of Jacob;
> That He may instruct us in His ways,
> And that we may walk in His paths."
> For instruction shall come forth from Zion,
> The word of the Lord from Jerusalem.
> (Micah 4:1–2)

The prophet is obviously speaking of a well-established central institution that already embodies a long history.

Can we work back to Solomonic times? I believe we can. In the first place, the Bible tell us that the Temple was in fact built by Solomon. If this is not conclusive evidence, at least it is entitled to some weight. Many biblical scholars believe that, as early as the time of the United Monarchy, royal records were already kept that were later used to compose biblical accounts. If this is true, then the biblical accounts of Solomon's Temple are well-nigh conclusive.

Moreover, the view that Solomon built the Temple is consistent with everything we know about the period archaeologists call Iron Age II (1000–586 B.C.), the period of the First Temple. Although we do not have much corroborating remains from the Temple Mount itself, this may well be because archaeologists have not been allowed to excavate there. But surprisingly similar details to Solomon's Temple *have* been found at sites where archaeologists have been permitted to excavate—at 'Ain Dara and Tell Ta'yinat; that is, the biblical description of the Temple fits well with other nearly contemporaneous temples. Moreover, there is nothing in the archaeological record that cautions us against concluding that Solomon built the Temple.

The biblical account also acknowledges that both architectural expertise and materials were supplied to King Solomon by the Phoenician monarch Hiram of Tyre. Why would any later Israelite king, making up a story like this about Solomon, include such belittling details if they were not true? That foreign help is acknowledged tends to confirm the reliability of the biblical account.

Similarly reinforcing are the biblical accounts of later Israelite kings (like Jehoash and Hezekiah) making repairs to the Temple. Contemporary inscriptions have convinced almost all scholars that royal records were kept at the time the description of these repairs were written. If these records were at all public, they are powerful evidence that there was a Temple to be repaired; no one would write about repairs to the Temple if there was no Temple there to be repaired.

In short, everything points to the existence of Solomon's Temple, and nothing casts a doubt upon it. We can confidently assert that King Solomon did indeed construct a Temple to the Lord on the site we know as the Temple Mount.

Notes

I. WHY THIS BOOK

[1] Carol M Meyers, s.v. "Temple, Jerusalem," in David Noel Freedman, ed., *The Anchor Bible Dictionary*, vol. 6 (New York: Doubleday, 1992), p. 350.

[2] Tovah Lazaroff, "Ross: Arafat Said Temple Was in Nablus," *Jerusalem Post*, May 15, 2002.

[3] www.worldnetdaily.com/news/article. asp?ARTICLE_ID=50637.

[4] Yassar Arafat. From *Al-Hayat Al-Jadida*, August 12, 2000. Quoted in "East Jerusalem and the Holy Places at the Camp David Summit," *MEMRI (Middle East Media Research Institute) Special Dispatch Series No. 121*, August 28, 2000.

[5] Yassar Arafat. Quoted in Eric H. Cline, *Jerusalem Besieged* (Ann Arbor: University of Michigan Press, 2004), p. 333.

[6] Nabil Sha'ath. From *Al-Ayyam*, July 27, 2000. Cited in Yigal Carmon and Aluma Solnik, "Camp David and the Prospects for a Final Settlement, Part I: Israeli, Palestinian, and American Positions," *MEMRI Inquiry and Analysis Series No. 35*, August 4, 2000.

[7] Mahmoud Abbas. Interviewed in *Kul Al-Arab* (Israel), August 8, 2000. Quoted in "Abu Mazen on the Peace Process," *MEMRI Special Dispatch Series No. 122*, August 29, 2000.

[8] "East Jerusalem and the Holy Places at the Camp David Summit," *MEMRI Special Dispatch Series No. 121*, August 28, 2000.

[9] Nadav Shragai, "A Campaign of Denial to Disinherit the Jews," *Ha'aretz*, May 11, 2004, p. 4.

[10] Ekrima Sabri. Quoted in Etgar Lefkovits, "1930 Moslem Council Guide: Jewish Temple Mount Connection 'Beyond Dispute,'" *Jerusalem Post*, January 26, 2001.

[11] Ekrima Sabri. Quoted in Charles M. Sennott, "History, Animosity Vie at the Temple Mount," *Boston Globe*, March 15, 2001.

[12] Hamed Salem. Quoted in Netty C. Gross, "Demolishing David," *Jerusalem Report*, September 11, 2000.

[13] Haim Watzman, "Antiquities Fraud: Reality Check," *Nature* 434, March 3, 2005, p. 13.

[14] Etgar Lefkovits, "Temple Mount Relics Saved from Garbage," *Jerusalem Post*, April 14, 2005.

[15] Gershom Gorenberg, "Digging In at the Temple Mount," *Jerusalem Report*, March 26, 2001.

[16] Richard Ostling, "Time for a New Temple?" *Time*, October 16, 1989.

[17] Jonathan C. Randal, "Israel Subdues Arab Protest in Jerusalem," *Washington Post*, May 14, 1988.

[18] Naomi Morris, "Is Peace Dead? Days of Bloodshed Between Israelis and Palestinians Darken Middle East Hopes," *Maclean's* (Canada), October 7, 1996.

[19] James Bennet, "Year of Intifada Sees Hardening on Each Side," *New York Times*, September 28, 2001.

[20] "Salah Calls for Intifada against Temple Mount Excavation," *Ha'aretz*, February 17, 2007.

II. DOME OF THE ROCK

[1] Miriam Rosen-Ayalon, *The Early Islamic Monuments of Al-Haram Al-Sharif, Qedem* 28 (Jerusalem: Hebrew Univ., 1989), p. 1.

[2] However, the dome fell after the earthquake of 1016, but was rebuilt. Many of the other elements in the building have been restored. Nothing of the original ceiling remains. Oleg Grabar, *The Shape of the Holy* (Princeton, NJ: Princeton Univ. Press, 1996), p. 79.

[3] It is unclear whether the conquest occurred in 636 or 638. See Grabar, *The Shape of the Holy*, p. 45.

[4] The rotunda may have been built somewhat earlier than the basilical church. See W. Eugene Kleinbauer, "The Anastasia Rotunda and Christian Architectural Invention," in Bianca Kühnel, ed., *The Real and Ideal Jerusalem in Jewish, Christian and Islamic Art*, Journal of the Center for Jewish Art 1997/1998, vols. 23/24, Studies in Honor of Bezalel Narkiss on the Occasion of His Seventieth Birthday (Jerusalem: Hebrew Univ., 1998), p. 140 at pp. 141–142.

[5] Quoted in Charles Coüasnon, *The Church of the Holy Sepulchre in Jerusalem* (London: Oxford Univ. Press, 1974), p. 14.

[6] Coüasnon, *The Church of the Holy Sepulchre in Jerusalem*, p. 35.

[7] F. E. Peters, *Jerusalem* (Princeton, NJ: Princeton Univ. Press, 1985), p. 154, quoting the *Breviarius*.

[8] Grabar, *The Shape of the Holy*, p. 54.

[9] Rosen-Ayalon, *The Early Islamic Monuments of Al-Haram Al-Sharif*, p. 7. See also Angelika Neuwirth, "The Spiritual Meaning of Jerusalem in Islam," in Nitza Rosovsky, ed., *City of the Great King: Jerusalem from David to the Present* (Cam-

bridge: Harvard Univ. Press, 1996), pp. 93–116, at p. 108; K.A. C. Creswell, "The Origin of the Plan of the Dome of the Rock," *British School of Archaeology in Jerusalem, Supplementary Papers* (London: The Council of the British School of Archaeology in Jerusalem, 1924), p. 25; Alistair Duncan, *The Noble Sanctuary: Portrait of a Holy Place in Arab Jerusalem* (London: Longman, 1972), p. 28; Josef van Ess, "'Abd al-Malik and the Dome of the Rock. An Analysis of Some Texts," in Julian Raby and Jeremy Johns, eds., *Bayt Al-Maqdis: 'Abd al-Malik's Jerusalem*. Part 1 (Oxford: Oxford Univ. Press, 1992), pp. 89–103, at p. 101; and Heribert Busse, "The Temple of Jerusalem and Its Restitution by 'Abd al-Malik B. Marwān," in Kühnel, ed., *The Real and Ideal Jerusalem*, p. 23, at pp. 27–28.

[10]Oleg Grabar, "The Umayyad Dome of the Rock in Jerusalem," in Oleg Grabar, ed., *Studies in Medieval Islamic Art* (London: Variorum Reprints, 1976), p. 33, at p. 55. See also Shlomo D. Goitein, "Jerusalem in the Arab Period (638–1099)" in Lee Levine, ed., *The Jerusalem Cathedra* 2 (Jerusalem: Yad Yizhak Ben-Zvi Institute, 1982), pp. 168–196, at p. 177.

[11]Creswell, "The Origin of the Plan of the Dome of the Rock," p. 25.

[12]Goitein, "Jerusalem in the Arab Period (638–1099)," p. 172.

[13]The inscription has been described as having a "strongly anti-Christian tendency." The relationship between the Dome of the Rock and the Church of the Holy Sepulchre "is a relationship *ex contrario*. The meaning is clear: The true successor of the Temple is not the Church of the Holy Sepulchre, but the Ḥaram al-Sharif." Busse, "The Temple of Jerusalem and Its Restitution by 'Abd al-Malik B. Marwān," p. 33.

[14]Busse, "The Temple of Jerusalem and Its Restitution by 'Abd al-Malik B. Marwān," p. 29.

[15]Grabar, "The Umayyad Dome of the Rock in Jerusalem," p. 60

[16]Some scholars, however, contend that Mamoun's failure to change the date was intentional. According to this school of thought, the change of name is to be interpreted as a symbolic act of taking possession. See Heribert Busse, "The Sanctity of Jerusalem in Islam," *Judaism* 17 (1968), p. 441 at p. 460. See also Grabar, *The Shape of the Holy*, p. 64.

[17]Meir Ben-Dov, *In the Shadow of the Temple* (New York: Harper & Row, 1982), p. 282.

[18]Rosen-Ayalon, *The Early Islamic Monuments of Al-Haram Al-Sharif*, p. 7.

[19]Saïd Nuseibeh and Oleg Grabar, *The Dome of the Rock* (New York: Rizzoli, 1996), p. 47.

[20]Rosovsky, *City of the Great King*, p. 109.

[21]John Wilkinson, trans., *Egeria's Travels to the Holy Land* (Jerusalem: Ariel, 1981), p. 182.

[22]Peters, *Jerusalem*, p. 155, quoting the *Breviarius*.

[23]Nuseibeh and Grabar, *The Dome of the Rock*, p. 47. But see Grabar, *The Shape of the Holy*, p. 48.

[24]Neuwirth, "The Spiritual Meaning of Jerusalem in Islam," p. 97.

[25]Amikam Elad, "Why Did 'Abd al-Malik Build the Dome of the Rock?" in Raby and Johns, eds., *Bayt al-Maqdis—'Abd al-Malik's Jerusalem*.

[26]Grabar, "The Umayyad Dome of the Rock in Jerusalem," p. 38.

[27]Oleg Grabar, in Nuseibeh and Grabar, *The Dome of the Rock*, p. 47.

[28]Nāṣir-i Khusrow, as described in Grabar, "The Umayyad Dome of the Rock in Jerusalem," p. 43.

[29]Elad, "Why Did 'Abd al-Malik Build the Dome of the Rock?" in Raby and Johns, eds., *Bayt al-Maqdis—'Abd al-Malik's Jerusalem*, p. 48.

[30]John Jarick, "The Temple of David in the Book of Chronicles," in John Day, ed., *Temple and Worship in Biblical Israel* Proceedings of the Oxford Old Testament Seminar (London: T & T Clark, 2005), pp. 365–338, at p. 380.

[31]Grabar, in Nuseibeh and Grabar, *The Dome of the Rock*, p. 51.

[32]Busse, cited in Neuwirth, "The Spiritual Meaning of Jerusalem in Islam," p. 489, n. 69.

[33]Van Ess, "'Abd al-Malik and the Dome of the Rock," p. 101. See also, Moshe Sharon, "Islam on the Temple Mount," *Biblical Archaeology Review*, July/August 2006, and Elad, "Why Did 'Abd al-Malik Build the Dome of the Rock?" p. 49; Busse, "The Temple of Jerusalem and Its Restitution by 'Abd al-Malik B. Marwān," p. 35.

[34]Grabar, *The Shape of the Holy*, pp. 73, 75.

[35]See Ora Limor, "The Place of the End of Days: Eschatological Geography in Jerusalem," in Kühnel, ed., *The Real and Ideal Jerusalem*, p. 13.

[36]Muqātil b. Sulāyman, cited in Edward Lipiński, *Itineraria Phoenicia, Orientalia Lovaniensia Analecta* 127 (Leuven: Peeters, 2004), p. 544.

[37]Yaron Z. Eliav, *God's Mountain—The Temple Mount in Time, Place, and Memory* (Baltimore: Johns Hopkins Univ. Press, 2005), pp. 78–79.

[38]Peters, *Jerusalem*, pp. 155–156. See the account of the anonymous sixth-century pilgrim in the *Breviarius*, in John Wilkinson, *Jerusalem Pilgrims before the Crusades* (Warminster, England: Aris & Phillips, Ltd., 1977), p. 60.

[39]S.v. "Golgotha," David Noel Freedman, ed., *Eerdmans Dictionary of the Bible* (Grand Rapids, MI: Eerdmans, 2000), p. 519.

[40]Palestinian Talmud, *Sotah* 20a, *Nedarim* 39b. See Rivka Gonen, "Was the Site of the Jerusalem Temple Originally a Cemetery?" *Biblical Archaeology Review*, May/June 1985, pp. 44–55, at p. 50 and p. 51. According to another tradition, Araunah's

skull was found even earlier—by the high priest Hilkiah who lived in the late seventh century B.C. See Palestinian Talmud, *Pesahim* 36b.

[41] Rivka Gonen, *Contested Holiness: Jewish, Muslim, and Christian Perspectives on the Temple Mount in Jerusalem* (Jersey City, NJ: Ktav, 2003), p. 123.

[42] "There is no doubt that the Haram was the site of the Solomonic temple." Grabar, "The Umayyad Dome of the Rock in Jerusalem," p. 38.

[43] S.v. "Jerusalem," in John L. Esposito, ed., *The Islamic World Past and Present*, vol. 2,(Oxford: Oxford Univ. Press, 2004), pp. 63–64.

[44] S.v. "Jerusalem" (Arab period), *Encyclopaedia Judaica*, vol. 9, p. 1408.

[45] Busse, "The Sanctity of Jerusalem in Islam," p. 461.

[46] Goitein, "Jerusalem in the Arab Period (638–1099)," quotation at p. 172. According to Oleg Grabar, what Umar wanted to see was the first *qibla*, the direction of prayer, fixed by the prophet, not the site of the Temple.

[47] Goitein, "Jerusalem in the Arab Period (638–1099)," p. 172.

[48] Busse, "The Temple of Jerusalem and Its Restitution by 'Abd al-Malik B. Marwān," p. 24.

[49] Busse, "The Temple of Jerusalem," p. 33.

[50] Busse, "The Temple of Jerusalem," p. 24.

[51] Busse, "The Temple of Jerusalem," p. 27.

[52] Busse, "The Temple of Jerusalem," p. 28.

[53] Grabar, "The Umayyad Dome of the Rock in Jerusalem," p. 40.

[54] Goitein, "Jerusalem in the Arab Period," p. 176.

[55] See Jerome Murphy-O'Connor, "The Location of the Capitol in Aelia Capitolina," *Revue Biblique* 101 (1994), p. 407 at p. 408.

[56] Grabar, "The Umayyad Dome of the Rock in Jerusalem," p. 41.

[57] Neuwirth, "The Spiritual Meaning of Jerusalem in Islam," p. 116.

[58] Busse, "The Sanctity of Jerusalem in Islam," p. 456.

[59] See Islamic text in Amikam Elad, *Medieval Jerusalem and Islam Worship* (Leiden and New York: Brill, 1995), p. 82, n. 100, which rejects this tradition.

[60] Busse, "Sanctity of Jerusalem," p. 456.

[61] Busse, "Sanctity of Jerusalem," p. 456.

[62] Busse, "Sanctity of Jerusalem," p. 457.

[63] Al-Musharraf b. al-Murajja, cited in Busse, "The Temple of Jerusalem and Its Restitution by 'Abd al-Malik B. Marwān," p. 32.

[64] Creswell, "The Origin of the Plan of the Dome of the Rock," p. 2.

[65] Grabar, "The Umayyad Dome of the Rock in Jerusalem," p. 42.

[66] Quoted in K. A. C. Creswell, "The Origin of the Plan of the Dome of the Rock," p. 2.

[67] This position of many scholars is acknowledged, but rejected by Shlomo D. Goitein, "Jerusalem in the Arab Period (638–1099)," pp. 176–177.

[68] Elad, "Why Did 'Abd al-Malik Build the Dome of the Rock?" p. 49.

[69] Rosen-Ayalon, *The Early Islamic Monuments of Al-Haram Al-Sharif*, pp. 6–7.

[70] See generally, Warren T. Woodfin, "The Holiest Ground in the World—How the Crusaders Transformed Jerusalem's Temple Mount" *Archaeology Odyssey*, September/October 2000, pp. 26–37, at p. 30.

[71] Raymond of Aguilers in Edward Peters, ed. *The First Crusade: The Chronicle of Fulcher of Chartres and Other Source Materials* (Philadelphia: University of Pennsylvania Press, 1971), p. 214.

[72] Myriam Rosen-Ayalon, "Jewish Substratum, Christian History and Muslim Symbolism: An Archaeological Episode in Jerusalem," in Kühnel, ed., *The Real and Ideal Jerusalem*, p. 466.

[73] Grabar, *The Shape of the Holy*, p. 142.

[74] Quoted in Woodfin, "The Holiest Ground in the World," pp. 31–32.

[75] See Jaroslav Folda, "Jerusalem and the Holy Sepulchre Through the Eyes of Crusader Pilgrims," in Kuhnel, ed., *The Real and Ideal Jerusalem*, p. 158.

III. THE INTERREGNUM

[1] According to one Arab account, it was Helena, Constantine's mother, who "made 'the Rock' the garbage dump of the area, and it passed into oblivion." Quoted in Priscilla Soucek, "The Temple of Solomon in Islamic Legend and Art," in Joseph Gutmann, ed., *The Temple of Solomon: Archaeological Fact and Medieval Tradition in Christian, Islamic and Jewish Art* (Missoula, MT: Scholars Press, 1976), p. 89.

[2] On the other hand, there is some evidence that certain installations like the stairway up to the Temple Mount supported by Robinson's arch were rather quickly dismantled. See Ronny Reich and Ya'acov Billig, "Another Flavian Inscription Near the Temple Mount of Jerusalem," *'Atiqot* 44 (2003) (English series), pp. 243–247, at p. 247.

[3] Hershel Shanks, "Archaeological Hot Spots: A Roundup of Digs in Israel," *Biblical Archaeology Review*, November/December 1996, pp. 52–56.

[4] Personal communication, Ronny Reich, the excavator.

[5] In the early fourth century the church father

Eusebius wrote: "It is possible to see with our own eyes the sad sight of the stones being taken from the Temple and the Holy of Holies of the past, to be carried to the temples of the idols and to the constructions for the public spectacle" (*Demonstratio Evangelica*, VIII, 3, 12).

[6] Bargil Pixner, "Church of the Apostles Found on Mt. Zion," *Biblical Archaeology Review*, May/June 1990, pp. 16–35, 60, at pp. 23–26.

[7] Pixner, "Church of the Apostles," pp. 22 and 25–28.

[8] Pixner, "Church of the Apostles," p. 60, n. 26. See also *Life of Constantine* 3.25 quoted in Magen Broshi, "Evidence of Earliest Christian Pilgrimage to the Holy Land Comes to Light in Holy Sepulchre Church," *Biblical Archaeology Review*, December 1977, pp. 42–44, at p. 43.

[9] Eusebius, *Life of Constantine* 3.25 in Broshi, "Evidence of Earliest Christian Pilgrimage," p. 43.

[10] Joseph Patrich, "The Early Church of the Holy Sepulchre in the Light of Excavations and Restoration," in Yoram Tsafrir, ed., *Ancient Churches Revealed* (Jerusalem: Israel Exploration Society, 1993), pp. 101–117, at pp. 103–104.

[11] Almost everything about this inscription is contested. The information I give is what I believe is the best and the most commonly accepted interpretation. The reading of John Wilkinson, "The Inscription on the Jerusalem Ship Drawing," *Palestine Exploration Quarterly*, vol. 127 (1995), is rightly rejected by Dan Bahat. See his review of Shimon Gibson and Joan E. Taylor, *The Archaeology and Early History of Traditional Golgotha* in *Biblical Archaeology Review*, July/August 1996, pp. 16–17.

[12] See Broshi, "Evidence of Earliest Christian Pilgrimage to the Holy Land Comes to Light in Holy Sepulchre Church," p. 43.

[13] See, conveniently, F.E. Peters, *Jerusalem* (Princeton, NJ: Princeton Univ. Press, 1985), p. 126.

[14] Dio Cassius, *Roman History* 69.12.1–2. For an argument denying that a temple to Jupiter was built on the Temple Mount, see G.W. Bowersock, "A Roman Perspective on the Bar Kochba War," in William Scott Green, ed., *Approaches to Ancient Judaism*, vol. 2 (Chico, CA: Scholars Press, 1980), pp. 131–141, at p. 137.

[15] The date of the founding of the Roman city (Aelia Capitolina) is a much debated question. The better view now appears to be that it was founded by Hadrian on his way back from Egypt in 130 A.D. See Hanan Eshel, "The Date of the Founding of Aelia Capitolina," in Lawrence H. Schiffman, Emanuel Tov and James C. VanderKam, eds., *The Dead Sea Scrolls Fifty Years after Their Discovery* (Jerusalem: Israel Exploration Society, 2000), p. 637.

[16] Mary E. Smallwood, *The Jews Under Roman Rule* (Leiden: E.J. Brill, 1976), p. 463.

[17] Benjamin Isaac, "Roman Colonies in Judaea: The Foundation of Aelia Capitolina," in Benjamin Isaac, ed. *The Near East Under Roman Rule* (Leiden: Brill, 1998), pp. 87–111.

[18] Benjamin Mazar, *The Mountain of the Lord: Excavating in Jerusalem* (New York: Doubleday, 1975), p. 237.

[19] But see, on the basis of negative archaeological evidence, Hillel Geva, "Searching for Roman Jerusalem," *Biblical Archaeology Review*, November/December 1997, pp. 34–45, 72 and 73, at pp. 41–42.

[20] Smallwood, *Jews Under Roman Rule*, p. 445.

[21] See Dan Barag, "The Table of the Showbread and the Façade of the Temple on Coins of the Bar-Kokhba Revolt," in Hillel Geva, ed., *Ancient Jerusalem Revealed* (Jerusalem and Washington: Israel Exploration Society and Biblical Archaeology Society, 1994), p. 272, at p. 276.

[22] See Jerome Murphy-O'Connor, "The Location of the Capitol in Aelia Capitolina," *Revue Biblique* 101 (1994), p. 407.

[23] Smallwood, *Jews Under Roman Rule*, pp. 459–460.

[24] P. Kyle McCarter, Jr., *Ancient Inscriptions: Voices from the Biblical World* (Washington, DC: Biblical Archaeology Society, 1996), p. 155.

[25] The view that the temple to Jupiter (and the other two Capitoline deities—Juno and Minerva) is located at the site of the Church of the Holy Sepulchre relies on Jerome's reports that a statute of Jupiter was on the site of Jesus' resurrection. Jerome Murphy-O'Connor reasons that it was not simply a statue, but that the Capitoline temple was also located here. He finds support for this position in the fact that neither the Bordeaux Pilgrim, who visited the Temple Mount in 333, nor Eusebius reports a Roman temple on the Temple Mount at the time of their visits. They would surely have reported it if such were the case, so the reasoning goes. The Bordeaux Pilgrim reports only two royal statues on the Temple Mount. "It is very unlikely that the pilgrim would have failed to report a Roman temple standing here [on the Temple Mount]." Jerome Murphy-O'Connor, "Where Was the Capitol in Roman Jerusalem?" *Bible Review*, December 1997, pp. 22–29, at pp. 25–27.

[26] Peters, *Jerusalem*, p. 143.

[27] Peters, *Jerusalem*, p. 144. See also Smallwood, *Jews Under Roman Rule*, p. 478.

[28] I am indebted to Ronny Reich for this text.

[29] Jerome Murphy-O'Connor, "Where Was the Capitol in Roman Jerusalem?" p. 26.

[30] See, for example, Gaalyah Cornfeld, *The Mystery of the Temple Mount* (Tel Aviv: Bazak, 1972), pp. 52–53. In his translation of the inscription, he omits the word Antoninus. Strangely, a guidebook of which Ronny Reich (who supplied me with an accurate translation; see endnote 28) is an author also made the mistake of attributing the dedication to Hadrian rather than Antoninus Pius. See

Ronny Reich, Gideon Avni and Tamar Winter, *The Jerusalem Archaeological Park* (Jerusalem: Israel Antiquities Authority, 1999), p. 35. Reich attributes the error to too many cooks in the kitchen. I am indebted to Philip J. King for confirming the translation.

[31] See Benjamin Mazar, *The Mountain of the Lord* (Garden City, NY: Doubleday, 1975), p. 20 and pp. 236–237.

[32] Orit Peleg, "Roman Marble Sculpture from the Temple Mount Excavations," in A. Faust and Eyal Baruch, eds., *New Studies on Jerusalem, Proceedings of the Seventh Conference* (Ramat Gan: Bar-Ilan Univ., 2001), pp. 129–131 (Hebrew). I am indebted to Eilat Mazar for this reference.

[33] Josephus, *Jewish War* VII.i.1, H. St. J. Thackeray, trans., Loeb Classical Library (Cambridge, MA: Harvard Univ. Press, 1976).

[34] Eilat Mazar, *The Temple Mount Excavations in Jerusalem, 1968–1978 Directed by Benjamin Mazar, Final Reports, Vol. IV, Qedem* (forthcoming).

[35] Michael Avi-Yonah, *The Jews of Palestine—A Political History from the Bar-Kokhba War to the Arab Conquest* (Oxford: Basil Blackwell, 1976), p. 188.

[36] Avi-Yonah, *The Jews of Palestine*, p. 194.

[37] Avi-Yonah, *The Jews of Palestine* p. 200.

[38] See on this entire episode, Jeffrey Brodd, "Julian the Apostate and His Plan to Rebuild the Jerusalem Temple, *Bible Review*, October 1995, p. 32, at p. 35.

[39] Peters, *Jerusalem*, p. 146, citing Sozomen.

[40] Peters, *Jerusalem*, p. 147.

[41] Peters, *Jerusalem*, p. 147.

[42] Personal communication from Ronny Reich.

[43] Avi-Yonah, *The Jews of Palestine*, p. 200.

[44] Mark Friedman, "Jewish Pilgrimage after the Destruction of the Second Temple," in Nitza Rosovsky, ed., *City of the Great King—Jerusalem from David to the Present* (Cambridge: Harvard Univ. Press, 1996), pp. 136–146 at p. 138, n. 6; The Bordeaux Pilgrim, *Itinerary from Bordeaux to Jerusalem*, vol. 1 (London: Palestine Pilgrims' Text Society, 1887–1897), p. 22.

[45] See, conveniently, Peters, *Jerusalem*, p. 136.

[46] Peters, *Jerusalem*, p. 144.

[47] Michael Avi-Yonah, *The Madaba Mosaic Map* (Jerusalem: Israel Exploration Society, 1954), p. 59.

[48] Yaron Z. Eliav, *God's Mountain—The Temple Mount in Time, Place, and Memory* (Baltimore: Johns Hopkins Univ. Press, 2005), p. 129.

[49] John Wilkinson, *Jerusalem Pilgrims Before the Crusaders* (Warminster, England: Aris & Phillips, 1977), p. 61.

[50] Matthew 24:2; Mark 13:2; Luke 21:6.

[51] Quoted in Hershel Shanks, "Excavating in the Shadow of the Temple Mount," *Biblical Archaeology Review*, November/December 1986, p. 20 at p. 32.

[52] Heribert Busse, "The Sanctity of Jerusalem in Islam," *Judaism* 17 (1968), pp. 441–462, at p. 451.

[53] Ibn al-Muradjdjā, folio 21b, described in Busse, "The Sanctity of Jerusalem," p. 451, n. 37.

[54] Christopher Rowland, "The Temple in the New Testament," in John Day, ed., *Temple and Worship in Biblical Israel* (London: T & T Clark, 2005), pp. 469–483 at pp. 480–481.

[55] Peters, *Jerusalem*, pp. 170–171, quoting from F. Conybeare, "'Antiochus Strategos' Account of the Sack of Jerusalem in A.D. 614," *English Historical Review* 25 (1910), p. 502 at p. 506.

[56] John Wilkinson, *Jerusalem Pilgrims*, p. 8.

[57] Peters, *Jerusalem*, p. 172; Michael Avi-Yonah, s.v. "Jerusalem," in *Encyclopaedia Judaica*, vol. 9, p. 1407.

[58] Peters, *Jerusalem*, p. 172.

[59] Peters, *Jerusalem*, p. 173.

[60] Avi-Yonah, *The Jews of Palestine*, p. 266.

[61] Wilkinson, *Jerusalem Pilgrims*, p. 8.

[62] Avi-Yonah, *The Jews of Palestine*, pp. 268–270.

IV. HEROD'S TEMPLE

[1] Mary E. Smallwood, *The Jews Under Roman Rule* (Boston: Brill, 1976), pp. 92–93.

[2] Babylonian Talmud, *Baba Bathra* 4a.

[3] Josephus, *Jewish War*, V.v.6.223, H. St. J. Thackeray, trans., Loeb Classical Library (Cambridge, MA: Harvard Univ. Press, 1976.

[4] Sulpicius Severus tells a similar story of a debate among the Romans after the fall of Jerusalem. Several participants advised against burning the Temple because it was a holy building more splendid than any in existence. It should be left intact, they argued, as evidence of the moderation of the Romans, while its destruction would publicize the cruelty of the Romans as conquerors. Rivka Gonen, *Contested Holiness* (Jersey City, NJ: Ktav, 2003), p. 77, citing Menahem Stern, "Jerusalem, the Most Famous of the Cities of the East," in Aharon Oppenheimer, Uri Rappaport and Menahem Stern, eds., *Chapters in the History of Jerusalem in the Second Temple Period* (Jerusalem: Yad Izhak ben-Zvi, 1980) pp. 257–270.

[5] Smallwood, *The Jews Under Roman Rule*, pp. 325–326. See Stern, *Greek and Latin Authors on Jews and Judaism*, vol. II, p. 348.

[6] S.v. "Josephus," *Encyclopaedia Judaica*.

[7] *Jewish War* VI, .iv.8, William Whiston, trans., *Josephus: Complete Works* (Grand Rapids, MI: Kregel, 1971), p. 581.

[8] Josephus, *Antiquities of the Jews* XV.xi.1–7, *Josephus: Complete Works*, Whiston trans., pp. 334–335.

[9] Josephus, *Jewish War* V.v.2.193–194, Thackeray, trans., Loeb ed.: Josephus, *Jewish Antiquities* XV.xi.5.417, Ralph Marcus and Allen Wikgren, trans., Loeb edition (Cambridge, MA: Harvard Univ. Press, 1969). The prohibition against the entry of gentiles is also referred to in the Mishnah (*Kelim* 1.8). For the prohibition in an earlier period, see Josephus, *Jewish Antiquities* XII.iii.4.145–146, Ralph Marcus, trans., Loeb edition (Cambridge, MA: Harvard Univ. Press, 1976). Levine tells us this was probably the normative rule "for generations, if not centuries." Lee I. Levine, *Jerusalem* (Philadelphia: Jewish Publication Society, 2002), pp. 68–69.

[10] Asher S. Kaufman, *The Temple Mount: Where Is the Holy of Holies?* (Jerusalem: *Har Yéra'eh* Press, 2004), n. 1, p. 6.

[11] P. Kyle McCarter, Jr., *Ancient Inscriptions—Voices from the Biblical World* (Washington, DC: Biblical Archaeology Society, 1996), p. 129.

[12] Some scholars have suggested that the differences between Josephus and Mishnah may be explained by the fact that they are describing the complex at different times. Martin Goodman, "The Temple in First Century CE Judaism," in John Day, ed., *Temple and Worship in Biblical Israel* (London: T & T Clark, 2005), p. 460. Leen Ritmeyer contends that the Mishnah describes the 500-cubit square Temple Mount of the First Temple period. Leen Ritmeyer, *The Quest—Revealing the Temple Mount in Jerusalem* (Jerusalem: Carta and the Lamb Foundation, 2006), p. 140.

[13] Mishnah, *Tamid* 3.8.

[14] See Kaufman, *The Temple Mount*, p. 10.

[15] Leen Ritmeyer, "Locating the Original Temple Mount," *Biblical Archaeology Review*, March/April 1992, pp. 24–45, 64 and 65.

[16] S.v. "Temple Mount," in *Encyclopaedia Judaica*, vol. 15, p. 965.

[17] Dan Bahat, lecture at a symposium on "Herod and Augustus," University College London, June 2005.

[18] Numbers 19 describes the procedure for slaughtering the red heifer before the Tent of Meeting. It is slaughtered "in front of the Tent of Meeting" (Number 19:4). The priest looks into the holy place, but cannot slaughter the cow there because the slaughter, paradoxically, defiles the priest; he is impure, even though the red heifer's ashes have a purifying quality. The holy slaughter thus occurs outside looking in. The same process is recapitulated when the Temple in Jerusalem is built. The slaughtering priest is outside the Temple compound but from a vantage point that allows him to look directly into the Temple and the Holy of Holies. The only place where this can be done is on the Mount of Olives. The entire Talmudic tractate Parah is devoted to the laws of the red heifer and reflects the fact that it is slaughtered on the Mount of Olives. See Mishnah *Parah* 3:6–7.

[19] Joseph Patrich, "Reconstructing the Magnificent Temple That Herod Built," *Bible Review*, October 1988, pp. 16–29 at pp. 17 and 18. For a somewhat different view, see Lee I. Levine, *Jerusalem* (Philadelphia: Jewish Publication Society, 2002), pp. 223ff. ("The discrepancies among the sources touch on nearly every aspect of the Temple complex.")

[20] S.v. "Jerusalem," in *The New Encyclopedia of Archaeological Excavation*, vol. 2, p. 736.

[21] Various calculations differ. Ronny Reich calculates only about 350 tons. Personal communication. Ritmeyer uses the same figure I have used. See Ritmeyer, *The Quest*, p. 137.

[22] Dan Bahat, "The Western Wall Tunnels," in Hillel Geva, ed., *Ancient Jerusalem Revealed* (Jerusalem and Washington: Israel Exploration Society and Biblical Archaeology Society, 1994), pp. 177–190, at p. 181.

[23] Ehud Netzer, *The Architecture of Herod, the Great Builder* (Tubingen: Mohr Sieback, 2006), p. 162.

[24] See Leen Ritmeyer, "Quarrying and Transporting Stones for Herod's Temple Mount," *Biblical Archaeology Review*, November/December 1989, pp. 23–42.

[25] Murray Stein, "How Herod Moved Gigantic Blocks to Construct Temple Mount," *Biblical Archaeology Review*, May/June 1981, pp. 42–46, at p. 45.

[26] No. 200 in L.Y. Rahmani, *A Catalog of Jewish Ossuaries in the Collections of the State of Israel* (Jerusalem: The Israel Antiquities Authority and the Israel Academy of Sciences and Humanities, 1994).

[27] See Stephen J. Adler, "Israeli Court Finds Muslim Council Destroyed Ancient Remains on Temple Mount," *Biblical Archaeology Review*, July/August 1994, p. 39; and Stephen J. Adler, "The Temple Mount in Court," *Biblical Archaeology Review*, September/October 1991, pp. 60–68, 72.

[28] Leen Ritmeyer, Book Review, *Catholic Biblical Quarterly* 67 (April 2005), p. 323.

[29] Etgar Lefkovits, "Temple Mount Relics Saved From Garbage," *Jerusalem Post*, April 14, 2005.

[30] Nadav Shragai, "A Campaign of Denial to Disinherit the Jews," *Ha'aretz*, May 11, 2004, p. 4.

[31] See Hershel Shanks, "Sifting the Temple Mount Dump, *Biblical Archaeology Review*, July/August 2005, pp. 14–15, at p. 15.

[32] Ritmeyer, *The Quest*, p. 214.

[33] Arutz Sheva, daily e-mail, March 31, 2005.

[34] Ritmeyer, *The Quest*, pp. 85–88.

[35] Ronny Reich, "Two Possible *Miqwa'ot* on the Temple Mount," *Israel Exploration Journal* 39, (1989), pp. 63–65.

36 See Levine, *Jerusalem*, p. 140.

37 Mishnah, *Kelim* 1:8.

38 Hershel Shanks, "The Siloam Pool—Where Jesus Cured the Blind Man," *Biblical Archaeology Review*, September/October 2005, pp. 16–23.

39 According to Jerusalem archaeologist Dan Bahat, the porticos were inspired by the previously existing eastern portico which survived the Herodian reconstruction because the wall line could not be extended. Lecture at symposium on "Herod and Augustus," University College London, June 2005.

40 Leen Ritmeyer believes this arch supported a stairway to the gate rather than the gate itself. See Ritmeyer, *The Quest*, p. 110.

41 Josephus, *Jewish Antiquities* XV.xi.5.411–415, Marcus and Wikgren, trans., Loeb edition.

42 Personal communication from Dan Bahat Ronny Reich agrees that the column was not intended for Herod's Royal Stoa.

43 Benjamin Mazar, "Excavations Near Temple Mount Reveal Splendors of Herodian Jerusalem," *Biblical Archaeology Review* July/August 1980, pp. 44–59, at p. 58.

44 Netzer, *The Architecture of Herod, the Great Builder*, pp. 170–171.

45 Aaron Demsky, "When the Priests Trumpeted the Onset of the Sabbath," *Biblical Archaeology Review*, November/December 1986, pp. 50–52, 72 and 73, at p. 52.

46 Babylonian Talmud *Shabbath* 114b; Josephus, *Jewish War* IV.ix.12.581–583, H. St. J. Thackeray, trans., Loeb Classical Library (Cambridge, MA: Harvard Univ. Press, 1979)

47 Demsky, "When the Priests Trumpeted the Onset of the Sabbath," p. 52.

48 Levine, *Jerusalem*, pp. 239–240.

49 For details, see Levine, *Jerusalem*, pp. 242–243.

50 The number of columns is not attested in the sources, but is based on a depiction on a coin from the Bar-Kokhba period and the painting of the Temple at Dura-Europos. See Patrich, "Reconstructing the Magnificent Temple That Herod Built," p. 19.

51 See Steven Fine, "The Temple Menorah—Where Is It?" *Biblical Archaeology Review*, July/August 2005, pp. 18–25, 62 and 63, at p. 24.

52 For a summary of the arguments and references, see David Jacobson, "Sacred Geometry—Unlocking the Secrets of the Temple Mount—Part 1," *Biblical Archaeology Review*, July/August 1999, pp. 42–53, 62–64 and "Sacred Geometry, Part 2," September/October 1999, pp. 54–63, 74.

53 Josephus, *Jewish War* V.v.8.238–245, Thackeray, trans., Loeb edition.

54 We do not reproduce here the models from the Holy Land Hotel (now in the Israel Museum) in Jerusalem and in the Convent of the Sisters of

Zion because they are inaccurate according to the latest scholarship. Pere Benoit has asserted that "The four 'towers' so impressively reconstructed in the models are also entirely without foundation." Pierre Benoit, "The Archaeological Reconstruction of the Antonia Fortress," in *Jerusalem Revealed* (Jerusalem: Israel Exploration Society, 1975), p. 87 at p. 89.

55 At one time, it was argued that the Antonia fortress was the site of the Roman praetorium where Jesus was condemned (John 19:13). This is no longer a viable argument. See Benoit, "The Archaeological Reconstruction of the Antonia Fortress," p. 87. A good case can be made, however, that Paul was taken to the Antonia (see Acts 21; 34–37; 22:24; and 23:10,16, 32) when he was arrested. The place where he was taken is variously translated in English as barracks, compound and fortress. See s.v. "Antonia, Tower of" in Paul J. Achtemeier, ed., *HarperCollins Dictionary of the Bible*, rev. ed. (San Francisco: HarperSanFrancisco, 1996).

56 Although it is open to debate as to precisely where the Antonia stood, the usual view is that it was on the site now occupied by the Omariyya school. See Benoit, "The Archaeological Reconstruction of the Antonia Fortress," p. 89.

57 Josephus, *Jewish Antiquities* XV.xi.4.403, Marcus and Wikgren, trans., Loeb edition.

58 Josephus, *Jewish Antiquities* XVII.vi.2.151–155, Marcus and Wikgren, trans., Loeb edition.

59 See, Shaye J.D. Cohen "Roman Domination: The Jewish Revolt and the Destruction of the Second Temple," in Hershel Shanks, ed., *Ancient Israel: From Abraham to the Roman Destruction of the Temple* (rev. ed.) (Washington, DC: Biblical Archaeology Society, 1999), p. 276.

60 See Menaham Stern, *Greek and Latin Authors on Jews and Judaism*, vol. II (Jerusalem: Israel Academy of Sciences and Humanities, 1980), p. 29; s. v. "Caligula," *Encyclopaedia Judaica*; s.v. "Caligula," David Noel Freedman, ed., *Eerdmans Dictionary of the Bible*; s.v. "Petronius." *Encyclopaedia Judaica*.

61 Cohen, "Roman Domination: The Jewish Revolt and the Destruction of the Second Temple," p. 277.

62 Cohen, "Roman Domination," p. 277.

63 Stern, *Greek and Latin Authors on Jews and Judaism*, vol. II, p. 374.

64 Josephus, *Jewish War* VI.i.1. 2–13, Thackeray, trans., Loeb edition.

65 *Jewish War* VI.v.1.271–272, Thackeray, trans.

66 *Jewish War* VI.viii.5.404–407, Thackeray, trans.

67 *Jewish War* VII.1, Thackeray, trans.

68 *Jewish War* V.iv.3.161–162, Thackeray, trans.

69 *Jewish War* VII.i.1.1–3, Thackeray, trans.

70 *Jewish War* V.iv.2.156, Thackeray, trans.

[71] *Jewish War* VI.iv.5.250, Thackeray, trans.

[72] Stern, *Greek and Latin Authors on Jews and Judaism*, p. 377. By contrast, Domitian adopted the name "Germanicus."

[73] Howard B. Brin, *Catalog of Judaea Capta Coinage* (Minneapolis: Emmett Publishing Company, 1986), p. 1. I am indebted to Robert Deutsch for this citation.

V. THE FIRST SECOND TEMPLE

[1] Carol Meyers, s.v. "Temple, Jerusalem," David Noel Freedman, ed., *The Anchor Bible Dictionary* (New York: Doubleday, 1992), vol. 6, p. 363

[2] For a maximalist view of the city's borders, however, see David Ussishkin, "Big City, Few People: Jerusalem in the Persian Period," *Biblical Archaeology Review*, July/August 2005, pp. 26–35, at p. 27. However, Ussishkin speaks only of the city's size, not its population. He does not contest the meager population of returnees.

[3] David Ussishkin believes that the wall of the returning exiles followed the line of the wall of the city at the time of its destruction by the Babylonians—a much larger city than is generally described. On the west, he would enclose the western hill. On the east, he would follow the old wall downslope from the wall Kenyon identified. But he does not question the small size of the population, nor the fact that almost all of these people lived in the old City of David. See Ussishkin, "Big City, Few People: Jerusalem in the Persian Period," pp. 26–35.

[4] A different version of the decree was preserved in the Persian archives and recorded in Aramaic in Ezra 6:1–4.

[5] D. Larry Gregg, s.v. "Alexander," in David Noel Freedman, ed. *Eerdmans Dictionary of the Bible* (Grand Rapids: Eerdmans, 2000), p. 40.

[6] Josephus, *Jewish Antiquities* XII.v.4.250, Ralph Marcus, trans., Loeb Classical Library (Cambridge, MA: Harvard Univ. Press, 1976).

[7] Ibid.

[8] Michael Avi Yonah, *The Jews of Palestine, A Political History from the Bar Kokhba War to the Arab Conquest* (Oxford: Basil Blackwood, 1976), p. 3.

[9] Menahem Stern, ed., *Greek and Latin Authors on Jews and Judaism*, vol. 1 (Jerusalem: Israel Academy of Sciences and Humanities, 1976), pp. 111, 115, 118, 216.

[10] Josephus, *Jewish Antiquities* XII.v.4.248–261, Marcus, trans., Loeb edition.

[11] Apion, referred to by Josephus in *Contra Apion*. See Stern, *Greek and Latin Authors on Jews and Judaism*, vol. 1, p. 409.

[12] Josephus, *Contra Apion*, II.7.81 and 86, H. St. J. Thackeray, trans., Loeb Classical Library (Cam-

bridge, MA: Harvard Univ. Press, 1976).

[13] Josephus, *Contra Apion*, II.7.92–96.

[14] Hillel Geva, s.v. "Jerusalem," *The New Encyclopedia of Archaeological Excavations in the Holy Land*, p. 723.

[15] Josephus, *Jewish War* V, iv.4.138–139, H. St. J. Thackeray, trans., Loeb Classical Library (Cambridge, MA: Harvard Univ. Press, 1979).

[16] 1 Maccabees 1:33.

[17] Leen Ritmeyer makes a distinction between the Ptolemaic Acra and the Seleucid Acra, the former north of the 500-cubit square Temple Mount and the latter south of it. Leen Ritmeyer, *The Quest—Revealing the Temple Mount in Jerusalem* (Jerusalem: Carta and the Lamb Foundation, 2006), pp. 201, 207–212. As Ritmeyer notes, the location of the Seleucid Acra is one of the "most debated," "most enigmatic" and "thorniest" of questions (p. 208).

[18] S.v. "Jerusalem," *New Encyclopedia of Archaeological Excavations in the Holy Land* , p. 723.

[19] Ritmeyer has recently expanded this argument in Leen Ritmeyer, *The Quest*, pp. 165–173 and *passim*. Archaeologist Dan Bahat vehemently disagrees with Ritmeyer's analysis. (Personal communication).

[20] See Erwin F. Reidinger, "The Temple Mount Platform in Jerusalem from Solomon to Herod: An Archaeological Re-Examination," *Assaph* (Tel Aviv University Studies in Art History), vol. 9 (2004), p. 29.

[21] There is considerable scholarly disagreement about the size of the cubit used in the Temple and on the Temple Mount, `amah in the rabbinic literature and *pexus* in Josephus. The different views vary between 40.6 centimeters and 66 centimeters. Perhaps the most widely accepted view is 56 centimeters, proposed by the Talmudic scholar Arye Ben David. As Joshua Schwartz has remarked, "Needless to say, a change in the length of the cubit affects almost all aspects of location and reconstruction [of the Temple on the Temple Mount]. It is not surprising, therefore, that there is so much disagreement in this matter." Book review of Asher Selig Kaufman's *The Temple of Jerusalem*, Part III (Jerusalem: Har Year'ah Presss, 2004), in *Biblical Archaeology Review* September/October, 2005, pp. 62–64, at p. 63. See also Ritmeyer, *The Quest*, pp. 170–173.

[22] This bend is also noted in Reidinger, "The Temple Mount Platform in Jerusalem from Solomon to Herod." It is also discussed, with citations, in Ritmeyer, *The Quest*, pp. 178–179.

[23] Dan Bahat disputes the existence of this bend (personal communication).

[24] Leen Ritmeyer, "Locating the Original Temple Mount," *Biblical Archaeology Review*, March/April 1992, pp. 24–45, 64 and 65, at pp. 37 and 43.

[25] On the other hand, Lee Levine contends that

"Rome was destined to conquer the East irrespective of internal Hasmonean politics." Even a unified stand by the fighting Hasmonean brothers would not have made a difference. Lee Levine, "The Age of Hellenism: Alexander the Great and the Rise and Fall of the Hasmonean Kingdom," in Hershel Shanks, ed., *Ancient Israel: From Abraham to the Roman Destruction of the Temple*, rev. ed. (Washington, DC: Biblical Archaeology Society, 1999), p. 264. Shaye J.D. Cohen takes the same view: "[W]e may be sure that in one way or another the Romans would have found a satisfactory excuse to exercise hegemony over the Jewish state." Shaye J.D. Cohen, "Roman Domination" in Shanks, ed., *Ancient Israel*, rev. ed., p. 266. Josephus, however, may take a different view: "For this misfortune which befell Jerusalem, Hyrcanus [II] and Aristobulus [II] were responsible, because of their dissension." Josephus, *Jewish Antiquities*, XIV.iv.5.77, Ralph Marcus, trans., Loeb Classical Library (Cambridge, MA: Harvard Univ. Press, 1976).

[26] Josephus, *Jewish Antiquities* XIV.iv.3.67–68, Marcus, trans., Loeb edition.

[27] Cohen, "Roman Domination," p. 269.

VI. SOLOMON'S TEMPLE

[1] While no stone can be positively identified, one recent researcher claims to have identified "the rock edge for the purpose of building construction as an indication of the Temple's location." See Erwin F. Reidinger, "The Temple Mount Platform in Jerusalem from Solomon to Herod: An Archaeological Re-Examination," *Assaph* 9 (2004), (Tel Aviv University Studies in Art History), p. 36. Reidinger speaks of this as the "'imprint' of the Temple on the Holy Rock," which is "clearly visible."

[2] Carol Meyers, "Jachin and Boaz in Religious and Political Perspective," *Catholic Biblical Quarterly* 45 (1983), p. 167.

[3] See Victor Hurowitz, "Inside Solomon's Temple," *Bible Review*, April 1994, pp. 24–37 and 50, at p. 33.

[4] S.v. "Showbread," David Noel Freedman, ed., *Eerdmans Dictionary of the Bible* (Grand Rapids, MI: William B. Eerdmans, 2000), p. 1216.

[5] Carol L. Meyers, "Was There a Seven-Branched Lampstand in Solomon's Temple?" *Biblical Archaeology Review*, September/October 1979, pp. 46–57, at p. 57.

[6] Hurowitz, "Inside Solomon's Temple," pp. 34–35.

[7] Edward Lipiński believes that Ahaz not only replaced the altar, but was responsible for redecorating the Solomonic Temple: The altar, the central feature of the Temple, was symbolic of all the decoration described in 1 Kings 6–7. Personal communication and see Edward Lipiński, *Itineraria Phoenicia, Orientalia Lovaniensia Analecta* 127 (Leuven: Peeters, 2004), pp. 506–507, n. 77.

[8] Hurowitz, "Inside Solomon's Temple," p. 34.

[9] Meyers, s.v. "Temple, Jerusalem," *The Anchor Bible Dictionary*, p. 355.

[10] Josephus, *Antiquities of the Jews* VIII.II.7, William Whiston, trans., *Josephus: Complete Works* (Grand Rapids, MI: Kregel, 1971), p. 173.

[11] James B. Pritchard, ed., *Ancient Near Eastern Texts Relating to the Old Testament*, 2nd ed. (Princeton, NJ: Princeton Univ. Press, 1955), p. 288.

[12] Ali Abu-Asaf, *Der Tempel von `Ain Dara*, Damaszener Forschungen (Mainz: Philipp von Zabern, 1990).

[13] In English, see John Monson, "The New `Ain Dara Temple—Closest Solomonic Parallel," *Biblical Archaeology Review*, May/June 2000, pp. 20–35 and 67, at p. 23.

[14] Monson, "The New `Ain Dara Temple—Closest Solomonic Parallel," p. 33.

[15] "[Solomon's Temple] certainly contained two pillars which may or may not have been free-standing." Ziony Zevit, *The Religions of Ancient Israel* (London and NY: Continuum, 2001), p. 341.

[16] But see Meyers, s.v. "Temple, Jerusalem," in the *Anchor Bible Dictionary*:

"Although some earlier studies comparing the Temple to the Assyrian *bit hilani*, with its two entryway pillars supporting a lintel, suggested otherwise, the pillars [of Yachin and Boaz] were probably freestanding. As such, they can be considered the gateposts flanking the entrance to the forecourt of God's house."

[17] Lawrence E. Stager, "Jerusalem as Eden," *Biblical Archaeology Review*, May/June 2000, pp. 36–47, at p. 47.

[18] Stager, "Jerusalem as Eden," pp. 37 and 47.

[19] Citations may be found in Hurowitz, "Inside Solomon's Temple," n.6, pp. 28 and 37.

[20] Hurowitz, "Inside Solomon's Temple," p. 28.

[21] Rivka Gonen, *Contested Holiness* (Jersey City, NJ: Ktav, 2003), p. 117, citing Louis Ginzberg, *The Legends of the Jews*, vol.V, (Philadelphia: Jewish Publication Society, 1913), pp. 125–127.

[22] John M. Lundquist, s.v. "Biblical Temple," in Eric Meyers, ed., *Oxford Encyclopedia of Archaeology in the Near East,* vol. 1 (New York: Oxford Univ. Press, 1997), p. 325.

[23] Baruch A. Levine, "On the Presence of God in Biblical Religion," in Jacob Neusner, ed., *Religions in Antiquity*, Studies in the History of Religions XIV (Leiden: Brill, 1968), p. 82.

[24] Hurowitz, "Inside Solomon's Temple," p. 36.

[25] Michael Fishbane, *Biblical Myth and Rabbinic Mythmaking* (Oxford: Oxford Univ. Press, 2003), p. 77.

[26] Scholars agree that Isaiah 40 and thereafter comes from a later period than the first 39 chapters.

[27] For an account of Mount Zion's peregrinations, see Bargil Pixner, "Church of the Apostles Found on Mount Zion" (The Odyssey of Mount Zion), *Biblical Archaeology Review*, May/June 1990, pp. 16–35 and 60, at p. 20.

[28] For a fascinating account of the beginning of time, see Jack M. Sasson, "Of Time and Immortality," *Bible Review*, Summer 2005, pp. 32–41, 52 and 54.

[29] Tractate *Kelim* 1, 6–9.

[30] See Andrew G. Vaughn and Carolyn Pillers Dobler, "The Probability of Forgeries: Reflections on a Statistical Analysis," *The SBL Forum*, March 15, 2005 [www.sbl-site.org/Article.aspx?ArticleID=372], and "Major New Forgeries Uncovered by Professor GBSTMT," *Biblical Archaeology Review*, May/June 2005, pp. 49–50.

[31] The most recent, as I write, and one of the most cogent, is Victor Sasson, "Philological and Textual Observations on the Controversial King Jehoash Inscription," *Ugarit-Forschungen* (Andre Caquot Festschrift), Band 35, 2003, copyright 2004, published 2005, p. 573.

[32] David Noel Freedman, Shawna Dolansky Overton and David Miano, "The 'Smoking Guns' Are Illusory," *Biblical Archaeology Review*, March/April 2004 [sidebar], p. 51.

[33] Chaim Cohen, Letter: "It's Biblical—Not Modern—Hebrew," *Biblical Archaeology Review*, May/June 2004, pp. 14–15, at p. 15.

[34] Ronny Reich, "Edom or Adam? New Reading Bolsters Case for Jehoash Tablet," *Biblical Archaeology Review*, July/August 2004, pp. 46–48, at p. 48.

[35] David Noel Freedman, "Don't Rush to Judgment," *Biblical Archaeology Review*, March/April 2004, pp. 48–51.

[36] See "Major New Forgeries Uncovered by Professor GBSTMT," *Biblical Archaeology Review*, May/June 2005, pp. 49–50 at p. 50.

[37] Kronfeld is a joint author, with Rosenfeld and Ilani, of a paper submitted to *Tel Aviv*, which replies to a paper in *Tel Aviv* by the IAA scientists.

[38] Personal communication.

[39] Philip R. Davies, "'House of David' Built on Sand: The Sins of the Biblical Maximizers," *Biblical Archaeology Review*, July/August 1994, pp. 54–55, at p. 55.

[40] Neils Peter Lemche, *The Israelites in History and Tradition* (Louisville, KY: Westminster John Knox, 1998), p. 38.

[41] Israel Finkelstein and Neil Asher Silberman, *The Bible Unearthed* (New York: The Free Press, 2001), p. 128.

[42] Finkelstein and Silberman, *The Bible Unearthed*, pp. 129–130.

[43] Finkelstein and Silberman, *The Bible Unearthed*, p. 133.

[44] See Alan Millard, "Half a Pot is Better than No Pot at All: The Role of Accident in Archaeology," *Buried History, the Journal of the Australian Institute of Archaeology*, vol. 40 (2004), p. 7.

[45] Jane Cahill, "Jerusalem in David and Solomon's Time—It Really Was a Major City in the Tenth Century B.C.E.," *Biblical Archaeology Review*, November/December 2004, pp. 20–31, 62 and 63, at p. 27. As noted above, however, this is not true with regard to the recent excavations at the Gihon Spring directed by Ronny Reich and Eli Shukron. See also Jane M. Cahill, "Jerusalem at the Time of the United Monarchy: The Archaeological Evidence," in Andrew G. Vaughn and Ann E. Killebrew, eds., *Jerusalem in Bible and Archaeology—The First Temple Period* (Atlanta: Society of Biblical Literature, 2003), p. 13 at pp. 55–56, 72.

[46] Finkelstein and Silberman, *The Bible Unearthed*, p. 132.

[47] Finkelstein and Silberman, *The Bible Unearthed*, p. 190.

[48] Finkelstein and Silberman, *The Bible Unearthed*, p. 238.

[49] Finkelstein and Silberman, *The Bible Unearthed*, p. 127.

[50] James Pritchard, ed., *Ancient Near Eastern Texts Relating to the Old Testament*, 2nd ed. (Princeton, NJ: Princeton Univ. Press, 1955), p. 308.

VII. BEFORE SOLOMON'S TEMPLE

[1] See, for example, *Sefer ha-Hinnukh* (13th century).

[2] S.v. "Tabernacle," in David Noel Freedman, ed., *Eerdmans Dictionary of the Bible* (Grand Rapids: Eerdmans, 2000). This Bible dictionary has no entry for "Tent of Meeting." While other standard reference works (*Anchor Bible Dictionary* and *HarperCollins Bible Dictionary*) do have an entry for "Tent of Meeting," they simply refer the reader to the entry on Tabernacle.

[3] Joshua R. Porter, s.v. "Tabernacle," in Paul J. Achtemeier, ed., *HarperCollins Bible Dictionary* (rev. ed.) San Francisco: HarperSanFrancisco, 1996). On the other hand, Egyptologist Kenneth A. Kitchen, finds parallels to the desert Tabernacle in Egyptian records of the Late Bronze Age of the second millennium B.C., but not in the Mesopotamian world of the first millennium B.C. He concludes, "All in all, the evidence makes it untenable to claim any longer that the construct of the Tabernacle is an Exilic fiction. To attribute the Israelite Tabernacle to Hebrew 'priestly' circles living in exile in Nebuchadrezzar's Babylon, six or seven centuries after such usages in our data, requires belief in some kind of magical telepathy that worked across nearly a thousand miles and several centuries! This may all be very well in science fiction, but real history indicates that the

Tabernacle tradition belongs to the Bronze Age Egypto-Semitic world, not to the Mesopotamian world of the mid-first millennium B.C." Kenneth A. Kitchen, "The Desert Tabernacle: Pure Fiction or Plausible Account?" *Bible Review*, December 2000, pp. 14–21, at pp. 20–21. In light of the clear resemblances of the Tabernacle to Solomon's Temple, which Kitchen does not discuss, I find his argument unconvincing.

[4] Porter, s.v. "Tabernacle," *HarperCollins Bible Dictionary*, p. 1088.

[5] The parallels Kitchen cites in the article mentioned in endnote 3 apply as much or more to the Ark of the Covenant as to the Tabernacle.

[6] See Siegfried H. Horn, "Why the Moabite Stone Was Blown to Pieces," *Biblical Archaeology Review*, May/June 1986, pp. 50–61.

[7] Israel Finkelstein, "Shiloh Yields Some, but Not All, of Its Secrets," *Biblical Archaeology Review*, January/February 1986, pp. 22–41, at pp. 40–41.

[8] Mishnah *Yoma*, 5.2.

[9] Asher S. Kaufman, "Where the Ancient Temple of Jerusalem Stood," *Biblical Archaeology Review*, March/April 1983, pp. 40–55, at pp. 53–54.

[10] On the possibility that Araunah might be a Hurrian/Hittite title, see Eric H. Cline, *Jerusalem Besieged: From Ancient Canaan to Modern Israel* (Ann Arbor: University of Michigan Press, 2004), p. 313, n. 9.

[11] Rivka Gonen, "Was the Site of the Jerusalem Temple Originally a Cemetery?" *Biblical Archaeology Review*, May/June 1985, pp. 44–55, at p. 55.

[12] Also called Early Bronze IV in another, for the most part abandoned, scheme of archaeological periodicity. Israel archaeologists often refer to the period as the Intermediate Bronze Age (IBA).

[13] Geza Vermes, *The Dead Sea Scrolls in English*, 4th ed. (Sheffield: Sheffield Academic Press, 1995), p. 360.

[14] Josephus, *Jewish Antiquities* I.x.2.179–182, H. St. J. Thackeray, trans., Loeb Classical Library (Cambridge, MA: Harvard Univ. Press, 1977).

[15] Josephus, *Jewish War* VI.x.1.438, H. St. J. Thackeray, trans., Loeb Classical Library (Cambridge, MA: Harvard Univ. Press, 1979).

[16] Ernst Axel Knauf, "Jerusalem in the Late Bronze and Early Iron Ages: A Proposal," *Tel Aviv* 27 (2000), pp. 75–90, at p. 78.

[17] Edward Lipiński also believes that the description in 1 Kings 6–7 refers only to the decoration of the Temple. In his view, however, Solomon built the basic temple, which was then redecorated by Ahaz with the decoration described in 1 Kings 6–7. See Edward Lipiński, *Itineraria Phoenicia, Orientalia Lovaniensia Analecta* 127 (Leuven: Peeters, 2004), pp. 506–507, n. 77.

[18] David Ussishkin, "Solomon's Jerusalem: The Text and the Facts on the Ground," in Andrew G. Vaughn and Ann E. Killebrew, eds., *Jerusalem in Bible and Archaeology—The First Temple Period* (Atlanta: Society of Biblical Literature, 2003), p. 103.

[19] This is the suggestion of Tel Aviv University biblical historian Nadav Na'aman in "The Contribution of the Amarna Letters to the Debate on Jerusalem's Political Position in the Tenth Century B.C.E.," *Bulletin of the American Schools of Oriental Research* 304 (1996), p. 17.

[20] Personal communication, July 8, 2005.

VIII. CONCLUSION

[1] See Moshe Sharon, "Islam on the Temple Mount," *Biblical Archaeology Review*, July/August 2006, p. 36–47 and 68, at p. 42

Illustration Credits

Alinari/Art Resource, NY—120

Antikensammlung, Staatliche Museen zu Berlin, Preussischer Kulturbesitz—129

A.M. Appa—135, 136, 137

Archives of the Temple Mount Excavations, Courtesy of Dr. Eilat Mazar—52 (top right), 52 (bottom)

The Art Archive/Collection Staatliche Glypothek Munich/Dagli Orti (A)—49

Meir Ben-Dov—52 (top left)

Bildarchiv Preussischer Kulturbesitz/Art Resource, NY—166

Adrian J. Boas, *Archaeology of the Military Orders* (London & New York: Routledge, 2006)—30

Werner Braun—80

British Museum/HIP/Art Resource, NY—106

Carta, the Israel Map and Publishing Company, Ltd.—21

Count Melchior de Vogüé—72

James Fleming—85 (bottom)

Volkmar Fritz—133 (middle), 133 (right; after Hugh Claycombe)

Marie-Henriette Gates—134

Geological Survey of Israel—151

Sonia Halliday and Laura Lushington—x

Sonia Halliday Photographs—13, 62

David Harris—35, 36, 37 (bottom), 47, 56, 64, 66 (top), 73, 78, 84, 93

David Harris/Bible Lands Museum—122

Aaron Horowitz/CORBIS—16–17

Israel Museum—32

Jewish Quarter Excavations/Hillel Geva and Avital Zitronblat—160

Erich Lessing—6, 19, 29, 34, 89 (top), 90, 96, 97, 104, 127, 128 (bottom left), 131, 132, 161

Maryl Levine—152, 153

Louvre/Réunion des Musées Nationaux/Art Resource, NY—55

Frederic W. Madden, *History of Jewish Coinage*—46 (bottom)

Garo Nalbandian—10, 11, 12, 20, 22, 24, 25, 28, 31, 44, 45, 50 (left), 50–51 (center), 51 (top right), 70 (bottom), 70–71 (top), 79, 83, 88, 94, 175, 178

Courtesy of National Numismatic Collection, Smithsonian Institution; photograph by Richard Doty—59

Ehud Netzer—95 (bottom)

Richard Nowitz—8, 38, 43, 77

Said Nuseibeh—14–15, 15 (bottom)

Palestine Exploration Fund, courtesy of curator Felicity Cobbing—164

Jacob Pinkerfeld—40 (right)

Bargil Pixner—40 (top left)

Svetlana Popović—23

Princeton University Press/Art Resource, NY—171

Private Collection/Bridgeman Art Library—168

Zev Radovan—3, 27, 46 (top), 76, 85 (top), 98, 102, 111, 126 (both), 128 (top), 128 (bottom right), 155, 157, 172

Ronny Reich, Gideon Avni, Tamar Winter, *The Jerusalem Archaeological Park* (Jerusalem: Israel Antiquities Authority, 1999)—51 (bottom right)

Dorothy D. Resig—viii, 18

Leen Ritmeyer—86 (top)

Reconstruction by Leen Ritmeyer—67, 75, 82, 86 (bottom), 89 (bottom), 91 (left), 95 (top), 99, 118, 124, 125, 138

Scala/Art Resource, NY—109, 112

SEF/Art Resource, NY—108, 110

Hershel Shanks—2, 37 (top), 41, 42, 74, 81, 91 (right), 116, 117

Suzanne Singer—87

Staatliche Museen zu Berlin/Bildarchiv Preussischer Kulturbesitz/Vorderasiatisches Museen—158

© The Trustees of the British Museum—113

Louis-Hugues Vincent—40 (bottom left)

Baron Wolman—100

Index